# GOD DID IT!

## The Story of
## Kansas City Youth For Christ

Vidy Metsker

WINEPRESS WP PUBLISHING

ISBN 1-57921-322-7 (HC)
ISBN 1-57921-323-5 (SC)
Library of Congress Catalog Card Number: 00-107200

# Dedication

*To the glory of our Lord Jesus Christ*
*Lovingly dedicated to our priceless family,*
*Our children, grandchildren and great-grandchildren.*
*To Al's sisters and my brothers and sister*
*And to all our extended families.*

*And*

*With profound gratitude to God*
*To all the fantastic men and women*
*who have worked on our staff through the years,*
*Those whom we have been privileged to serve,*
*And each person who has faithfully supported our*
*ministry over the years.*
*I wish I could list every name.*
*I love you!*

# Acknowledgments

As I sat writing this book on my computer, I had to chuckle. My little laptop that I can carry in its case on an airplane has more power, speed and storage space than the huge main-frame computer we bought for YFC in 1982—not that long ago. That computer and software cost $150,000 and required a private room with its own special air-conditioning unit. How technology has advanced! I doubt that I could have completed this without my computer.

I give my heartfelt thank you to all who have helped in so many ways to make this book become a reality.

Our children and their spouses, Martha and Don, Marilyn and David, and Ronnie and Susan were invaluable for reading my rough manuscript and offering their helpful suggestions.

Martha especially worked tenaciously with me for innumerable hours reading, and re-reading—to the extent of literally dreaming about it and losing sleep. And she went through myriad of pictures with me trying to find the right ones. Her encouragement and prayers were priceless.

Our oldest grandson, Topher Philgreen, for all his help, especially on the new ministry. He helped me write Chapter 38 and Appendix C. Thank you, Topher.

Our granddaughter, Michelle Gann, rescued this 77-year-old grandma every time I hit snags on my computer.

She was a great teacher!

And our friend, Ryan Bilyeu, who patiently helped my computer work for this "dummy."

Jeanette Gardner Littleton, who is now senior editor at *Moody Monthly,* kindly gave her precious time to edit this book for me. Jeanette and I have been co-workers since she was a freshman in high school while she was active in KCYFC. She is like family.

I also thank Joann Peake Johnson for her help in proofreading and my publisher, Athena Dean, of WinePress Publishing and my project manager, Tammy Hopf for their help, patience and encouragement.

# CONTENTS

# Introduction

Writing this book has been an emotional journey—full of laughter, tears, and loneliness without my sweetheart. This pilgrimage through the past 50 years was full of joys and heartaches, victories and trials, successes and failures, spiritual conquests, following God's leading, times of embarrassment—but always, God was in control.

I felt God's definite leading in this project. Each day I asked His Holy Spirit to fill me and write through me.

I have been moved many times to tears of rejoicing as I have reviewed the miracles we saw God do through the years in our midst. Truly, these experiences have not been of our making, but the hand of God at work. How good God has been to let us be a part of His work.

It is my desire—not only that this be enticing reading—but also that it will be a ministry, speaking to the heart of each reader. It may speak to some about trusting God more. Some may be inspired to be better parents or spouses. May some be challenged to follow in Jesus' steps and present their body to Him for service. I trust some will learn the joy of giving.

I pray that everyone will realize the importance of *always* making the gospel clear and simple for all to understand.

It is my prayer that any who do not know Jesus as Savior will, as they read, ask God for forgiveness of their sin and become a child of God.

Yes, this is the story of Al's and my fifty years of ministry together—but it also includes our family—because, you see, our family was a vital part of our ministry. Through the years Al's brother and sisters and their families have played vital roles in the ministry. Their extended families are still involved. My mother and daddy, brothers and sister and their families were also intrigal parts helping in a wide variety of ways through the years. Now many of those in our extended family are on the mission field or serving the Lord here at home.

In the middle of this project, I became disheartened. That morning, in desperation, I prayed:

"Lord, please give me something right now to encourage me. I'm to the end. I can't go on. I'm depending only on You to help me."

Then as I read His Word, He gave me the encouragement I needed.

> "Because the Lord God helps me I will not be
> dismayed. Therefore I have set my face like a flint
> to do His will and I know that I will triumph."
> (Isaiah 50:7)

I wrote that verse in large bold type on my computer and printed it out. Then I posted it right above my computer to be a constant reminder. God truly does meet our every need.

Through the years multiplied hundreds of people have worked for us. Each one was like a member of our family. Untold thousands of teenagers have been born into God's family through this ministry. Each one holds a special place in our hearts. We remember fondly all the guest preachers, singers, and entertainers of various kinds who have been a vital part of our ministry.

I wanted to tell each of their stories because they are precious to us. I have struggled with what I could leave out. It hurts me to leave anyone out but to fit this into one volume it was necessary. Fond memories of each of you are held deeply in my heart. Thank you for being a part of our lives.

# FOREWARD

Heroes. We read about them nearly every day in the paper. Men and women who, in a blink of an eye and without regard for self—take courageous action ... usually in a moment of rescue.

What is a hero? A servant. One who is obedient. One who gives his or her life away.

In Chuck Colson's book "<u>Loving God</u>" I love what he wrote. (Zondervan Publishers)

> "It is not what we do that matters, *but what a sovereign God chooses to do through us.* God doesn't want our success; He wants us. He doesn't demand our achievements; He demands our obedience. The kingdom of God is a kingdom of paradox, where through the ugly defeat of a cross, a holy God is utterly glorified. Victory comes through defeat; healing through brokenness; finding self through losing self". (pg 25). . . . "What God wants from His people is obedience, no matter what the circumstances, no matter how unknown the outcome." (pg 36)

Obedience and servanthood—two dynamic components of a hero. These two words mean—to love—to have compassion ... expecting nothing in return. It means giving when no one says thank you. It means forgiving those whom won't forgive us. And it even means coming early and staying late when no one else notices. Service, prompted by duty.

Does Jesus call us to be heroes? NO! He calls us to be available. He calls us to be obedient. He calls us to love Him with all our heart, soul, and mind and to love our neighbor as ourself. He calls us to absolute abandonment. It is through Him that we can become heroes.

This book is the life story of two heroes—my parents. They were available and understood absolute abandonment. And today thousands upon thousands around the world can look back to the moment that God touched their lives through the ministry of Youth For Christ in Kansas City.

Today at YouthFront (the new name of Kansas City Youth For Christ) our staff of over 80 servant leaders are keenly aware of their rich heritage. Many of us learned under the direction and leadership of my mother and father. Their impact on our early years of ministry continues to drive us today in the YouthFront mission: to bring youth into a growing relationship with Jesus Christ.

God is honoring the faithful hard work of the ministry that was founded in 1943 as today we excitedly stand on the verge of explosive growth. Calls literally come daily into our offices from New York, South Dakota, California, Cuba, Hungary, Alaska, Hong Kong, Spain, Italy, Pennsylvania … much like the Macedonian call to Paul, "Come on over and help us." The need is as great as it was in the 40's … young people who  desperately need a Savior. Those of us on the Leadership Team at YouthFront find it hard to sleep at night—God is orchestrating something awesome.

Even as I write this there are over 100 schools in the Kansas City area with a Club121—our on campus, student-lead, student-initiated, church based evangelistic Club. Just two days ago, Brittany Hills Middle School had their first meeting of this school year. An excited 130 students packed the school-room before school began. And, when the Gospel was presented, 24 students trusted Christ as Savior!

That's when I think of Mama and Daddy and others who faithfully listened to God and were obedient to reach young people with the Gospel—in the youth ministry movement that exploded in the 40's. Many of those saints are now in Heaven … and I believe they are cheering us on and last Tuesday they had a party in Heaven—rejoicing over those 24 teens who trusted Christ as Savior.

Yes, *God Did It*! And He continues to do it, today!

I hope this book challenges you to faithful obedience and absolute abandonment to Jesus Christ. And then, as we can say about my parents, Dr. Al and Vidy Metsker—"may all who come behind us find us faithful."

Ronnie Metsker, President

YouthFront
formerly Kansas City Youth For Christ

# CHAPTER 1

# American Farm Boy

We're here, boy. Get out! You're on your own now," snarled the driver as his truck lumbered into the Kansas City Stock Yards. "Be on your way. I've got to get these cattle unloaded."

Al grabbed his tattered bag containing everything he owned and jumped to the brick street below. With the sun barely peeking over the bluff, panic stabbed the confidence of this 18-year-old. He had never been more than 50 miles from his farm home in Central Kansas. It didn't matter that he had worked with cattle all his life, the stench in the stockyards was so pungent he almost choked.

His heart pounded! Fear? Yes. And excitement! The 200-mile ride across black, uncertain territory in a bumpy cattle truck with a grouchy driver wasn't the entrance of a millionaire. You see, that was his purpose in coming to Kansas City—to become a millionaire.

For a brief moment he was lost in his dream. *Someday he would ride in a chauffeur driven limousine. His home would be an elegant mansion with uniformed servants awaiting his commands. He would be known by all and be respected by the most elite society. No more of the meager living he had known growing up. He would shower his parents with all the luxuries they never knew. And he would help other people who were in need.*

He knew he could do it and he would!

## Al's Early Years

On a blistering hot day—July 21, 1921—there was no waiting for the doctor to arrive. The "I can do it myself" attitude of this newborn baby boy should have warned his mother that he would become a natural leader. Alfred Earl Metsker was born at the farm home of Mabel and Oran Metsker near Toronto, Kansas, the third of four children—two boys and two girls. From the time he was a toddler his lively, inquisitive antics kept his mother hustling.

Farm life demanded that each family member be busy doing important jobs—the responsibilities increasing with age. The children never got "time off" from everyday chores—milking cows morning and evening, feeding hogs and chickens and gathering eggs.

As a boy Al never knew what "store bought" toys were. He invented his own. His creativity inspired him to make anything he wanted from junk machinery parts, bailing wire and whatever intrigued him.

Their home had no electricity—merely kerosene lamps to carry from room to room. The only running water was when they ran to the well and got it! A path "out back" led to the only toilet they knew. It was conveniently supplied with an old Sears and Roebuck or Montgomery Ward catalogue. Who could afford toilet tissue?

But, Al grew up with the most precious commodity of all—love. Even though the Metskers knew no extravagances, the family was close and everyone worked together to accomplish what had to be done. There was no time for foolishness.

As the children finished chores, the smell of smoke from the wood-burning stove drew them to the kitchen. The tantalizing aroma of crispy fried pork chops, mounds of mashed potatoes and creamy gravy Mother had just put on the table made them scramble to their chairs. A simple prayer of thanks preceded their "diving in."

After chores, dinner and homework, everyone dropped exhausted into bed so, at daybreak, they could start all over again. No wonder kids didn't get into trouble; they didn't have time.

"My little fix-it man" is what his mother called Al. He thought things through logically, constantly figuring easier and better ways.

Laundry was done by hand. When a washtub sprang a leak, Al figured how to correct the problem and then fixed it for his mother. When a gate was left open the pigs got out, so he fixed the gate to close automatically. He built a wagon from things he found laying around so he could carry a bigger load of stove wood instead of an armload at a time. He was a "doer."

Sometimes in the summer after the chores were done Al and his brother, Lowell, would wade and skip rocks in Fancy Creek. When they got a little older they went skinny dipping or fishing in Walnut Creek.

### The Dirty Thirties

That black day that the stock market crashed, on October 24, 1929, came when Al was eight years old. The Great Depression caused stocks to lose more than 40% of their value resulting in a weak economy. This catastrophe caused banks to close leaving many people frightened and bankrupt. Thirteen to fifteen million people became unemployed—25% of the work force.

Panic struck much of the nation as businesses failed and thousands of people were left homeless. Poverty became a way of life for many. But the crash didn't make that much difference to Al's parents because they had nothing in the bank to lose. They did suffer when prices on the crops and cattle they raised to sell dropped to new lows.

"At least we don't have to worry about food," Al's mother cheerfully pointed out. "We have milk, eggs and garden vegetables. We can butcher a pig and a cow for meat. We have a lot to be thankful for." They sold eggs and cream in exchange for sugar, flour and other items the farm didn't produce. Their clothes were few and had often been patched.

## One Room School

Al's first seven years in school were in a one-room schoolhouse heated with a pot-bellied wood stove. He could never fake knowing his lesson since he was the only one in his class. He had to answer all questions.

At daybreak each morning he hopped out of bed, pulled on his overalls and scurried to the barn where he helped milk six to fourteen cows. Especially on cold wintry mornings, he wolfed down a steaming hot breakfast of eggs and pancakes or oatmeal and biscuits his mother had waiting for him. He had no time to dawdle before hustling off to school.

Al usually walked the two miles to Triumph School, but sometimes he rode his horse, Prince. His motivation to hurry home from school was to arrive just as his mother was taking hot bread or cinnamon rolls out of the oven. She made bread nearly every day in a wood-burning cook stove. He could devour those tasty morsels as they came hot from the oven along with a big glass of creamy milk!

When in high school, the ten-mile trip on a rugged dirt road in a horse-drawn buggy to Eureka High School was tedious. The buggy seat held only two. Because Al was the youngest, his brother, Lowell, and sister, Leona, sat on the seat and he rode standing on the back. Anger sometimes welled up inside him because he didn't think it was fair. But he held his tongue thinking *Someday I'll get even.* Years later, he realized that experience helped prepare him for times, as an adult, when he felt something was not fair.

## Drought And Grasshoppers

Right on the tail of the Great Depression two other tragedies struck the central states. First was the plague of grasshoppers. Huge swarms of grasshoppers swept the country stripping every stalk of corn, every green leaf off plants and trees, leaving no crop and very little to eat. When you went outside it was difficult to walk without stepping on the plethora of insects. Your skin stung when grasshoppers smacked into you as they jumped.

The next year came the great drought. Blistering sun with temperatures above 100 degrees day after day marked the summer of 1936. Long periods of no rain created a dust bowl everywhere. Gusty winds stirred the dust into a hazy atmosphere that made the sun appear—in the middle of the day—white like the moon. Nothing would grow. Vegetation dried up. Livestock shriveled with little to eat or drink. Good food for people was even scarce. Everyone was convinced the end of the world was coming.

Finally, rain came and things started turning around.

## High School

High school days were not fun for Al. He had to work to stay in school. During his last two years of high school he and his younger sister, Alta Mae, rented a room in Eureka where they lived during the week, going home only on weekends. He had just one pair of pants he wore every day. When he went home on weekends his mother would wash them for the next week. To pay his rent he worked in a grocery store/gas station. Consequently, he could never even attend football and basketball games, much less participate in them.

In 1936, President Franklin D. Roosevelt organized the

National Youth Authority (NYA), a government program in which needy youth could work for pay.

Al applied and was given the responsibility to clean certain parts of the high school. While he was sweeping the gym, basketball players walked through making snide remarks and snickering about his menial tasks. His face flushed with embarrassment and anger. But in his heart he determined *Just wait, I won't always be doing this. I'll work hard and get someplace!*

## Near Tragedy

"Come on, Prince, let's go!" Al whooped, as he jumped onto Prince bareback, galloping into the pasture to round up the cattle for milking. Suddenly startled by a rabbit, Prince jumped sideways and Al was tossed through the air into a patch of cactus—striking his head on a rock.

His mother was in the garden picking lettuce for  dinner when she saw Prince gallop into the barnyard without Al. Distressed, she gathered the others to help. Frantically searching the countryside, they finally found him walking around dazed. A concussion had disoriented him. They walked him back home, picked the cactus stickers out of his clothes and skin and bandaged his cuts. Soon he was back to normal.

This is when 14-year-old Al began to think about  eternity. *What if I had been killed when my head hit that rock?* The thought frightened him.

He asked his mother, "How can you know you'll go to heaven when you die?" She didn't know how to explain it to him.

Distraught, he asked his teacher the same question. She didn't have an answer either. It seemed that no one could answer to his satisfaction. That question plagued him for years.

By high school graduation, Al knew he did not want to stay on the farm. *There has to be something better,* he pondered. All their hard work had yielded his family nothing but a meager living. He had bigger dreams.

One day, grungy with sweat and dust, he trudged in from the field and saw a stranger dressed in a suit. The representative from Central Business College in Kansas City greeted him.

"I came to offer you a scholarship to our school," the stranger proposed. "You can attend our college, deferring tuition payments until you have a job." He promised to find a home where Al could work for room and board. The final promise was that the college would help him find a job when he was ready.

Al was excited! It sounded too good to be true! *This is my chance to leave the farm and become wealthy,* Al contemplated.

## Arriving in Stockyards

Coming back to reality in the stockyards, Al was stunned with the brutal fact: *I don't have any idea where I am or where I should go.*

He gazed up at the skyscrapers, his mouth gaping in disbelief. Even though it was scary being all alone in this big, strange place, he was determined to not be intimidated.

His "home" would be with a middle-aged Jewish couple who had no children—except their dog—that indeed was their child. His job was to bathe and walk the dog, chauffeur his boss-lady, wash the car, do grocery shopping, do some cooking and cleaning. His boss was very demanding, looking down on him as a servant. For weeks Al had no time for anything but going to school, studying, and pleasing his boss.

Al was happy to start a new life. But homesickness overwhelmed him. At times he wanted to just give up and go back to the farm. He missed the open country and his horse. He missed his mother's homemade bread and her hugs.

A good student from the beginning, he learned shorthand quickly and his typing was fast and accurate. In those days for a man to be an Executive Secretary was considered a good position.

Although his sister, Leona, had come to Kansas City before him and now had a job, Al could hardly get away from his "house job" to see her. Leona had made friends who had taken her to Central Bible Church. She had heard the gospel and had received Jesus as her Savior.

Some of Al's classmates also attended the same church. At lunchtime they shared Bible verses and their experiences with the Lord while they ate brown-bag lunches. Al was drawn to them. He watched them. They radiated joy. He was beginning to wonder what made them different.

That same hunger to know how to get to heaven was still troubling him. He knew he lacked what these kids had. Finally, he was able to go to church where he saw Leona.

There, Dr. Walter L. Wilson's preaching held him spellbound. The Bible came alive the way he read it. He spoke with such wisdom and compassion. His audience was captivated by his stories and teaching.

Dr. Wilson preached from the Bible clearly—things Al had never heard before.

"All have sinned and come short of the glory of God." (Romans 3:23)

"The wages of sin is death but the gift of God is eternal life through Jesus Christ our Lord." (Romans 6:23)

He stated that even though we are all sinners, God loved us so much He sent His Son Jesus to earth to take our death penalty for us. All we need to do is receive Jesus into our heart, ask Him to forgive us our sin, and He will give us eternal life.

After listening to Dr. Wilson's messages for several months, on Easter Sunday night, 1940, conviction overwhelmed Al. Rushing home after church, he knelt beside his bed and prayed for Jesus to forgive him for his sins and give him eternal life.

He instantly became a new person! Ecstatic joy flowed over him! Now he knew he was on his way to heaven. "…old things have passed away and all things have become new." (2 Corinthians 5:17) Almost immediately he had a burden for the teenagers he had gone to high school with. He wondered if they would hear about Jesus as he had.

He hungered for the Word of God. Each week he longed for Sunday to come when he could go hear a message from God's Word and have fellowship with other Christians. He soon became active in the youth group.

The events of the last few months were about to make drastic changes in the course of his life.

# CHAPTER 2

# Vidy

A blustery north wind fetching feathery snowflakes seemed a perfect setting for the day before Christmas Eve. But it didn't provide much of a welcome for the doctor trudging through the drifts into the tiny home of Paul and Lucille Hughes in south Kansas City. After delivering a little baby girl the doctor insisted: "I need a name for the birth certificate."

It seems there was a controversy. A daughter born two years earlier had been named for her two grandmothers, Olive Elizabeth. Daddy now wanted this one to receive an old family name that had been passed down for several generations—Elvira.

"Well, if you insist on naming her that, you can just give her the other name, too!" Mother said, resigned.

The doctor offered, "My name is George. How about calling her Georgia? I can't leave without completing this birth certificate and I must go!" So it was. Georgia Elvira. That was my noble entrance into this world on December 23, 1923.

Shortly after my birth the homesteaded farm of Daddy's grandparents was divided among the survivors. So we moved to Daddy's inherited land where he built a house. This was in the Rosedale district of Kansas City, Kansas. During the next five years two brothers, Paul Tucker and Earl Lee completed our family.

"Elvira" was hard to say so my two-year-old sister called me "Sister." Soon the rest of the family shortened my name to the "Vi" in the middle of Elvira. Somewhere along the line the "dy" was added so around home I answered to "Vidy." At school I was Elvira. I hated it—especially when some of my best friends couldn't pronounce it correctly. When I graduated from high school I declared, "I will never tell my real name again." And I didn't for many years.

Ours was a loving family with wonderful parents who taught us traditional morals. A coal-burning stove in the living room provided heat for our three-room house in the winter. We were happy to have running water in the kitchen and electric lights. A private "path" led to our two-hole privy at the back of our large lot. We weren't concerned that we lived in a small house. Bath time on Saturday nights meant putting a round galvanized wash tub in the kitchen and pouring in a couple of inches of warm water heated in the teakettle.

Dinner together every evening was a fun time. Daddy always repeated the same prayer before we ate: "Our Father, thank you for this food. Bless us. Amen." Simple. But it gave us respect for God. I loved to save stories to tell at the dinner table so everyone could hear. Daddy was strict on table manners. "Please" and "Thank you" were necessary words for us.

We were taught all the basic skills in life, plus more—like sewing, cleaning, and cooking for the girls and building and mechanics for the boys. We were encouraged to always continue to learn. I am so thankful my parents considered these things important.

Because my birthday was in December, I started kindergarten four months before my fifth birthday so I was always the youngest in my class.

Every Sunday morning Daddy polished our shoes to a shiney gloss while Mother helped us get ready. Then off we went to Sunday School at the local Methodist Church—each with a nickel to put in the offering. I learned all the stories in the Bible. I knew about Adam and Eve; Joseph and his coat of many colors; Noah and the Ark; Jonah and the whale. I even knew about Jesus' birth—although I didn't know what a virgin was. I knew He died and rose again and walked on the water and performed miracles. But, to me, these were only stories. I never questioned "Why?" I believed the Bible just because I was taught to believe it—even though I didn't understand what it said.

My mother's parents lived on a small farm near Edgerton, KS and we kids loved to stay with them. Our grandpa, whom we called "Poppy," was a strawberry farmer. Each May the strawberries started to ripen about the time school was out. We packed our bags and headed for the farm. Poppy paid us kids three cents for picking a quart box. He was a hard taskmaster. His rules were that you could not step on a plant or put any rotten berry in the box and you had to pick *every* ripe berry. No matter how hard I tried, turning over every leaf; Poppy's piercing eyes could find berries I missed. Picking berries for hours at a time on your knees in the hot sun was hard work, but we took pride in how many boxes we could pick.

Grandma taught me to make my first dress at age eight. My fabric was printed flour sacks. I proudly wore my new dress to the neighbors' house when we helped cook for wheat threshers. I still have the quilt she taught me to make at age nine. I cut and sewed all the pieces by myself, using her treadle machine but she helped quilt it—in fact she probably did most of the quilting.

Grandma also taught me to bake my first pie—made from rhubarb out of their garden. My piecrust was flaky like Grandma's. At a Campfire Girl cake-baking contest when I was 12, I received the blue ribbon.

During the depression "hobos" were common because of lack of work. These were not necessarily lazy or bad men—but were decent men looking for work. Hobos would hop on a freight train and travel trying to find work. Often they would go to a house and ask for food.

"Could you spare a bite to eat?" the hobo asked my mother when she answered his knock on the door.

"Let me see if I can find something," she answered. "You can sit here on the porch." She never invited them in but, even though we didn't have much, when a beggar came to our door asking for food, Mother always found something to fix for them. This taught us, by example, to give.

By the time I was a teenager, Daddy had enlarged our house, including a bedroom, bathroom, and a basement with a furnace. We finally got a telephone! High school days were great! My friends were the "in" crowd at school. I was elected to several offices; had parts in plays and was in the marching band.

"Your mother is pretty!" my friends told me. I was so proud! She was PTA President several times while we were in school so she was very visible. While we were in high school Mother and Daddy were usually around—working in the refreshment stand at football games and wherever they were needed in other activities.

A new pastor, Rev. Werner, came to our church about this time. Taking a special interest in the youth, he started youth meetings on Sunday evening. He led the meetings and was always the speaker. Afterward, he joined us at someone's house for fun. We kids thought he was nice, even though his hair was turning gray. But he made me mad when he told us we were sinners. I believed that if the good we did outweighed the bad we would go to heaven. I thought I was a pretty good girl and was doing fine, thank you.

"I'm not going back to church," I told my mother. "I don't like what Rev. Warner says."

"Try it a little longer," she encouraged me. So I complied.

After a while the Holy Spirit opened my eyes to the truth of God's Word. One Sunday I was really under conviction. The next day walking to school with a friend who had already been saved, I said, "What do you think? Should I pray for Jesus to save me?"

"Sure, go ahead. I did," she urged. That was all the encouragement I needed.

All that week I was miserable waiting for Sunday to come. I thought I had to be in church to receive Jesus and could hardly wait for Sunday.

That Sunday evening, February 27, 1938, I asked Jesus to come into my heart and forgive my sin. God took away the fears I had grown up with—of being burned in a fire, of drowning, and of being molested or captured by a bad man. He replaced my fears with His perfect peace. I was filled with a joy I had never known before. This was a life-changing experience. Soon my whole family knew the Lord.

Some of the old timers in the church wanted Rev. Werner out! So when he left we asked him, "Where can we go to hear preaching from the Bible like yours?" He sent us to Central Bible Church at 31st and Main, Kansas City, Mo.

We still did not own a car so we walked several blocks to the streetcar and transferred twice to go to church across town. This required an hour of travel each way for both morning and evening church. It was well worth it for the spiritual food we received.

We learned that Dr. Walter L. Wilson, a godly young physician, had organized this church around 1930. His remarkable Bible teaching was practical and relevant to everyday living. His greatest gift though was personal evangelism. His uncanny ability to turn any situation into a witnessing experience made him an incredible soul winner. Well known nationally as a Bible teacher and conference speaker, he had authored many Bible study books plus others that recounted his witnessing episodes.

Our family had not been attending Central Bible Church long when a new girl started coming. Since she had no family in town we invited her home for Sunday dinner. It became a habit for this girl, Leona Metsker, to come home with us.

"My brother, Al, graduated from high school and is coming to Kansas City to go to business school," she told us one Sunday as I was entering my junior year. I didn't tell anyone but I was eager to meet this country boy.

# CHAPTER 3

# Our Love Story

Al and I saw each other for the first time several months after his sister, Leona, told me about him. No sparks flew between us, but we promptly became friends. Al, along with Leona, became a friend of our whole family, coming home for dinner on Sundays when he could get away from his job. Al and I started sitting in church together and spent moments together as time permitted.

He was happy to finish school and start a job so he had more time for personal pursuits.

The ministry outreach possibilities at the church were almost limitless. Al and I both joined teams that ministered in nursing homes, rescue missions, orphanages, and jails. Not only did we young people have fun being together; we were developing our talents while serving the Lord.

## Here Am I

Over the Labor Day weekend—September 1940—a young evangelist, Clifford Lewis, taught a Bible Conference at church. At one of the meetings he spoke on Romans 12:1-2: "I beseech you therefore, brethren, by the mercies of God, that you present your bodies a living sacrifice, holy, acceptable unto God, which is your reasonable service. And be not conformed to this world: but be transformed by the renewing of your mind that you may prove what is that good, and acceptable, and perfect will of God."

The Holy Spirit used his stirring message to convince many of us young people to totally surrender our lives to God. Al and I both committed our lives to Christ that night. Al wanted so desperately to give himself to God that he went forward after the service and literally lay on the altar symbolic of sacrificing his body. From that time, our compelling desire was to follow in Jesus' steps.

In our most fanciful imagination we would never have dreamed what our relationship to that young, single evangelist would be in years to come!

## The World Scene

> "You're in the Army now
> You're not behind the plow
> You'll never get rich digging a ditch
> You're in the Army now"

These crafty words fit a catchy tune everybody was singing.

It was a psychological release from the heavy burden of war we all felt.

England and France were at war with Germany, and the United States was tooling up for defense. Most young men were being drafted for the military service including Al's brother, Lowell.

Exactly one month after Lowell entered the army, on December 7, 1941 Japan made a surprise attack on Pearl Harbor. United States declared war on Japan, Germany and Italy. Now the war was far-flung on various fronts, including the South Pacific, North Africa and much of Europe.

Al was a little younger so had not been called yet, but knew it was inevitable soon.

Lowell left his 1932 Plymouth for Al to drive.

"Hey, Al!" I flashed a friendly smile and sparkling eyes. "Could you take some of us in your car to the City Union Mission for a meeting Saturday night?"

He was thrilled to be asked.

At the mission we sang and gave our testimonies for those

homeless men but the preacher didn't show up. Mrs. Bulkley, Director of the mission since her husband's death, said, "You're going to have to preach, Al."

"Not me!" He objected. "I can't preach. I never have."

"You'll do just fine, honey," Mrs. Bulkley insisted, shoving his Bible into his hand and pushing him onto the platform.

What could he do?

He supported his shaking body with the rickety pulpit trying to remember exactly what he had heard Dr. Wilson preach. Breathing a prayer for "HELP" in his heart, he told the simple plan of salvation the best he could. Afterwards, men came for counseling and Al felt the surge of joy that comes from being used by God. That is how he started preaching.

## Al's First Job

Secretary to the President of Mid-Continent Airlines was his first job after Al finished his school. It was a fairly new company so he was entering on the ground floor. A year and a half later Mid-Continent became Braniff and moved their headquarters to Minneapolis. Al refused the offer to move to Minneapolis because he couldn't stand the thought of leaving his friends and the church.

By this time Al and I were spending quite a lot of time together. He started taking me home last after going on gospel team meetings together. It was fun just being together and we couldn't find enough time to talk to each other. We always ran out of time. At first we were just good friends. That began to change.

In January 1942, we started dating seriously. Winsteads Drive-In became our regular stop for one of their famous steakburgers and yummy frosty malts. A skyscraper soda for two was the most fun! (Yes, the original Winsteads on the Country Club Plaza that is still popular with teenagers today! Only "curb hops" came to your car and took your order back then.)

Now that he had a good job Al bought his first car, a 1936

black 4-door Buick Century. He was so proud of his "two-ton chariot" and loved to take me places in it. On Sundays we went to Sunday School and Church. We usually ate Sunday dinner with my family. During the afternoon we went to the park, the zoo, or almost anyplace where we could just be together. Then we returned to youth group and evening church.

Monday evening we took classes at Kansas City Bible College. Wednesday was prayer meeting at church. Thursday night we ministered someplace with the gospel team. Friday was a Bible study and Saturday nights were always busy with a church youth activity. That left only Tuesday night that we didn't go out together. That night we spent on the phone. We had so much fun. All of our time together was spent in church or some Christian activity. We were best friends. "Toots" was his special name of endearment for me. I liked it.

Being about the only fellow not in the army, Al became the male leader for the youth group. While leading the youth activities, God burdened him to reach further than the confines of the church. This bashful country boy was being transformed into the dynamic, motivated, charismatic leader he would be through his life.

## We're Engaged!

I was 19 on December 23, 1942. Two weeks later Al invited me to a special dinner date the next Saturday. It would be a wonderful evening—just the two of us. I suspected the reason for this special date.

But, he was like a little boy who couldn't wait to give his mama her birthday present. On the way home from prayer meeting on the preceding Wednesday evening, Al parked on a tree lined road, put his arm around me, told me he loved me and asked me to marry him. He just couldn't wait for Saturday! As part of the proposal he said, "God may call me to Africa as a missionary so don't say 'Yes' unless you are willing to go with me."

This was a moment I had dreamed of! There was no question in my mind. I loved him and I also had dedicated my life to God. Wherever He led we would go!

Al expected to be drafted into the army at any time, so we decided not to get married until after the war.

"I don't want you to be a war widow if anything should happen to me," he declared. We hated to say "good night" so we often sang—in our off-tune harmony—a line of the popular song, "Two sleepy people in dawn's early light, and too much in love to say 'good night'." Then we laughed.

"A little talk with Jesus makes it right, all right...." we heard the male quartet sing over the radio.

One Sunday afternoon Al and I were sitting in his two-ton chariot in Swope Park. Our regular Sunday afternoon routine was listening to "Young People's Church of the Air." A young evangelist, Percy Crawford, had started the national, weekly radio broadcast from Pennsylvania. There was nothing like it. The program had lively music by the male quartet and Percy preached a short powerful message.

Yes, we were sitting there in the park cuddled up in the front seat. The policeman didn't know we were listening to a gospel service. We weren't doing anything wrong.

"Move on!" he snapped. "You can't park here!" What he meant by "park" was not exactly what we were doing—but we obediently accommodated him.

## Criticism

As President of the youth group, Al later booked Percy Crawford and his quartet to come to Central Bible Church for a one-night youth meeting. The place was packed with around 500 people. Al was the emcee. The quartet sang lively gospel songs for 40 minutes. Then Percy preached a dynamic 20-minute gospel message. Forty-two young people came forward to receive Jesus that night. Al and I were ecstatic! This was his first taste of being in evangelism—which led to his starting Singspiration, the forerunner of Kansas City Youth For Christ.

Al felt honored when he was invited to attend the Deacons' and Elders' meeting the next Wednesday. He expected to be commended for generating a meeting where 42 young people were saved. Instead, they confronted him.

"What do you mean having a meeting like that with so much frivolous music and foolishness and only 20 minutes of preaching?" they scolded him.

He was speechless! He thought the meeting had been a wonderful success. How could the leaders be critical of winning people to Jesus? The men presented no encouraging words like: "We know your motives were good, but we believe you goofed." They only leveled harsh, critical accusations. He felt so rejected, alone and hurt. But in his heart he knew what he had done was right in God's eyes.

He learned how cruel people can be. Little did he know, at this point, that there would be other times in his ministry that he would be misunderstood, rejected and hurt for doing what he knew God wanted him to do.

Dr. Wilson was out of town so was not at this meeting. Later, he assured Al of his support for what he had done. Dr. Wilson traveled around the world speaking. In years to come, after we started Singspiration, he constantly suggested people or talent Al should book. Dr. Wilson was always a great encourager and mentor—a great man of God!

## Uncle Sam Wants You!

Al's heart pounded as he opened a letter from Uncle Sam just four months after our engagement.

"Greetings! You are requested to be at the Ft. Leavenworth induction center at 6 A.M. on May 26 for your physical examination and swearing in."

We had expected the summons, but were not ready for it. I went to work that morning where I was a secretary at the North American Bomber Plant, a defense industry. Al, by this time, worked there also on the airplane production line.

The war was the turning point for all of our generation, forcing us from national complacency to total involvement in conflicts in areas of the world that previously we had only vaguely known about. Our nation's commitment in these wars touched every family in many ways. All plans for the future were put on hold.

About 1:30 P.M. I received a personal call at work—an unheard of thing in those days. I was frightened. It was Al calling from Ft. Leavenworth. "I was rejected!" he shouted.

I knew I must be hearing wrong. He was physically a perfect specimen of an all-American farm boy.

"They found a calcified spot on the X-ray of my lung." he continued. "Because of the possibility of it becoming active TB, they rejected me and said they would call me back in six months for another X-ray." We couldn't believe it. (Now, we believe it was the providence of God. He never had any lung problems.)

My emotions flip-flopped. On one hand I was excited that I didn't have to say "good bye" at this time but was terrified by the possibility that he may get TB, which was then a life-threatening disease.

By that evening he had thought it through. "Let's get married NOW!" he begged.

"We can at least have six months together." We decided to set the date for one month from that day—June 26. My parents agreed, if a consultation with a medical doctor gave them fair assurance that TB was not a strong possibility. We were excited! But I was overwhelmed at the thought of preparing for a big wedding in such a short time.

# CHAPTER 4

# Beginning Life Together

## First Singspiration

I'll carry this box of songbooks and you bring those programs," Al told me as we unloaded the props and supplies we needed for our first Singspiration. We had worked hard to get everything ready for this historic night.

The "songbooks" were mimeographed words to gospel choruses that we had stapled into bright blue cardboard covers. We had booked talent for the program as well as a song leader, a speaker and pianists.

It was Saturday, June 19, 1943, one week before our wedding. Our first Singspiration was held in a downtown service men's center. There was no way to know how many people would show up. We had put our ad in *The Kansas City Star* and spread the word through our friends and invitations to church youth groups. Then we prayed.

The enthusiasm of one hundred fifty youth who gathered to sing and praise God that night elated us. No one imagined that this was the birth of what would become one of the nation's most effective local youth ministries—the result of Al's and my burning passion to reach young people with the gospel.

A Sing-along was a major part of the program, so having a good song leader and pianist was vital. We chose Darrell Freleigh (pronounced "freely"), a young local pastor and graduate of Moody Bible Institute, to be our song leader. His enthusiasm, creativity, and contagious "Pepsodent smile" (as Al called it) combined with his golden tenor voice was unbeatable. Al always said, "Darrell can get singing out of an old pine stump."

We sang contemporary choruses and some well-known

hymns. When Darrell led the hymns they were lively. One of his innovations was when we sang "One Day!"

When we came to the chorus that says: "Rising, He justified freely forever," he joshed; "My name—Freleigh—is in this song but it is for all of us. When we get to that word, each of you insert your own name instead of mine." What a jumble! Everybody laughed! For nearly every song, he had some kind of fun variation! You had to pay close attention or you might goof up.

Captivating special music, testimonies and a skit provided "entertainment with a purpose" before the short gospel message and invitation. Bob Shaper, our friend and a student at Bob Jones University, was the speaker. Our joyful reward was when several were saved at that first Singspiration.

Enthusiasm was rampant.

"This was fun! Let's do it again!" those who attended begged.

We announced the next one for one month later to be held in the Wornall Road Baptist Church.

"Bring your friends next month," Al challenged the crowd. "Get all the youth from your church—but also bring unchurched friends, and pray for them."

Not even a seed of an idea in our minds revealed how that evening would change our lives.

How could we produce a rally just one week before our wedding when we had such a short time to prepare anyway? I don't know. When I look back, I wonder how we possibly did many of the things we did. Youth. Determination. Hard work. Faith in God. Those are my only explanations.

### We're Married

"Right here's a clean spot to drink," Bob Shaper, Al's best man, joked as he handed the dirty cup of water to Al who thought he was dying of thirst. It was our wedding night and Al was in the little back room of the church with the groomsmen, waiting for the ceremony to begin. The un-air-conditioned church was jammed with around 500 people on that hot Saturday evening, June 26, 1943. Dr. Walter L. Wilson married us in a beautiful ceremony followed by a garden reception in my parents' yard.

We were such faithful church attendees, it never entered our mind that we could miss church the next morning. So we were there. Sunday evening we were there also. We both had to be back on the job on Monday morning. There was no time for a honeymoon in this war-torn time. We felt privileged to even be able to get married. Many couples had to wait until after the war.

Housing of any kind was difficult to find so we felt especially blessed to rent a little house. The 83-year-old landlady lived in the basement of this quaint little house that was filled with ancient furnishings. We were extremely happy. Our strong feelings were that all our married life should be a continuation of our courtship. We determined that nothing would change in the way we loved, honored, and respected each other. We wanted our honeymoon to last a lifetime. And it did.

Gasoline rationing made car pools necessary. Only one out of six people was awarded gasoline ration stamps for transportation to work. The times of our separate shifts plus working in distantly separated buildings made riding together impossible. Al's ride came at 5:30 A.M. and mine came at 6:30. We worked nine hours a day, six days a week. Everyone did during the war. Those 54 hours actually required 66 hours counting travel time each way.

The pace was exhausting.

Preparation time for the Singspiration was hard to find. Phone calls. Printing. Mailings. Booking talent. We were bogged down! The solution? I quit my job so I could work on Singspiration during the day, thus relieving both our loads. Al and I would discuss what needed to be done, then I did it while he was at work. A great idea!

When we married, we chose Matthew 6:33 for our life verse.

"But seek ye *first* the kingdom of God and His righteousness, and all these things shall be added unto you." (emphasis added) To us it meant to put God *first* in all we did, looked at, listened to, thought about, planned, said, or dreamed—in every area of our life. We tried to live our lives daily with this measuring stick.

Shortly after we were married, Al and I started the Navigator memory course. This blessed us. Nothing takes the place of hiding God's Word in your heart. Once committed to memory, God promised to "bring it to our remembrance" when we needed it.

## Mother's Cancer

In April 1942, when Al's mother was only 48, she had radical breast cancer surgery performed at the Eureka Hospital. Six weeks of X-ray treatments in a Wichita Hospital left her nearly debilitated.

Her condition continued to worsen and the kids went home to see her as often as possible. Traveling 200 miles in those days was a major trip. Gas rationing made it even more difficult. They didn't have a phone, so besides visits, mail was our only communication. By the time Al and I were engaged Al's mother was pretty well confined to bed and had a caregiver to help her.

A week after our wedding, we drove with his sisters and brother-in-law to Al's parents' farm near Eureka, KS. Tears cut furrows through his mother's cheeks when we modeled our wedding clothes for her. Our hearts broke because we knew she would not be with us long.

Just two weeks later, we were all gathered around her bed in the living room of their little farm home, and sorrowfully watched her take her last breath. As hard as it was, we were thankful that her long months of terrible suffering were ended and we knew she was at peace in heaven.

We especially hurt for Al's dad, who would live way out in

the country by himself. But he wasn't a quitter and he was soon back in the Eureka Methodist Church singing bass in the choir.

## Our First House

"We're going to have a baby!" we excitedly told our land-lady a year later.

"You have to move out. I'm not having a baby around here." In her senile mind she didn't understand that it would be months away. She was getting crotchety.

It's amazing how the Lord uses circumstances in our lives to get us where He wants us. He seemed to say to us: "Don't throw your money away on rent any longer. Start an invest-ment in a house."

We found a cute little two-bedroom house with a basement for $3,750. For a down payment, we borrowed money from my parents and Al's dad. Monthly payments were $27.50. We moved shortly after our first anniversary—but we didn't have much to move since our other place had been furnished.

We found a used kitchen stove for $10. My mother bought a card table and two chairs at a second-hand store for $1 each. My parents had an old bed they gave us. The living room was bare except for a folding canvas cot covered with a pretty comforter that was a wedding gift. That was it!

But, we were happy as two kids playing house! This was our own little home and we loved it! Other furnishings were added as we could afford them.

I continued to work hard handling all the details of the ministry under Al's direction. Our house was often filled in the evenings with friends who came to help make posters. We learned to silk-screen posters to display in stores and churches.

On other nights people would be all over our floors stuff-ing envelopes, stamping and sorting mail. Sometimes the gang would have a planning meeting or make decorations for an event. We had no leisure time—but we loved what we did!

Because the living room was often too small, we expanded it by removing a partition between the living room and front bedroom. Then we dug—by hand with a shovel and wheelbarrow—a 12'x24' addition on our basement and laid concrete blocks for the walls. On this foundation Al built another bedroom and enlarged the kitchen. This was Al's first building project. My dad gave him direction and taught him all about building. The larger basement made room for a ping pong table. What an improvement to our little house!

This was only the beginning!

# CHAPTER 5

# Singspiration Grows

Although Singspiration spawned from the youth group at Central Bible Church, we were determined that it would be denominationally neutral, yet work together with all Bible-preaching churches. Al longed for unity and cooperation between churches. Until now, mostly jealousy and criticism of each other prevailed. God used our ministry to bring churches together.

The crowd more than doubled for our second Singspiration held at the Wornall Road Baptist Church. Linwood Presbyterian Church was the scene of our next one. Richard Halverson, a new Wheaton College graduate who would later become Chaplain of the U. S. Senate, had recently become assistant pastor there. Dick and Al became buddies and Dick was a great booster and encourager.

For several months we moved our Singspiration from church to church in an effort to not show partiality. Soon we realized it was almost impossible to effectively communicate a change of location each month to crowds that had grown to more than one thousand.

After much prayer, serious thought and consultation with others, Al formed an executive committee of seven reliable young people from seven different denominations—his next step in uniting churches. The purpose of Singspiration was to reach out with the gospel to the unchurched, get them into a Bible-believing church, and to provide a wholesome place for Christian youth to go on Saturday nights with an emphasis on evangelism and spiritual growth.

Al was still employed in defense work—now head of the accounting department at Pratt and Whitney Aircraft Engine

Plant. His experience in accounting would prove valuable in years to come. He was a good businessman.

After a few months, we started having Singspiration downtown every Saturday night in the Grand Avenue Temple at 9th and Grand. Although the Grand Avenue Temple was a Methodist Church, it was considered a neutral auditorium. Rent was $50 a week. The pastor, Dr. Philip Bohi, was very cooperative and friendly. His teenage daughter received Jesus at one of our meetings. Transportation by car during the war was difficult to find. Because public transportation went downtown from every area of the city, it was a good location.

A room at the front of the auditorium was open for informal prayer before every Singspiration. Everyone was welcome but especially all staff and program personnel. It was a "come-when-you-can-leave-when-you-must" prayer time. Al made the announcement:

"Hey, Kids! Don't forget to come to the prayer meeting before Singspiration every Saturday night. We pray in the room to the right of the stage. Remember, PRAYER CHANGES THINGS!"

Al was a fireball emcee who started every rally by running with all his might onto the stage and shouting his welcome. "This is Kansas City Youth For Christ. Let's stand and sing!" This became a tradition. His enthusiastic introductions, spirited applause, and contagious smile made every performer a winner! Certain things became his trademarks in those beginning days—like wearing bright ties, red socks, brown and white wing-tipped shoes and classy sport coats. That was high style then. He insisted I starch his shirts stiff and iron them smooth. Every Saturday I pressed his pants with a firm crease. His shoes were always shined. He felt it was important to always look sharp.

Our fast-paced programs had a theatrical flair and burst with variety as we used spotlights, curtains and fan-fares. The auditorium exploded with applause during the evening often calling for an encore. Applause was unheard of in churches in those days.

Our service men, in the Army, Navy, Marines and Air Force, were affectionately honored at every Singspiration as we stood and sang a song written for the time:

God bless our boys wherever they may be,
God bless our boys on land or on the sea,
Or in the air, we follow with our prayer,
God bless our boys! God bless our boys!

This song was followed with a passionate prayer for safety and God's blessing on all servicemen. Tears often flowed freely as people remembered their loved ones or friends who were away at war. People never knew when they would get word that their loved one had been killed.

Singspiration always ended with a gospel message and an invitation for those who did not know Jesus as Savior to receive Him and be born again. Al made it clear: No matter the subject of the message or what clever or heart-tugging illustrations were used, one thing must always be included—a simple explanation of the gospel. If the gospel was not explained clearly, how could we expect people to make that decision? We allowed no compromise!

Since we had both grown up in churches where the gospel was not preached, we were determined to never have a meeting of any kind without giving God's plan of salvation clearly—including an invitation for people to be born again.

Al's question was simple. "Did you ever see a salesman tell all about his product or service and not draw his presentation to a conclusion? What would be his purpose? There has to be a reason for what you do—or why do it? I am a salesman. I sell Jesus—eternal life. How futile would it be if I never made a sale? I ask God to use me to win people to Jesus. I pray believing. He promises to answer. I preach expecting people to respond positively to the gospel by the power of the Holy Spirit. I believe what Jesus said."

"If you ask anything in my name, I will do it." (John 14:14) Al almost never preached without people coming to Christ. He didn't preach in his own strength but in the power of God.

Every party, hayride, banquet—no matter what the occasion—for our fifty years of ministry this was our policy. Al called it "a party with a purpose." God blessed. Not even a dozen times in all those years did we have a meeting without salvation decisions. This is not to our credit but God's. He promised that His Word would not return void. The Holy Spirit is the one who convicts and draws all men to God. We are exhorted only to be faithful to proclaim God's message.

The glorious climax of every Singspiration was when many came to the prayer room. A counselor personally talked to and prayed with each one to lead them to Jesus.

This brought the need for the first thing Al organized after the Singspiration.

## Soul-Winning Class

One of our biggest burdens was our desire to make sure people had assurance of their salvation. At many churches, if an invitation was given and someone came forward, he or she was merely voted into the church. No one showed the person scripture verses explaining how to become a child of God. We feared that thousands of "church members" had not experienced the new birth.

But how can you share with someone else what you don't understand yourself?

So Al developed what he called a Soul-Winning Course. The simple plan used several Bible verses with explanations to help people understand how to accept Christ.

This goes back to Al's theory—if you have a strong decision, you'll have a strong Christian. If the decision is weak, spiritual growth will be slow.

Al first taught this Soul Winning Class in 1944 to 40-50 eager learners in a large home in central city. The purpose was two-fold—to train counselors for our prayer room on Saturday nights and to help them become personal witnesses in their everyday life.

He believed bringing a new baby into God's family was every bit as serious as a physical birth so it was important that there be no casualties. We prayed that every convert would go home with complete assurance of his or her salvation and become a growing Christian.

Through the years teaching the Soul Winning Course has been a staple of our ministry. It was our goal that every teenager involved in KCYFC learn how to lead their friends to Christ using the proper Scriptures. A large percent have done this.

Eventually the name changed to Basic Counseling Course and then to Basic Training for Evangelism—but it is the same course. Scores of thousands have taken and used it. The whole premise is "Teens telling teens!"

## First Baby

Saturday night, a little past midnight, we arrived home after finishing all the details at the end of a great Singspiration. More than 25 teenagers had come to the prayer room where they prayed to receive Jesus as their Savior. We were evaluating all that had happened that evening and feeling contentment from the way we saw God work.

Suddenly we realized it might be time to call the doctor. After discussing the situation with him, Dr. Singleton told us to hurry to the hospital where he would meet us. When we arrived a nurse was waiting with a wheelchair for me. She told Al to sign me in and she would rush me to delivery. Before long a darling little girl, whom we named Martha Jane, was born—November 20, 1944. We were ecstatic!

Having a baby didn't keep me from continuing my ministry

responsibilities. By the time Martha was a few weeks old, I bundled her up in her buggy and pushed her six blocks to the bus stop. A gas station owner kindly let me park the buggy at his station while I took the bus downtown. My stops for ministry business included the printer and *The Kansas City Star* newspaper. The buggy was waiting for the return trip.

## Step of Faith

All this time God was working in Al's heart. He desperately wanted to work full-time in the ministry. We prayed earnestly about it. But the war was still in full swing and he was required to work in a defense job.

Between all the work he did in the evenings and weekends and what I did, we were really working full-time in the ministry. Several of our pastor friends encouraged Al to quit his job and devote full time to reaching teenagers.

Because they were grateful for our outreach to teens, a group of pastors wrote letters to the Draft Board telling them that Al would be more valuable for the good of our country in youth ministry than working in a defense plant. They asked for a permanent deferment for him to go into the ministry full-time.

We prayed continually that God's will be done.

Al told his boss what the pastors had done. "If I get the deferment I will quit and go into the ministry full time."

"That would be a foolish mistake," his boss tried to convince him. "If you stay I'll get a good increase in salary for you."

"No amount of money will keep me from making this move if I get the opportunity." Al knew it was the devil's trick to try to entice him with money. As usual, Al knew what he wanted and he wouldn't give up until he got it.

But the draft was not our only obstacle. What would we live on? He had a family to provide for now. So he formed an Advisory Board of influential Christian businessmen who shared his vision to be financial advisors.

We cheered, cried, and shouted for joy when the letter of deferment from the draft board arrived in early May 1945.

The amount of salary the Advisory Board felt the organization could handle was only half of what his defense job paid. It would be tough, but we were willing to trust God to supply our needs as He had promised in His Word. We were convinced we should take this step of faith.

We stood on promises in God's Word: "My God shall supply all your needs according to His riches in glory by Christ Jesus." Phil. 4:19 and Matthew 6:33 "....all these things shall be added unto you." and many others. We stepped out by faith with no security from anyone but God. He was all we needed.

A few days later, the phone rang.

"This is Torrey Johnson in Chicago, Al," the voice announced, with his excitement flowing through the phone, "I've been hearing good things about your ministry there. I know you're having large crowds and that many churches are involved. I praise the Lord for all those kids that are being saved!"

Torrey Johnson was a young, fireball preacher who had started a similar ministry in Chicago. He would later become the first President of Youth For Christ International.

"Al," he continued, "Youth ministries like yours are springing up all over the country. So we're going to have a meeting to pull all these organizations together and you've got to be there!"

He gave Al the details of the organizational convention to be held the second week of July at Winona Lake, Indiana (near Chicago). The big meetings would be held in the Billy Sunday Tabernacle.

"Sell your car! Sell your house! Mortgage your wife! Do whatever you must do to make it! You've GOT to be there!"

Torrey's enthusiasm was infectious.

We were stunned. Our heads were spinning. How could we afford this trip? But it was the chance of a lifetime. We had to go! We started praying and dreaming. God's timing is so perfect! If that call had come before his deferment, we couldn't have gotten away. Al wanted me to go with him so my mother cared for our seven-month-old Martha.

## Second Anniversary

Before our trip to Winona Lake, we took another big step of faith. We rented the beautiful Kansas City Music Hall for a "Victory Rally" to celebrate our second anniversary on May 19, 1944. This beautiful auditorium seated 2,600—twice the number we usually had on Saturday nights. What an exciting rally it was!

"FUN IN TEEN SINGING" was a headline in the *Sunday Kansas City Star*.

> "Teenage enthusiasm and full-throated song vibrated along the walls and rolled down the aisles of the Music Hall last night when 2,600 young voices blended in a Singspiration. The young people gave their answer to both the juvenile delinquency problem and "what to do on Saturday nights" with wild bursts of "Onward Christian Soldiers," and "In the Sweet By and By."

The caption under a picture of a sea of bright teenagers standing and holding hands read: "At one point the youthful singers were solemn and silent for a moment as they held hands and dedicated themselves to better, fuller Christian lives."

The Paseo High School band played a 20-minute concert before leading into "Onward Christian Soldiers" when the R.O.T.C. Color Guard marched in with the flags. The program included a girls' quintet, a trumpet trio, and "Dr. I. Q." roaming through the audience with a roving mic asking clever questions. Dr. John Brown, Sr., founder and president of John Brown University, was the main speaker of the evening. A number received Jesus as Savior. God blessed and it was a true VIC-TORY Rally!

## Youth For Christ International Born

Al quit his job just in time to take off for the great meeting at Winona Lake. We rode the train to Chicago and transferred to another going to Warsaw, Indiana, near Winona Lake. When we got off the train at this small-town station, a jovial older man greeted us.

"Hi, I'm Homer Rodeheaver. Would you like a ride to Winona Lake?"

We were flabbergasted! Homer Rodeheaver had been the world renowned song leader/music director for the late Evangelist Billy Sunday for 20 years. "Rodey," as everyone called him wrote music, played trombone solos, sang, and directed choirs. We were honored to be driven the three miles by this distinguished gentleman.

Every well-known Christian leader and minister of the day was there—the Presidents of Wheaton College, John Brown University, Bob Jones University, Moody Bible Institute, Bible Institute of Los Angeles, Taylor University, Northwestern Schools, etc.

All the great Bible Conference speakers such as Dr. M. R. DeHaan, Dr. Donald Barnhouse, Dr. Harry Ironside and others were there.

Others were there who would become well known within a few years, like Billy Graham, Cliff Barrows, George Beverly Shea, Bob Cook, and many others. Leaders of youth ministries like ours from Detroit, Portland, DesMoines, Los Angeles, San Diego, Grand Rapids, Indianapolis, and others came. It was a rare, great gathering of God's servants. And we were privileged to be a part!

Winona Lake Conference center was open all summer. Christian people from across the country came regularly for Bible Conferences. This week, however, was the biggest ever.

Probably three or four thousand people attended the evening rallies.

The Billy Sunday Tabernacle was a rustic high-roofed frame building with a sawdust floor and sturdy wooden benches that seated 5,000-6,000. Open windows on three sides provided air circulation. The huge stage could hold a 750-voice choir or handle dramatic productions. Bright flags from all states and some foreign countries adorned the stage.

We never knew Billy Sunday, but his ministry was legend. His home was there and his wife, "Ma Sunday" they called her, invited us to their home, which was like a museum full of pictures and memorabilia. Even though she was quite old by this time she was a gracious hostess. She came the short distance from their home to the tabernacle for all our evening rallies.

All the leaders at the convention were "race horses"—motivated people. What a thrill to be a part of organizational plans. The business meetings during the day were held in the Westminster Hotel on the campus. Often, when an important decision was to be made these dedicated men stopped and called on God to give direction. Many times a day, we stopped to pray.

The leaders talked about youth movements of bygone days like YMCA, Christian Endeavor and Epworth League. They pointed out that some organizations had started as strong evangelistic movements and gradually lost their original passion until they had become merely athletic or service organizations.

"We would rather this organization die than for it to lose its fire," they all vowed.

The name chosen for the new organization was Youth For Christ, International.

The leaders felt that if the name of Christ was included, it would safeguard its falling away.

Many of the wives spent their time together in various activities but I was so involved in our ministry Al wanted me with him. I attended every business meeting and prayer meeting with him. Several other wives were involved as I was but not many. I was so happy to be able to serve the Lord with Al and share in the victories. One of the most memorable parts of each annual YFCI Convention was the all-night prayer meetings. Peter Dyneka, President of the Slavic Gospel Mission, was in charge. A little roly-poly Russian fireball, he became famous for his enthusiastic quote: "Little prayer, little power. Much prayer, much power!" The prayer meetings started around 10:30 after the evening Rally and lasted until the wee hours of the morning. We were all on our knees praying all that time—not just talking about prayer.

Dr. Bob Cook, who became the second YFCI President, often stood and walked around through the crowd loudly proclaiming: "Talk to God in the first person. 'Lord, forgive *me*'—not *us*. 'Lord, help *me*'—not *us*. Name your failures to God. Get real with God." He helped bring revival to everyone's heart during those prayer meetings—an unforgettable experience.

Al was elected to the Board of Directors that very first year and became vice-president of Mid-Central States—Kansas, Missouri, Nebraska and Iowa. At times Oklahoma, Colorado and Wyoming were included. This was a volunteer job performed from the heart. His responsibility was to help start ministries in this area. He contacted churches and leaders searching for local men to carry the burden of reaching young people with the gospel in their cities. As Area VP (after the end of gas rationing) he traveled thousands of miles a year. But, he always was aware that the Kansas City ministry took first priority. We were thrilled as ministries sprung up in scores of both large and small cities in our area. This was the beginning of KCYFC being a missionary organization because we never received any financial aid from YFCI or the local areas Al helped.

The fellowship, challenge, and blessing we received each year at the YFCI conventions motivated us to reach higher goals.

# CHAPTER 6

# New Name — KCYFC

We came home from that first convention more fired up than ever. We had filled notebooks with clever and innovative ideas we could incorporate into our programs. God was our leader and we were out to reach all the young people in Kansas City and the surrounding area with the gospel of Christ.

After the convention, we changed our name to Kansas City Youth For Christ and gradually started to call our Saturday night gatherings "Rally."

Now that we worked full-time, some of our dreams started to become realities. Al rented a small suite of offices on the top floor of the Temple Building alongside the Grand Avenue Temple where our Rallies were held. He used to joke, "I'm a big shot now. I have hundreds of people working under me." His first secretary, Bertie Roberts, the daughter of a Presbyterian minister, carried a huge load. Now that Al and Bertie were on the job, I no longer did the routine details I had carried since the beginning.

## Rally

The auditorium was filled every Saturday night with 1,000-1,200 enthusiastic youth. When there was a special program we could crowd in about 1,500 by putting chairs in the aisles, in front and on the back of the stage.

Al almost never missed emceeing a Rally. I believe sick headaches were his "thorn in the flesh." If he got one on Saturday, it never kept him from doing his job at the Rally. He got ready and I drove him to the Rally. When he arrived the headache miraculously left. As soon as the invitation was over, the headache would return. This happened many times through the years. God was faithful! Al was persistent and would never give up.

I also was at every Rally except when I was in the hospital for the birth of a baby or if one of our children was sick. The teenagers loved our kids. From when they were small, teens carried them around before and after the Rally. When they got in grade school, the teens included them in their crowd.

We always enjoyed taking our children with us—but when we had three small ones, it was a real treat for us when we occasionally had a sitter or when my parents kept them. We had an evening alone—with 1,200 teenagers.

Bill "Hi" Johnson was one of our two spirited song leaders. "Hi" was his nickname because he was six feet, nine inches tall—almost a foot taller than Al. Al jested, "Hi and I are the long and short of it!"

George Philgreen and Mary Shaper played the twin grand pianos. Nelson Reagan, a young Baptist minister, played a comical quizmaster, Dr. IQ, who roamed through the audience generating lots of laughs. Bill Baum, a German-born Jew who had escaped from Nazi Germany to the United States, and had become a born-again Christian while serving in the U.S. Army, did a witty segment called "Slogan of the Week." Being of small stature, curly hair and a mustache gave him a whimsical aura. His German/Jewish/English accent along with clever illusions and object lessons made his part a favorite.

Fast moving. Variety Packed. Teen music. Enthusiasm. These words described our Rallies—all building to the end goal of presenting the gospel. The climax of the evening was when scores of youth came forward at the gospel invitation!

## We Win!

On May 7, 1945, Germany surrendered unconditionally to the Allied forces (VE Day), but the war with Japan was in full force. Japan accepted terms of surrender (VJ Day) on August

14, and peace was declared at the signing on the 15th! It was a happy time for everyone when our young men returned from military service.

## High School Bible Clubs

Our hearts became increasingly burdened to reach more teenagers. As we prayed, the Lord seemed to say, "Go where they are!" Al decided we must reach into the schools.

He talked to some of the high schoolers about it. One who was especially interested was Judy Raby, a student at Central High School. She was one of several carloads of teens who went with us to the Second Annual Convention of YFCI in July 1946, at Medicine Lake, MN, near Minneapolis. We all got so motivated at the convention; the trip home was spent making plans for starting High School Bible Clubs in the fall. Incidentally, after high school graduation, Judy went to Bible School and became a missionary to Japan. God has tremendously blessed her efforts there for nearly 50 years. She has had a great witness to very influential officials in the government.

When we got home from convention, we called together teenagers we knew from every high school and presented our burden and plan. Each teen was to contact all the Christian kids from his or her school and get them involved. We found mothers or other interested adults to help. Since this was near the beginning of the electronic age, "beam" was a much-used word. "Youth on the Beam" became the name of our clubs. Their nickname was YOB Clubs. As clubs started, kids from other schools wanted to start them in their schools. The Clubs met in a room in the school usually before or after school. A few met during the lunch hour.

The Saturday night Rally was the gathering point for the teenagers across the city. They looked forward to every

Saturday evening when they saw friends from other schools. We encouraged the clubbers to bring unsaved friends from school to the Rally – thus drawing in many teenagers who needed to hear the Gospel.

"Teach the teenagers how to be a leader and then let them do it," Al insisted. Our motto was "Teens telling teens" not only with the Basic Counseling Course, but also with teens bringing their friends into the Clubs and Rallies.

We appointed officers for each Club who formed a committee to put together the Club program each week. Normally, programs consisted of someone leading singing, another playing the piano, someone singing a solo or playing an instrument, a testimony, someone making announcements and a short message from God's Word. A telephone committee reminded teens to come and a greeting committee made sure of a friendly atmosphere.

One of our fundamental precepts was "Involvement is the key to success" the slang of which is "Use 'em or loose 'em." This works in every area of ministry!

Bible Clubs were booming. It was a great way to reach out. Our very first Bible Club convert was Vera Mae Alleman at Shawnee Mission Rural High School – which later became Shawnee Mission North. Vera Mae's father, business teacher at the school, had previously started Inner Circle, a fellowship of Christian students there. He became sponsor of Shawnee Mission YOB Club. Vera Mae remained active in YFC and eventually spent many years as a missionary in Mexico.

Through the years, Al received invitations to become YFC Director in other cities. But, believing God had called him to Kansas City, he refused the offers. Al strongly believed you should drive down your stake where God calls you and stay there. He believed that every time you move, it is like starting over.

"You build a relationship with people, businesses, churches, and pastors that establishes you as a leader in the area," he emphasized. "When you move to another location, you must begin again."

### Third Anniversary

The summer of 1946 was packed with activities!

Al's faith was big! He contracted for the Municipal Auditorium Arena for June 1 for a big third anniversary celebration. This was our first attempt at filling 10,000 seats.

We arranged for churches and other YFC ministries to come in delegations and hang a banner over their section of reserved seats. The arena was filled with 10,000 people.

The Westport High and Paseo High bands combined to play a 30-minute concert at 7 P.M. before Al excitedly ran onto the stage screaming "This is Kansas City Youth For Christ — Let's stand and sing!" Everyone rose to their feet as the 6-foot, 9-inch "Hi" Johnson stretched his arms a full seven-feet directing the huge crowd singing

"Christ For Me."
Yes, it's Christ for me,
Every day as I go my way,
It is Christ for me!"

Every Rally started with the crowd singing this followed by a good time of audience singing. On this special occasion, George Beverly Shea presented a mini concert including his own composition, "I'd Rather Have Jesus."

A highlight of the evening was when six little 6-year-old boys dressed in white suits and baker's hats carried a 2'x4' birthday cake the whole length of the arena as everyone sang "Happy Birthday to YFC." Two of those little boys were Donnie and Ronnie Philgreen (Yes, Don who married our Martha) and Chuck Johnson, Hi's son.

Gil Dodds, who held the world's record for the indoor mile, ran an exhibition mile around the arena with several high school track stars—of course outrunning them.

Five concert grand pianos Al had rented from Jenkins Music Company made quite an impressive sight on the stage! The exceptional performance of five artists playing together was rare.

Dr. Torrey Johnson, founder and President of YFCI and an extraordinary evangelist preached a dynamic message. Many came to receive Jesus as Savior.

## Campspiration

Two weeks after the Super Rally we had our first "Campspiration" at Camp Fellowship on Lake Afton near Wichita, Kansas. This was a typical primitive campground. The "chapel" was a roof over our heads and the seats were wooden benches. A swimming pool was the only recreation facility. Baseball games, tug of war, three legged races and such were our creative "fun" activities. During that, our first week of offering a camp experience, 150-200 attended.

The dining room and kitchen were in a Quonset hut—popular at that time for inexpensive buildings and used mostly in the military. I was in charge of the meals—three a day for the whole week. I planned the menus, bought the food and got volunteers to help me. We used this campground for several years. This was the beginning of an annual Campspiration which grew in numbers each year.

T. W. Wilson, a terrific young evangelist from Dothan, Alabama, who would later become personal assistant to Billy Graham, was the speaker. T.W. became a favorite with our crowd. We booked him often for Rallies and for several years he was our main camp speaker.

When T.W. was in town he spent quite a lot of time in our home. Our little Martha was almost two and tried to say T.W. It came out "P. Bub." So this became our pet name for him.

I have to relate one story on T.W. One night before we left

our house for the Rally he told Al a story he was going to use in his message. He often practiced his message on Al before he preached it. Hours later, after the rally he asked Al, "What did you think of that story I used tonight?"

Al just laughed and laughed. "You didn't ever tell it! You told me at home before we went but you didn't use it in your message." That was another standing joke between us for years. After he joined the Billy Graham team, he could not come often but he remained one of our favorite people.

In 1947, KCYFC took on their second missionary project. We raised the money to send T.W. Wilson along with the Couriers for Christ male quartet from Moody Bible Institute to Ireland for a six-month evangelistic missionary journey. They flew out of Kansas City. A crowd of more than a thousand gathered at the airport to send them off. T.W.'s wife, Mary Helen, and his mother came for the send-off. Just before they got on the plane the whole team plus local leaders knelt beside the airplane and prayed. This was in the days when you walked onto the field and climbed steps to enter the plane. A memorable experience for everyone!

Because it was air-conditioned, we moved our weekly Rallies to the 2,600-seat Music Hall during the summer. We had a great time when Billy Graham was our speaker at the August 3rd Rally. The August 10th Rally with Cliff Barrows was outstanding. Both were huge Rallies with scores receiving Jesus as Savior.

The next month, September 1946, is when we started Bible Clubs in the high schools. (As I have mentioned previously.)

In October, we had Billy Graham and Cliff Barrows back for a banquet, which we had in the basement banquet hall of Linwood Presbyterian Church. It was a great evening. After his message, Billy asked those who wanted to dedicate their lives to the Lord to stand. We no longer have the records of decisions made in those early days, but we constantly hear from people who tell us about their decisions at those meetings.

One was Margaret Bechtel (Baldwin) who would later be involved in our ministry in various ways. With a journalism degree, she wrote articles for the Conquest magazine which we began in 1980. She produced several news format programs for TV-50, after the station began in 1979. And she held a host of other volunteer jobs.

Jack Hamilton, a good friend from Central Bible Church, who had just returned from military service also dedicated his life to the Lord that night. He and his wife, Marijean, immediately involved themselves in our ministry. Jack often told Al how burdened he was to serve the Lord full-time in the Bible Club ministry. He knew how badly Al needed help. YFC had no money to hire him but he, Al and others prayed about it. A few months later Jack came on our staff by faith to help work with the teenagers and establish more Bible Clubs.

## Another Girl

Our next trip to the hospital was on December 17, 1946. God blessed us with another darling baby girl whom we named Marilyn Jo. We now had two cute little girls and felt especially blessed by God!

When Al and I started our family we prayed diligently that God would give us wisdom as parents. Our burden was stated in I Timothy 3:5: "If anyone does not know how to manage his own family, how can he take care of God's church?"

We knew if we had trouble with our children, people would never trust us to minister to theirs. We dedicated our family to God and claimed His promise in James 1:5-6 "If any of you lack wisdom, let him ask of God, that gives to all men liberally, and upbraideth not; and it shall be given unto him. But let him ask in faith, nothing wavering."

We constantly prayed for our children, their relationship to Christ and for wisdom to be good parents. The praise all goes to God—none of our children ever went through a rebellious time and we always had a fantastic relationship with them.

Thankfully, both Martha and Marilyn received Jesus as their Savior just before their fourth birthdays. Even though they happened two years apart, their stories are almost identical

They knew how excited we were when they heard us talk about teenagers who had made decisions for Christ. They understood the importance we placed on this decision. But we did not urge them. It was totally their response to the Holy Spirit. Both of them came to us in their own time and told us they wanted Jesus to wash away their sin. What a joy it was to lead our own daughters to Christ!

As the Area Vice-President for YFCI, Al traveled thousands of miles to many cities and towns helping set up Rallies and clubs. In his travel, he always tried to make it home at night. Many times I sat up until two or three o'clock sewing or ironing while waiting for him. When it got extra late, I feared an accident had happened so searched out the window watching for the encouraging sight of headlights approaching while pleading to God for Al's safe return.

I was a good seamstress and loved to make cute little dresses full of ruffles and bows for our little girls. By the time Marilyn was one and Martha was three, I dressed them alike much of the time and put bows in their curly hair. My heart swelled with pride when even strangers in stores bragged about how cute they were. Many times I was asked if they were twins. It was great fun having those two cute little girls!

Another reason I sewed all our clothes was because we could not afford to buy them. We pinched every penny but sacrificing was no problem to us since we had grown up during the depression. We believed God had called us to the greatest mission field in the world—the American teenager!

From the time we were saved Al and I have been staunch believers in the biblical principal of giving. We gave because we *wanted* to—not just because God **said** to.

We believed: "*You can give without loving but you cannot love without giving.*" When you love God, you can't keep from giving to Him. Another of our beliefs was: "*You cannot outgive God.*"

Shortly after I received Jesus as my Savior at the age of 15, I worked in my uncle's insurance office after school for $2.50 a week. I gave 50 cents or 20% of that to the Lord. Did I miss it? NO! Because God gives back with interest. That is the way Al and I always gave—way beyond 10%. Even when our salary was only half of what an average person made, we gave heavily to God. We proved God's promise to be true: "Give and it shall be given unto you, pressed down, shaken together and running over shall men give unto your bosom." (Luke 6:38) So many verses spoke to us.

"Whoever sows sparingly will also reap sparingly, and whoever sows generously will also reap generously. Each man should give what he has decided in his heart to give, not reluctantly or under compulsion, for God loves a cheerful (hilarious) giver." (2 Corinthians 9:6-7)

"One man gives freely, yet gains even more; another withholds unduly, but comes to poverty. A generous man will prosper; he who refuses others will himself be refused." (Proverbs 11:24-25)

Our hearts ached for those who never learned the JOY of giving. Oh, how much they miss!

## Quizzing

We had challenged the teens to carry their Bible to school on top of their stack of books as a witness. They learned to lead their friends to Christ in our Soul Winning Course. Now we were dreaming of a way to inspire them to more thoroughly study God's Word.

Jack Hamilton was a great idea person. He and Al together made quite a team!

One day Jack said, "We need to make a game out of studying God's Word—make it fun and exciting!" They discussed patterning it after basketball. Finally, they came up with the idea of Bible Quizzes. The quiz program began at the beginning of the 1947 school season.

We assigned books of the Bible for the teenagers to study. Certain verses were "memory verses" which meant the teens must quote them perfectly. Each school could have seven players at a time on their team. Extras could be used as substitutes, just like in basketball. Teams sat on a bench facing the quizmaster. When the quizmaster asked a question, as soon as a teen knew the answer, he or she jumped to his or her feet. A panel of judges decided who jumped first and that teen could give the answer. If the answer was correct, points were awarded to the team's score. If a quizzer jumped before the question was completed, the quizmaster stopped and the quizzer had to finish the question before answering.

Quizzes were between schools, which led to a tournament at the end of the school year. It worked. Scores of teens memorized great portions of the Bible. Eventually quiz teams got uniforms to distinguish their team. After a few years an electronic seat was designed so a light indicated to the quizmaster who was the first to jump. This was more accurate.

After our quiz program had been going several years and Bible Clubs had started across the nation, YFCI leaders realized the value of Bible Quizzing and implemented it in clubs across the country. For years it was a large part of the YFCI Conventions.

⋙⚔⋘

In 1957 at the Rally in Grand Avenue Temple, where we met except in the summer, Westport and Shawnee Mission North High School teams were quizzing over the book of Matthew for the city championship. The book of Matthew was the material. One of our quizzers, Don Philgreen, (who later became our son-in-law) had spent the afternoon memorizing the begats in Chapter 1 because he knew the rest of the book. In the middle of the quiz, Club Director Bob Kraning who was the quizmaster said: "Question. Who begat...?"

Don jumped. Groans erupted from the audience.

"If I quote the whole chapter, will it count?" Don pled.

Astonished, Kraning looked to the judges for a decision. What could they do? Their decision? If he can do it, he deserved the points.

The audience didn't breathe as Don quoted the whole first chapter of Matthew with all the begats – perfectly!

The crowd exploded with wild cheers, whistles and applause! Heads wagged in disbelief.

Years later a number of denominations implemented Quizzing into their church youth programs. Many of these are continuing today.

# CHAPTER 7

# YFCI Board Meeting

Usually twice a year for the next 20 years or so, Al traveled to different cities for YFCI board meetings. A significant one was in January 1947, because of what happened on the home front while he was gone. First a little background. We had been alternating song leaders for the Rally between Hi Johnson and Darrell Freleigh. Recently Hi had told Al that he wanted to lead singing *all* the time or not do it at all.

We had not agreed to this, so while Al was in Tampa, Florida for this YFCI board meeting, Hi went to our businessmen friends to complain. He warned them that he would go across the state line to Kansas and start his own Singspiration and asked for their support. This was threatening to us because Al had done all he could to popularize Hi.

I called Al in Tampa and told him what was happening. It concerned him greatly. He wrote me the next day:

> As soon as I heard the news from you, I talked to Torrey (Johnson, president of YFCI). Torrey told me to wait until I get home to do anything. Maybe the talk is more potent than the action . . . There is only one thing to do and that is to PRAY!

The next day he wrote:

> Darling, it works! I've seen the impossible happen right here in front of my own eyes. Those businessmen may stop supporting us because of Hi calling on them but they are not our source—God is our source!
>
> God has been literally dumping oceans of blessing on me this week and I know the devil is using this to get me

69

down. Bless God! I've got a vision of our work in Kansas City and the Mid-Central Region and that vision can't be stopped as long as God is in it!

Last night I felt too bad to write, so I took some aspirin and went to bed. When the fellows came in two hours later they woke me up, so I got up and prayed for a whole hour—and did I get blessed! In that prayer I asked almighty God to take care of the Hi situation. I'm trusting God for the answer. God is giving me great peace. My only worry is that it will upset you and our staff before I get home. Poor Bertie, [his secretary] she is so conscientious and takes everything on her own shoulders. Try to bolster her up all you can. Tell her I said to pray every time she gets loaded down with cares and just hang on until I get home and we'll talk about it.

God has spurred me on so I have prayed all week that He would help me to translate my renewed vision to the board. I've prayed for those who can't catch the vision—for God to take them away!

I love all these guys more than ever! Torrey and Dave Morken are going to China and the Philippines. Bob Cook is going to England! We raised $5,200 toward their trips right here. Praise God!

It's hard to realize how little old good-for-nothing me could be in fellowship with God's very best—Boy!!!! I'm feeling on top of the world and this problem is not going to get me down!

Please pray for me as I go to Sarasota to preach Sunday that God will give me souls for His kingdom. "Not by might, nor by power, but by my spirit, saith the Lord." (Zechariah 4:6)

There is no competition in the Lord's work. There is more to be done than all of us put together could possibly get done. A letter the next day said:

God has sent me here to prepare me spiritually for the *job* and also for the *jolt*. I believe if we can keep our feet clean and our eyes on Jesus that a real victory is coming!

When Al walked off the airplane from Tampa, more than two dozen friends were at the airport to welcome him home. Some of the guys boosted him to their shoulders and carried him through the airport showing him their love and support.

Hi did, in fact, announce that he was going to Kansas City, Kansas and start his own organization. His meeting place would be less than five miles from Grand Avenue Temple where we held our Rallies. So we gave him a big send-off, gift and all, at our Rally following God's instructions in Luke 6:27-28. "Love your enemies, do good to those who hate you, bless those who curse you, pray for those who mistreat you." I doubt that any of the general public ever knew there was a problem.

A few of our crowd who came from Kansas City, Kansas transferred to his Singspiration, but our crowds slumped only for a few weeks and we were back as large as ever. We praised the Lord for those Hi reached with the gospel. After a while, he closed his teen ministry and became a successful pastor.

When we celebrated our 40th Anniversary, we received a nice letter from Hi saying in part:

> Our heartiest congratulations on forty years of Christian service. Memories flood our minds of those early days in the Municipal Auditorium. It's wonderful to know God has recorded all that's done to His glory and that He forgives our many mistakes. Love you more than words can tell! Hi

### Fur Coat

About this time what I considered a "crisis" in my personal life appeared. Because I had always had trouble keeping warm in the winter, I had bought myself a fur coat when I started my first job. It was so cozy, I vowed to never wear anything but a fur coat again. By this time the fur had worn off around the bottom of the sleeves and down the front. In fact, there were several tears in the skins. I needed a new coat. Now, I was married to a poor minister. I prayed before I went downtown shopping but still, I did not find a fur coat I could afford.

Discouraged, I came home, went to my bedroom and fell on my knees.

"Dear Lord," I pleaded. "You know I need a new coat. You have promised to supply all my needs. You also said you would give me the desire of my heart. So, I'll just leave it with You. Either You'll have to show me a coat I can afford or You'll have to take away my desire."

What do you think He did? Right! He changed my desire! Was I unhappy? No! Did I feel rejected? No! And my life has been extremely happy! I have never desired a fur coat again and I don't feel badly about it. That was a good lesson for me to learn early in our ministry.

## God—Kicked Out

Everything was growing so fast, more Bible Club Directors were needed. Gene French, Jerry Klippert, and Jim Whitby were added to our staff. They were all local young men who left their secular jobs to serve the Lord. We had Clubs in nearly all the high schools for miles around. Teens were being saved and growing spiritually.

Then the devil stuck in his ugly head in the form of atheist Madelyn Murray. She viciously fought for atheism and against Christianity. She was upset that her son, Bill, who was in high school, was occasionally subjected to prayer in school. Her brazen crusade to do away with anything Christian went all the way to the U. S. Supreme Court. In 1948, the court broke the longstanding traditions of our forefathers by putting the Bible and prayer out of the schools.

That threw us into a tailspin. It was a disastrous time.

"If you take God out of the schools," Al preached, "you can't keep evil from coming in." That is exactly what happened.

But Al was not one to be defeated easily. He believed a solution existed for every problem. As we prayed about what to do, the answer God gave him was to have mobile chapels.

The teens were motivated, too. Members of these first Clubs creatively figured out how to help raise money to buy school buses. Three large buses were bought and painted red and white in a design that set them apart from others. Large lettering on each side read: HIGH SCHOOL BIBLE CLUBS "MOBILE CHAPEL". Two front seats next to the door were removed and a piano was installed. Club Directors drove the buses to a different school each morning before school and each afternoon after school. The big red and white buses were a familiar sight parked in front of area high schools for several years. Teens arrived 30 minutes before school for the morning Bible Clubs. In the afternoon, they streamed from school for their meeting.

The meetings were the same as before—teens doing everything on the program except messages by the Club Director or other guest speakers. Teens could certainly not be secret believers because the whole school could see who entered the bus. It was not as convenient as the previous system, but it worked well. New kids continued to come and be saved. Even amicable teachers dropped by sometimes.

Probably the biggest hindrance was driving those buses in cold and icy weather.

Those poor Club Directors had to be dedicated to arise very early, go to the bus location, get it started and drive across town, arriving at school before anyone else. Sometimes the buses were difficult to start on cold, wintry mornings. But they served the purpose and were certainly better than quitting.

Ministries in other cities heard about our Bible Clubs and wanted us to help them get started. One day in 1949 Club Director Jack Hamilton, told Al, "I am so burdened that the rest of the country have High School Bible Clubs, I feel God is leading me to go help them start."

Oh, how we hated to see him leave. But, also feeling the burden for teens across America, we reluctantly bid him farewell.

Jack went first to Des Moines, then to Detroit, and Portland. He was eagerly accepted as he taught how to reach teenagers in the high schools. Eventually, YFCI realized the value of the clubs and hired Jack as the National Bible Club Director, freeing him to work across the nation. Thus the Bible Club movement became nationwide and teenagers were being reached by tens of thousands. Those were exciting days!

Our three buses with three Club Directors could reach only so many high schools so we started looking for an alternative. More parents became volunteers.

After a time Clubs started meeting in homes, community buildings, church parlors or any location that seemed convenient. Some clubs met before school, others after school and many met in the evening. Each club decided which was best for them.

## City-Wide Crusade

Our first venture organizing a citywide evangelistic crusade was in 1949. Al called on pastors, inviting them to be on a committee to sponsor this big crusade with us. A large number joined us. We rented Music Hall for one week

Dr. Jesse Hendley, a young southern evangelist, preached dynamic messages for eight nights straight. Crowds filled the 2,600-seat Music Hall, and every night scores of people came to Jesus. Pastors were thrilled with the results and continued to be our good supporters—working together with us on many occasions. Converts were funneled into participating churches.

## Club City Council

Each of the Bible Clubs' four officers—president, vice-president, secretary and treasurer—were automatically members of the City Council. These students were the cream of the crop! Several times a year the City Council met on a Sunday afternoon. Officers were elected from the City Council members.

At these meetings, these sharp teens shared about programs

or activities that worked well in their club as ideas for other clubs. Victories and numbers of decisions in their clubs were reported. They, with the Club Directors, discussed and made decisions on a wide variety of activities and programs. The Club Directors promoted coming activities and charged the kids to be even more dynamic leaders.

The City Council gave the teens experience being leaders and helped them learn to be creative. Some were elected to high offices in their high school.

## Year Books

Almost every year from 1948 through 1962 we produced a yearbook. A Club Director led a group of teenagers who planned, designed, took pictures and produced the whole book, which was very similar to those offered by high schools. Instead of pictures of different classes it contained pictures of Clubs in each school across the city. The yearbooks also included pictures and information of Rallies, Club and citywide YFC activities. It showed pictures of teen leaders and their accomplishments, quizzes, winners of talent contests, action shots of camps, conferences, and parties—serious pictures and fun collages. Most of the year books had pictures of a girl elected Year Book Queen.

The book was dedicated to someone each year—usually a staff member.

The students and Club Directors had a good time producing these yearbooks and they became great keepsakes.

At Rallies and other activities the students met kids from all across the city who became their best friends so, to many, this book was more valuable than their school yearbook.

But we finally had to stop producing them because it became financially unsound.

## Week-End Conferences

Weekend conferences were usually held twice a year and provided a time to get really close to the teens.

In both the fall and spring of 1950, we had weekend conferences at the Nazarene's Lakeview Camp at 77th and Antioch in Overland Park

I remember the conferences well because I was the head cook. A number of wonderful mothers volunteered to be my helpers. We cooked everything from scratch. About 250 teenagers attended plus adult helpers. No cold cereal for breakfast. It was bacon, scrambled eggs and biscuits. Our biggest meal was a full turkey dinner. We roasted and carved eight turkeys for that meal.

I also remember the spring conference well because it was the last of April and our baby had been due (we thought) on March 15. He still hadn't arrived. But, there I was, big as a truck, heading up the cooking.

### At Last, a Son

Dr. Singleton told me to walk a lot. With 3- and 5-year-olds, to take long walks was difficult. So in the evening sometimes Al would put our girls in the car and drive along slowly beside me as I walked. (Strollers didn't exist in those days.) About eleven o'clock one evening, our girls were asleep so we put them comfortably in the car to ride along. Al was driving beside me with the car window open and we were talking while I walked down Prospect near our home. A police car started following.

"Is that man bothering you, lady?" he shouted to me.

"No, it's just my husband," I responded. We must have looked pretty stupid.

After following a while I guess he decided we were not having trouble so he moved on.

Finally, on May 9, Ronnie made his appearance — and were we happy! We were not only happy to get him here at last, but that God had given us a son! We now had our two sweet daughters and a wonderful son.

## Young Preachers' Club

This was the era of dynamic preaching. Dr. Bob Jones, Sr. and Dr. John Brown, Sr. were two of the older dynamic preachers. Now coming along were Billy Graham, Bob Pierce, Torrey Johnson and many others just starting out. Dr. Bob Jones had a preacher's club at his university in North Carolina and was producing terrific young preachers.

In 1949, using Dr. Bob's preachers' club as a pattern, Al started his own Young Preacher's Club. He was a natural-born teacher. He liked nothing better than to teach others what he had learned. His prayer was that those he taught would do even better than he. Each young man with whom he worked was a Timothy to him.

Al started his Young Preacher's Club with just a dozen or so but it grew to 150-200 coming to his sessions each year. He taught them how to prepare a message with a purpose. He said, "You never peach just to fill time. Have a goal in mind and shoot for it. Study your audience. Use an illustration or funny story at least every seven minutes."

He taught them to use fitting gestures, facial expressions, changes in voice volume and tone, movement, objects, anything to give variety and interest — to hold the audience's attention and get the point across.

"But most important," he emphasized, "you must study and memorize God's Word." He underscored the necessity for the teens to live dedicated lives, separated from the world.

He told them to write in the front of their Bibles:

**"This book will keep me from sin, or sin will keep me from this book."**

**"The Word of God does the work of God"** was a point he pounded home.

Another slogan he had for them was:

**"Be ready to preach, pray, sing or die on a moment's notice."**

He was a master at giving a gospel invitation. This was one part he never missed teaching. He cringed if the invitation was not presented well. He compared not giving a good invitation to a salesman who didn't close the deal.

Many of Al's young preachers became dynamic preachers and teachers who became pastors, missionaries and teachers.

### Teen Talent Contests

One of our goals was to develop teens' talents. We used lots of teenagers on the Rally and in Clubs. An outlet for their talents provided an incentive to develop them. We also gave teens help in presentation and provided the encouragement to make them want to succeed.

Again, with the idea of making a game of it, we started teen talent contests in 1950. It was amazing how much talent we uncovered.

Categories included male and female vocal solo; (you couldn't judge them against each other and, anyway, it made more winners); Vocal group (could be duet, trio, quartet or whatever); Instrumental solo; Instrumental group; Piano (included playing a solo, accompanying a vocal soloist, and playing for crowd singing); Song leading; Preaching; and Drama (monologues or group sketches). When we discovered good talent we provided opportunities to serve the Lord with their talent. We realized that if a talented person didn't have opportunities in a Christian atmosphere to use their talents, they would go into the world to be used.

We loved to show support to our teens when they had leads in their high school musicals and dramas by attending. We felt they were our own kids! Many have continued to use those talents throughout their lives.

Because Al was YFCI Mid-Central Region Veep, we started having regional camps each summer at John Brown University. Regional contests were a part of camp. Each city brought their winners to compete.

Eventually, YFCI realized the value of all three programs we initiated: Clubs, Quizzes and Talent Contests, that were adopted into the national program. This, of course, made competition even more challenging. Kids who won locally went to the regionals, then on to the national contest. We always took a full slate to these national contests and brought home quite a few trophies.

We believed many of our contestants were the best. Sometimes when they took second or third in the nationals, we were terribly disappointed—but we got our share of winners. And we were proud of them.

# CHAPTER 8

# Escapade with Billy Graham

Hi, Al. This is Billy."
It was in June of 1949. When Al answered the phone he heard Billy Graham's voice.

"Al, I have a big favor to ask of you," Billy continued. "My Uncle Tom who lives in Tahlequah, Oklahoma died. I promised him I would come preach his funeral when he died, no matter where I was. I'm starting a crusade in Altoona, PA tomorrow so I don't have much time."

"I'm sorry to hear about your uncle," Al consoled.

"Al, Bev and I are flying to Kansas City and I need you to charter a private plane to take us to Tahlequah as soon as we arrive. And I want you to go with us." He gave details of when they would arrive in Kansas City. ("Bev" he referred to was George Beverly Shea the great vocalist who later joined the Billy Graham Evangelistic Association.)

It wasn't easy to find a plane readily available on such short notice but Al made arrangements and was at Executive Aircraft waiting when Billy and Bev arrived on a commercial flight. They quickly took off for Tahlequah, but in central Kansas they encountered a bad storm.

"We can't fly through this," the pilot warned. "We can go around it but I'm not sure I know the way."

"That's no problem," Al announced. "I know Kansas like the back of my hand. I'll navigate." So the pilot turned off course to miss the storm. All was going well when the pilot panicked, "We're getting low on gas! This extra flying has used a lot."

They started looking for an airport where they could re-fuel—but to no avail.

"Let's find a level field to land on and we'll get gas from a farmer," Al suggested.

It maybe wasn't the best solution—but it was a lot better than running out of gas. They found a field and negotiated a bumpy landing, dividing a herd of frightened cattle. Billy got out to stretch his legs as a scared heifer calf ran furiously trying to be reunited with her mother. Billy, thinking the calf was chasing him, sprinted with all his might toward a fence screaming: "A bull is after me! A bull is after me!" Al just about died laughing because he knew the calf was as scared as Billy.

The farmer, flabbergasted by the landing in his field, darted with his barking dog to investigate the bizarre incident. Obligingly, he drained gas from his storage tank and thankfully the airplane was able to lift off from the pasture. Soon the men were on their way again. The little Tahlequah runway was a welcome sight. A waiting car whisked them to the church where the funeral had already begun. The little church was packed with the overflow crowd peering in through the windows.

When Bev sat down at the old upright piano to accompany himself, he was chagrined to hear the tinny, out-of-tune sound — but he continued singing, making the best of it. The people were delighted to have them there. How often do two celebrities of their caliber come to a place as small as Talaquah? After Billy preached they rushed back to the plane for the return trip. When they were airborne the pilot said to Al, "You know how to fly, don't you?"

"Sure!" Al fibbed.

"Here, you fly it a while and I'll navigate," he continued.

Al took hold of the stick and immediately took a nosedive.

"Are you sure you know how to fly?" Billy apprehensively questioned Al.

"Sure, I just have to get the feel of this plane." Al answered with confidence. After a while the pilot took back the controls and they arrived back in Kansas City with no more incidents. I am surely glad I didn't know about any of this until it was over because Al had never had a single flying lesson!

# CHAPTER 9

# Merv Rosell Crusade

Since the evangelistic crusade the summer before with evangelist Jack Shuler in the Music Hall had been such a success, we decided to have another – only more aggressive. For this one Al booked the 12,000 seat Municipal Auditorium.

For months Al tackled the details for a 1950 Greater Kansas City for Christ Crusade. He rallied together pastors to join forces. To muster the participation of more than 75 pastors from such a wide spectrum of churches was a celebrated event. This would be the largest evangelistic effort in the area since the Billy Sunday crusade in 1926.

We held counseling classes in churches across the city for members who wanted to lead people to Jesus at the end of the meetings.

Communism was a frightful curse in the world at this time. Al's constant message to rally people behind the cause of winning young people to Christ was:

"Two great opposing forces are making a bid for the youth of the world. We're challenged with the responsibility of giving these young people the Christian principles that will stem the tide of "isms" creeping in.

"American youth want more than just churchianity," he pointed out. "We do not persuade them merely to 'join' a church, but challenge them as the early Americans, to have a dynamic faith which will keep them strong against the inroads of false theory. Young people are ready to be challenged with Christianity which is real rather than ritualistic and virile enough to combat the wild promises of communism."

This was a huge step of faith — but faith is about the only thing 29-year-old Al had in large supply. It took enormous faith to sign the expensive nine-day contract for the Municipal Auditorium. The crusade would run Saturday, July 22 through Sunday, July 31.

Al preached: "**PRAYER IS THE ANSWER.** We must all pray.
*The place of prayer is at the foot of the cross.*
*The posture of prayer is humility of heart.*
*The power of prayer is faith.*
*The person of prayer is the Lord Jesus Christ.*"

Prayer meetings were held in homes and churches all over the city.

Strategies devised unprecedented measures to make Kansas City "Christ conscious." We enlisted several thousand volunteers to be involved. The Kansas City area was zoned for systematic "house to house" personal evangelism. Every doorbell was to be rung communicating the message about the crusade. In addition, every residential telephone would "ring for Christ" as a corps of trained workers invited every household to come to the crusade. Lawn signs blossomed in the front yards of thousands of homes indicating family and friends' participation in the interdenominational Crusade.

Music played an important role. Church and school choirs combined under the direction of Darrell Freleigh. The entire south end of the arena balcony was filled with the 1,000 voice choral ensemble.

"Involvement is the key to success!" was again one of Al's primary principles. We had learned that several things are accomplished by grass-roots involvement:

> *People are blessed when they feel a part of the organization or event.
> *Each person can reach only a certain number of people. The more you have working, the more you will reach.
> *Those who are involved will be talking advertisements as they share with their friends and others.

Arrangements were made for chartered buses. Billboards and newspapers carried extensive advertising. We intended to make this an event everyone—not just church people—was talking about.

Merv Rosell, a captivating, 38-year-old evangelist from California, played his saxophone and preached with power. His constant flashy smile, his deep compassion for everyone, and his zeal for preaching the gospel were contagious. He communicated a burden for the lost to the audience, telling them:

"When you see a drunk Sailor out here leaning against a lamppost, don't say: 'That dumb guy, why doesn't he wise up?' Instead, you should have compassion and say, 'If only he knew Christ as his Savior!'"

Each evening he admonished the 10,000-12,000 present to go out the next day and ask those they saw: "Do you know Jesus?"

Al loved to do what he called "firsts" in things he planned. This was no exception.

Every Sunday afternoon for years, Dr. Charles E. Fuller had broadcast his "Old Fashioned Revival Hour" live from Long Beach, Calif. over nearly 800 network and short-wave radio stations around the world. For the "first," Fuller brought his radio staff to join us in the Kansas City Municipal Auditorium and broadcast in front of 12,000 people over KMBC radio. This was fed to the other 800 stations. That was a provocative feat in those days when broadcast capabilities were more primitive. It was tremendously successful. The whole Christian world knew about the crusade here as Dr. Fuller asked all who were listening from around the world to pray. "Pray for revival in Kansas City," he announced.

The Old Fashioned Revival Hour Quartet sang every evening with Rudy Atwood tickling the ivories as only he could. Hilding Halverson, Merv's energetic song leader, was a major part of the musical program.

From the very first meeting the arena was packed. Scores came forward at the gospel invitation each evening. This record-breaking series of meetings had front-page coverage in *The Kansas City Star and Times* nearly every day of the crusade. It quoted the young evangelist:

"At the foot of the cross, love cancels hate; faith cancels fear and sin is canceled by salvation through the blood of Christ."

The results were too great to stop at the end of our contract. When Al begged for an extension, city officials agreed to let us use the auditorium for an additional week to August 6—postponing a cleaning and painting job in the arena.

Another day, *The Star* read:

Fifty pastors were introduced on the "feature preacher" night. Each one gave a one-sentence statement of his opinion of the effect of the meeting. [It quoted several.]

"This crusade has meant more to Kansas City than anything that has happened for years," Dr. D. A. Holmes, pastor of the Paseo Baptist church, said.

Dr. Alvin G. Hause of the Bales Baptist church, said, "It is bringing the greatest spiritual awakening Kansas City has ever seen".

The largest delegation present that evening was a group of 800 from the First Assembly of God church at 3100 East 31st Street where Dr. A. A. Wilson was pastor.

More than 1,000 persons went forward last night after Dr. Merv Rosell called for persons between 16 and 39-years-old whom "are willing to let God lead you, even if it may cost your life?"

"God has chosen you," he said to the audience. "You may say. 'But I have no talents with which to serve the Lord.' God only expects you to have one talent, and that is faithfulness."

Then as they gathered around the platform, Dr. Rosell said: "I'm scared to death too many of you are coming forward. I'm worried that some of you might not be taking this seriously."

At the end of the extension the unprecedented response demanded more time.

On Saturday, August 5, *The Kansas City Star* read:

> "A group of seventy-nine ministers, representing nineteen denominations and organizations, met for breakfast and voted unanimously to support continuing the campaign."

But it wasn't quite that easy. Al took a delegation of pastors with him to confer with the City Manager and the painting contractor. Al reasoned with the contractor:

"If we raise the money to pay overtime to your men, would you delay starting your work another week?"

After serious thought, the contractor agreed. A definite answer to prayer!

That night when Al told the crowd of the agreement, they enthusiastically gave an extra offering to cover painters' overtime.

Hundreds of lives were changed during those awesome three weeks. Even today, 50 years later, we can point to many of those converts who have become Christian leaders.

God honored our faith and hard work. Witnessing God uniting pastors and churches from all denominations to work together in an evangelistic effort was a fulfillment of our dreams and prayers. Seeing a bond of genuine love emerge was thrilling. We were constantly humbled as we saw God work such mighty miracles.

This crusade took place when Ronnie was only nine weeks old but I was sitting on the front row every night holding our new little baby. After Al finished emceeing and Merv was on to preach, he usually came down and sat with me. Al was always so attentive. All through the years when we were at Rallies or church, he would wink at me and smile from the platform. How do you think that affected me? I never had a doubt about his devotion to me! *I highly recommend men give their wives that kind of attention.*

## Larger House

When the big crusade was over we turned some attention to a personal matter.

"How long can we manage in this house without more room?" I wondered. We could barely fit a baby bed into our bedroom and the two girls filled our other small bedroom.

"This would be a good time for us to make a change," Al reasoned. "The market is right."

A two-year-old Cape Cod house on an acre lot near 69th and Nall was our answer. Beyond 69th was mostly pastures. In fact, Overland Park was not yet an incorporated city.

We sold our house in Kansas City, Mo. for $7,500—exactly double what we had paid for it seven years earlier. Our equity enabled us to swing the deal for $13,200 with more than double the floor space. Monthly payments on our 20-year loan were $68.

How excited we were to move in January of 1951 when Ronnie was eight months old.

## Miracle—Daily Radio

"Brother Epp, this is Al Metsker." It was a long distance call to Lincoln, Nebraska. "I want to come pick the brains of an expert."

"Hi, Al. I don't consider myself an expert but what can I do for you?"

"God has laid it on my heart to start a local daily radio program and I want to learn from you." Al continued. Arrangements were made for the two men to meet in Lincoln.

Al always felt the need to learn from successful people. He could think of no one better to consult than our dear friend, Theodore Epp, founder and daily teacher on the "Back to the Bible" radio broadcast. He was, I believe, the only one in the country who had a daily gospel program broadcast nationally at that time.

Al's trip was educational and inspiring as Brother Epp shared all he had learned about being successful on radio. What a no-nonsense, dedicated, kind man he was. Al was thrilled with what he learned.

Buying time for a daily religious program on a radio station in Kansas City appeared to be impossible. Every station manager told Al "No!." But he was determined. WDAF was his first choice because it had the strongest signal and was considered the premier station.

"We have never sold to religion." the manager told him. "We *give* time now and then on a Sunday morning, but we never *sell* to religion."

Al gave his rebuttal. "Maybe you have never done it before, but now is the time to start. I'm working to try to save our teenagers. You know how troubled they are. Delinquency is rampant. What is going to happen to our country if we don't do something?"

Their conference was pretty intense as Al tried to convince him how important it was for us to be on the air. He was impassioned and let his burden be known.

"Well, let me talk it over and think about it a few days," the manager finally conceded. They set an appointment for Al to come back a week later. Al assured him that many people would pray about this.

Al felt like Joshua. He had a battle to fight and he intended for God to give him the victory!

"Do not be afraid; do not be discouraged. Be strong and courageous." (Joshua 10:25) Verses like this gave him strength.

"God is our source and prayer is our weapon," he proclaimed.

Communication with friends, kids in clubs, churches and anyone he met was his first job. An all-night prayer meeting was set for the night before his next appointment.

Those who cared came from all over. They prayed all night that God would overrule and give us the airtime.

"Call unto me, and I will answer you, and show you great and mighty things, which you know not" (Jer. 33:3) is the promise they claimed.

When morning came others left. Al went to the restroom, splashed water on his face, shaved and walked boldly into the general manager's office.

"You can buy the time, Al," was the welcome greeting he received. Al wanted to shout but contained his emotions enough to calmly say,

"Thank you. I am thrilled but not surprised. You see, a large group of our people prayed all night last night and we knew that God would answer our prayer."

This was before WDAF had tape recorders. It was before wire records. It was the day of "live" broadcasting or recording on a platter. So Al and his musicians went to a downtown recording studio twice a week to make the programs—three one day and two the other, to fill a week.

On May 7, 1951 at 6:30 A.M. we launched a daily 15-minute radio ministry to reach people in the Mid-Central area with the gospel. The format of the "Youth For Christ Hour" was piano and vocal music, victory stories, announcements and prayer requests about YFC activities, and a 5-7 minute challenging message from God's Word.

We inherited WDAF's large audience that covered a 300-mile radius. Our varied audience included everyone from doctors and lawyers to factory workers and farmers. Soon our mail response was huge. Some of the letters made us chuckle.

"I have a radio in my barn" wrote one, "and listen while I'm milking my cows. They give more milk while listening to your broadcast."

A businessman wrote "If I'm not through with breakfast by the time you go off the air, I'm in trouble..."

Another explained: "I listen while driving to work and if I'm at 13th and Grand by sign-off time, I'm right on schedule."

God sent a colorful gospel pianist, Albert Lane, from Bangor, Maine, to be on the radio team. Albert had traveled with an evangelist for years but was eager to settle down so he moved his family and made Kansas City his home. Because his early experience had included playing background music for silent movies, he was adept at improvisation and exhibited exciting variety in his arrangements. When he played "Master, The Tempest Is Raging," you would almost shiver with the howling winds; be startled by the lightening flashes; shake with the rumbling thunder; and feel the spray from the waves clapping against the shore. Then, as intense as the storm, came the calmness of "peace be still" when the storm was over.

When he played before crowds, applause for him brought the house down and many times called for an encore.

Another of his imaginative performances was to play a song in many different languages. Pretending to turn a switch under the piano between versions, he played the same song in Japanese, Russian, French, German, Hawaiian, and the American Indian always ending with patting his hand over his mouth as he made a noise the way kids often played "Indian." It was amazing! The crowd went wild! Sometimes he would don the headdress of the nation's song he was playing.

Al and Albert were known for a few cute routines they did together, like pretending to be a little girl singing: "Mommy told me something a little girl should know, it is all about the devil and I learned to hate him so..."

Soon, Al and Albert were in great demand for gospel meetings and crusades in large and small towns all over Kansas, Missouri and Nebraska. Al loved to go to the small towns because nearly the whole town would come to the meetings. They were like celebrities in small towns. It was not uncommon for him to lead 15 to 50 to the Lord each night in these rallies.

One evening they had a rally in the little Methodist Church in Toronto, Kansas, where Al grew up. The church was packed—including some of his relatives. His cousin, Betty, received Jesus as her Savior that night along with 17 others. He was so blessed!

How many stories I could tell! I must share one that made us cry and praise God.

One Monday night Al and his music team went to Lane, Kansas, for a meeting. After Al preached 19 teenagers came forward and he led them to Jesus. Among them was a 16-year-old boy named Jim. After they had prayed, Jim talked to Al a while. He was so happy to be saved. The next Friday Al received a letter from Jim's mother.

> Dear Al,
>
> Thank you for coming to Lane Monday night and preaching. You remember Jim whom you led to Jesus? I am his mother. Jim was in a hunting accident on Tuesday and was accidentally shot and killed. My heart is broken but thanks to you, he's in heaven with Jesus. Don't ever quit leading people to Jesus.

Experiences like those were so precious that Al just couldn't turn down opportunities to preach the gospel. What a tragedy it would have been if he had refused that call to travel into Kansas to share the gospel and give an invitation.

The friendships that emerged from those encounters lasted through the years. The broadcast continued 31 years—however it moved to different stations.

Albert Lane was on our staff for 25 years when he retired at age 66.

## Jack Cousins

During the Merv Rosell crusade in August 1950, a sharp young guy from John Brown University, Jack Cousins, started frequenting our place. He was a natural born promoter and just kind of pushed his way in. By 1951, "Cuzzy" had his own office and was helping with many details.

Soon Cuzzy was booking Rally talent. He did promotional work. Befriended pastors. Helped service other YFCs in our Mid-Central area. In general, he lengthened Al's arms. We named him Field Representative for the Mid-Central area under Al's direction, thus freeing Al of many responsibilities so he could devote more time to the Kansas City ministry.

Al had organized the pastors of the city into what we called Evangelical Ministers Fellowship. One of Cuzzy's main focuses was to become a friend to pastors and help them realize we are here to cooperate with them and be an arm of the church. Cuzzy was loved and respected greatly by ministers.

CHAPTER 10

# Great Gatherings

### "Jam For Sermon"
### "Youth for Christ Rally Fills Arena, and About 2,500 Listen Outside"

The above was the main headline on the front page of the June 19, 1951 *Kansas City Star*. A 5" x 7" picture of the huge crowd dominated the front page. The story read:

> There could be a question as to whether the word "super" was a strong enough adjective for the Youth For Christ eighth anniversary Rally last night in the Arena of the Municipal Auditorium.
>
> A banner stretched above the top row of seats at the south end of the big hall described the rally as 'super.'
>
> Sgt. Neal Faler of the police traffic and safety division, holding the doors against the masses who sought entrance after even the standing room was gone, was certain that the banner needed a bigger and better word.
>
> Such an outpouring has never been seen in the Thirteenth Street block between Wyandotte and Central. Never before has any certain set of proceedings inside the big hall been carried by loudspeaker to 2,500 persons who jammed the sidewalks and crowded back into semi-darkness of the grassy rectangle across the street north of the auditorium.
>
> Perhaps never before have from 2,000 to 3,000 others returned to their homes because they had no hope of getting inside and because they did not care for the rigors of standing in a space where only catch-as-catch-can rules applied.

The big voice of slender, handsome Billy Graham, evangelist who is perhaps the top name in religious crusades nowadays, boomed through the loudspeakers mounted on top of the Music Hall marquee. He could be heard at Twelfth and Wyandotte streets, two blocks away, preaching the old-fashioned, the orthodox, the fundamentalist kind of religion which permits no compromise with the Holy Word.

Inside the hall every seat was filled, and standing listeners lined the outer aisle around the Arena or sat on the floor. There were more standing be hind the boxes, above the highest tiers of the second balcony, and the overflow formed a sparse ring in the lobby. Perhaps seventy-five more found chairs in the hallway behind the stage at the south end of the Arena, their view blocked by the back of the stage.

You could get any guess on the size of the inside crowd, but Arena officials were confident there were at least 13,000. There would have been more but for the fire regulations. The doors were closed at 7:30, fifteen minutes before the start of the rally. Sergeant Falter stood guard at the entrance to keep more from entering.

It had been intended to keep the doors locked until 6:30, but because of the immensity of the throng outside, the doors opened at 6 o'clock. This audience which had waited outside swarmed in. It seemed that in a matter of minutes the place was filled. Still they came, until officials were forced to declare a halt.

We had anticipated an overflow so had set up the sound system to the outside. While Al took care of things inside the Arena, Club Director Gene French led the overflow outside in singing gospel choruses. Jack Cousins took Billy Graham outside to speak to the overflow crowd. The newspaper article continued:

Graham, tall, slender, earnest—32 years old—carrying a bright red Bible, addressed those who stood on the sidewalks and across the street. He delivered an abbreviated version of the message he was to give inside.

While Graham was speaking outside, Al Metsker, 30-year-old Director of KCYFC was warming up the inside crowd. He related the story of KCYFC and how it had grown in it's eight years. An offering was taken without fanfare. In a quiet voice Metsker asked for all to give sacrificially; all that is given above the actual expenses of the rally would go toward furthering the KCYFC work, he said.

"When you give your money, you will see it again," he said. "Only instead of money, that which you will see will be the precious souls your money helped to save."

After more music Graham spoke: "Will God spare America?" He wondered if perhaps it was not already too late. "In no city in America", he said, "had he found a group of young people as devoted, as consecrated, as those here in KCYFC."

After the message more than 250 persons came forward to profess Christ as Savior.

This Super Rally was a fantastic way to celebrate eight years of winning teenagers to Christ. God, indeed, had been so good and had blessed abundantly!

## Stewart Hamblen

"I'm just a traveling salesman of God" asserted Stuart Hamblen from the stage of the Municipal Auditorium. "I've got the best product of all!" He held up his Bible and pointed at it with his other hand. "There, friends, is the greatest spot remover you ever saw!"

Over 10,000 people listened as the big, tall, cowboy singer—who had been a rodeo champion, professional boxer, and race horse trainer—told how God changed his way of living.

"I used to be an alcoholic," the former movie and television star confessed in his husky-voiced, rambling style. "I mean the kind that would wake up in some other city and not remember how I got there from my home in Hollywood."

Stuart Hamblen was our guest at a big Rally on January 19, 1952. Two years before, he had attended Billy Graham's crusade in Los Angeles and had a dramatic conversion that rocked the city.

"I knelt down and accepted Christ," Hamblen said. "Yes, I walked down the sawdust trail, if you want to call it that."

Since that rally more than two years before, he had toured the nation, Mexico, and Canada giving his testimony.

Stuart had composed more than 200 songs during his 20 years in show business. But the lyrics of his new songs had changed. "It Is No Secret What God Can Do," was his first Christian song to hit the national best seller list. Before singing it that night, Hamblen explained how he happened to write it.

"I was talking to an old friend one night after I quit drinking. He asked me if I was really serious about giving up alcohol. I answered 'Yes.'"

"You mean to say you don't even want a drink?" the friend asked.

"Yes, I can honestly say I do not. It is no secret what God can do."

That phrase stayed with the friend and later in the evening he suggested Stuart write a song based on it. Before Hamblen went to bed that night he had written the song.

## YFCI Convention in Kansas City

The annual convention of YFCI was always at Winona Lake, Indiana but they also had a Mid-Winter Convention in various cities. Kansas City was the location on March 8-16, 1952. All the well-known leaders descended on Kansas City for this great event in Music Hall. Cuzzy played a significant role in preparing details.

Business meetings during the day were followed by public Rallies in the evenings. Those leaders who were not involved in the KC Rally each evening scattered for evening rallies in Topeka, Osage City, St. Joseph, Fort Scott, Clay Center, Marion, Newton, Salina and Emporia. Arranging all these meetings was no small job.

We felt honored to host this great convention and probably would not have survived without Cuzzy's help.

### Jack Shuler

In July of that year (1952), we held another big evangelistic crusade in the Municipal Auditorium with Jack Shuler, a young handsome fireball evangelist from California. Cuzzy relieved our load by working with pastors and promotion. An average of 8,000 people attended each evening and hundreds of people received Jesus as Savior. It was a great success with terrific results.

YFCI officials had been so impressed with our outstanding job of organizing the Mid-Winter Convention in Kansas City the year before, that they asked to borrow Cuzzy to help them. So for several months in 1953, Cuzzy went to Japan where he prepared for YFCI's Tokyo World Congress. We were glad to loan him for this worthy cause but were very happy when he returned.

With those big events behind us, we were ready to start on our next project.

# CHAPTER 11

# First Headquarters

Now, almost eight years after we rented our first office, even though a room had been added to our office suite, we were still crowded. Something had to be done.

When YFCI formed, they made a policy that YFC organizations should not own property. They reasoned that Young Men's Christian Association (YMCA) had started as an evangelistic ministry and had evolved into a sports and service organization. They felt that not owning buildings would be a safeguard against the same erosion.

Our philosophy was that you throw your money away when you rent, while you could be building equity by buying. Besides, finding rental property to meet our needs was difficult. So in 1953, we decided to break with the YFCI policy and look for property.

We bought our first Headquarters Building—a big old brick mansion on an acre of ground with huge oak trees at 4500 Walnut Street in Kansas City, Missouri. The location was great—across the street from the Conservatory of Music and one block off Main Street in the Country Club Plaza. We converted several rooms into offices. In the dining room we put our grand piano and Hammond Organ as it became our radio recording studio. By now, WDAF was using wire recorders. An adjacent butler's pantry became the control room holding recording equipment. The large basement room was a great meeting place for Bible Quizzes, Soul Winning Classes, City Council meetings, and other small meetings. It was a busy place! The kitchen was left intact.

## Directors' School

It was no secret that Al trained staff well. Our staff members were constantly lured away by sunny offers from other cities. This was terribly disheartening and frustrating to us because it was difficult to build our own program when we had to constantly train new workers. Actually, I guess it could be considered a compliment also, that the men Al trained were in such demand. After a few years, Kansas City guys were working all across the nation.

As an alternative, Al made an offer to YFC Directors across the nation: "Choose a sharp young man from your area and send him to me to train. I'll teach him and send him back to you."

This started happening. One or two at a time, young men came to Kansas City for six weeks of training. Al spent one-on-one time teaching them. During those six weeks we involved them in every aspect of the ministry so they could learn first-hand all we did.

This required so much effort for what was being accomplished, Al decided better use of his time would be to dedicate two weeks to teach a group. Thus the Directors' School was born. A date was set and announced for all who wanted to apply.

We took care of all the participants' expenses after they got here—another missionary project. Friends volunteered to house them and we fed them their meals.

Al taught them everything they needed to know about programming, stage presentation, how to run clubs, public relations, fund raising, follow-up, office procedures, setting up a board, and much more. On-the-job training included involvement in Bible Clubs, Quizzes, Rally programming, etc.

When he realized the numbers who wanted to come were great, he invited the YFCI President Bob Cook, Kelly Bihl, Jack Hamilton, Ted Engstrom, and other YFCI leaders to come and help teach. Finally it became a YFCI school held here.

Twice a year, fifty to eighty young men would come for two weeks of intensive training. Al set the schedule and taught about half the classes because he could "show" as well as "tell." He actually took them into our bookkeeping office and "showed" them how. They were taken to clubs to "see." They observed the Rallies. Everything was here to see.

The first Directors' School was held in our new Headquarters building.

As the head cook, I became accustomed to seeking bargains. I visited the wholesale grocery warehouse for better prices. I asked the manager at a wonderful smaller bakery what they did with their leftovers at the end of the day. Rather than throw them away I talked them into giving the surplus to us. So every evening at 9 o'clock I picked up delicious sweet rolls, dinner rolls, bread, etc. In every class was a fellow who prided himself in making coffee each morning. So they had orange juice, coffee, milk, cereals and sweet rolls for breakfast on their own.

I arrived to start preparing lunch after I dropped our girls off at school. Ronnie, who was only three that first year of the YFCI training school, spent the day at the headquarters with me. Martha and Marilyn arrived after school and helped set tables, peel potatoes, or whatever they could do. In every class a different young man would become a special friend to each of our girls. They got lots of attention. They loved it.

Vividly in my memory are two "catastrophes" I faced during these schools. Ronnie was three; Marilyn was seven and Martha was nine. We had about fifty fellows from across the country and a couple from foreign countries for that Directors' School. When I returned one afternoon from picking up our girls at school, we hurried in to work on dinner. I must not have gotten the car securely in "park."

"Your car is in the fish pond!" someone shouted a few minutes later.

Blood rushed to my head and I started shaking! What had I done?

But Al hurried to comfort me; "Everything is alright. No one got hurt and that's all that matters."

The car had rolled a few feet forward, the front wheels landing in an 18-inches deep former fishpond in the yard. There was no water in it. Was I embarrassed! A bunch of the strapping guys attending the Director's School and some high school boys who were there for a quiz practice considered it a lark to lift the car out.

Another day I opened a 10-pound canned ham to prepare for a meal. The can slipped and cut the pad off my left ring finger—leaving it hanging by a fragment. Squeezing it tightly to stop the gush of blood, I ran to find help. Al rushed me to emergency at St. Luke's Hospital, which fortunately was near by. Sixteen stitches by the emergency room doctor put the finger back together. But I couldn't let the pain stop me from finishing the meal for those 50 hungry guys. To this day, that finger pad is off-center. Definitely no one has a finger print like mine. Each day was a new and exciting adventure!

I'm embarrassed—but when I consider that I was only 30 years old and carrying all those responsibilities, it relieves my shame a little.

As a result of these Directors' Schools, Rallies began all across the country with leaders who had been trained how to do it. Directors' Schools were held twice a year for years.

## Home For Dinner

Al was a good Daddy. No matter how busy his schedule, he was always home for dinner. In fact, he preached that to his employees.

"Even if you have a meeting in the evening," he admonished, "go home and eat dinner with your family. Don't let anything rob you of that time with them."

Our children made a production of welcoming him home. When he called to say he was leaving the office, I would cheer:

"Daddy's on his way home!" That was their cue to run or get on bicycles, or skates and scurry to the corner to meet him.

They were welcoming the "king." He played with them until dinner was on the table.

He had built a huge, 16-foot swing set in our back yard. With that high a swing you could swing wa-a-a-ay out.

"Run under me, Daddy!" they would yell. And he did. He could keep two of them going "high" at the same time. That swing was used a lot—even by teenagers—for years!

As they got a little older, croquet and badminton provided lots of fun along with various kinds of ball. When we had a free evening we played together as a family. Ping-Pong in our basement was great for the wintertime. And we loved to play all kinds of board games. We were a great game family, which created closeness.

The rural atmosphere where we lived didn't last too many years because developers came along. One offered to pay us $1,000 if we would sell 100 feet off the back of our lot. After selling it we still had a 110'x200' lot and we used the money to finish the other bedroom and bathroom upstairs.

Once again God provided for our personal needs as we sought to put Him first in our lives.

## New Building

After we had been in our 4500 Walnut Headquarters three years, the city reversed the zoning on our property and made it retroactive—a decision that was illegal. Al was so mad because it was "big money" with city government on its side. They wanted to demolish the beautiful mansion and build a revenue-producing hotel on the site. We were being discriminated against but didn't have the money to fight. Al was so upset he determined to move out of the city.

Just one mile west—one block beyond state line into Kansas—he found three acres with a little old brick bungalow on Rainbow Boulevard. God was again proving to us that He works all things for our good. This would give us more ground on a premiere roadway and we would no longer have to deal every day with Kansas City, Mo. politicians. The new property would be in the little town of Westwood, Kansas in booming Johnson County. They welcomed us.

We sold 4500 Walnut at a profit, giving possession quickly to negotiate a better price. Central Bible Church rented us a little house next to their church for our temporary office. The puzzle was where to put the recording studio. Al always found an answer.

This answer turned out to be our living room and Ronnie's bedroom. Our furniture was pushed aside and in came the Hammond organ with its two big speakers and the grand piano. Ronnie's bed moved over to make room for the recording equipment. When it came time to make radio broadcasts we who "lived" there had to either leave or sit quietly. Ronnie loved it when Club Director Bob Kraning doubled as the soundman because Ronnie would go out and sit in Bob's MGA sports car that was parked in our driveway, uttering little-boy motor noises and making-believe steering while broadcasts were being recorded.

At the same time we sold 4500 Walnut, we bought the 4715 Rainbow property and demolished the little house on the land. Al designed a custom-made headquarters building that would fit our needs perfectly and be more economical to maintain. The 90x50 foot brick building was built on a concrete slab and contained twelve offices, a radio recording studio and control room, a reception area, furnace/storage room, kitchen and a multi-purpose room that would seat 300.

Everyone got in on the act. We printed little leaflets that looked like a brick and said, "BUY A BRICK." The other side explained that the project was KCYFC's new Headquarters building. Teenagers canvassed their neighborhoods, talked to their church friends, walked the business areas asking, "Buy a brick?" as they held out their jar, collecting quarters. They thought it was a ball!

Volunteers helped with the construction with Al overseeing it all. The bricklaying was contracted. Ronnie, being only six, thought he was helping when he went with his Daddy.

One Saturday at lunchtime all the volunteer workers loaded into cars and headed for a drive-in. When they arrived they realized Ronnie was not there. Al, thinking he had ridden with someone else, frantically drove back to look for him—only to find him playing on a big dirt pile with his toy earthmoving machine. He hadn't even realized they were gone.

Ninety days after construction started, September 1956, fifty young men arrived from across the country for Directors' School with the routine starting all over again. Our new Headquarters was just a block away from our girls' school making it very handy.

Were we heavenly minded or what? Our building was on *Rainbow* and our phone number was *Skyline* 1700. That was when prefixes were words instead of numbers. So we named our multi-purpose room the *Skylight Room*. It had skylights in the ceiling.

This facility greatly enhanced our ability to minister effectively. All our regular activities except for camps, retreats, Rallies and Clubs were held at our headquarters.

## Martha, a Teenager

Our children had been attending a Christian school. When Martha started the seventh grade, Marilyn the fifth and Ronnie the second they entered public schools.

Martha entered seventh grade at a new school in our area, Milburn Junior High. Although she did not have friends there yet, she decided to start a club. First, she called all the churches in the school area and obtained the names of their students who attended Milburn. Then she contacted those kids and invited them to a planning meeting. From this nucleus the YFC Club was started and she found some instant friends. That was a huge undertaking for a 13-year-old to call strangers and sell the Bible Club idea. She single-handedly got that club started. We were proud of her ingenuity, hard work, and dedication.

Although I had been involved in the ministry all these years, this was my first time being a Sponsor. What fun! I learned that all you have to do is LOVE those kids and show them you CARE and it's easy to win them and guide them. We had children in Milburn Junior High for eight years so I had lots of experience working with those teens.

Our motto for the clubs was "Teens telling teens." We were making leaders who could communicate. I encouraged my junior highers and taught them how to make enthusiastic announcements during the meeting. I helped them learn how to give their testimony without stammering so it would influence others. Through the club planning meetings, I taught them how to organize and how to plan a well-rounded meeting.

"You can help a teenager only to the extent that you know him or her personally," was a principle Al practiced and taught. I spent lots of time with these teenagers.

Of course, cookies, popcorn and other snacks were plentiful. What teenager isn't hungry when he comes home from school? I'm thankful for Carole Barnhart and other mothers who often helped me with transportation and snacks. Those were fun and rewarding years. What a thrill it was to lead many of those kids to Jesus and watch them grow.

I motivated as many of them as possible to be Bible Quizzers. Once a week after school we had quiz practice. Some studied and memorized more than others, but they all learned God's Word. When Martha was in the eighth grade, a young man named David Lewis was in the seventh, and he attended all of our events. In fact, he was the son of Clifford Lewis, the evangelist who preached in the meeting when Al and I dedicated our lives to the Lord. Besides Martha and David, I had some other good quizzers and our practices were exciting. This was before most of the modern translations were done so we were quizzing over King James Version. I often used the Amplified Bible and Phillips translation in our practices to help them understand difficult verses. Marilyn was in the sixth grade and was always there for the practices. Even though she wasn't old enough to be a team member, she liked to practice with us.

## Film Library

At that time gospel films were big. More than four big producers had several new films coming out each year. The films were very popular in YFC and churches. We rented them for our own use until we decided to start our film rental library in 1956. We purchased copies of more than 300 gospel films to rent as a service to churches and other Rallies in the area. They became a great evangelistic tool.

Cuzzy had the responsibility of keeping our Film Library running smoothly. Each time a film was shown it had to be cleaned, repaired, and shipped to the location of its next showing.

Usually high school boys were hired to clean, repair and deliver or mail the films for rentals.

The film library was a service to area churches and organizations that used them, and to us it was another way for us to help spread the gospel.

# CHAPTER 12

# More New Activities

## Formal Banquets

For quite a few years our formal banquets were the big social events of the year for hundreds of teens. Their social lives are vitally important. We believed Christian teens could have as much fun in their social lives as those in the world—only without regrets.

2 Corinthians 6:14-18 directs: "Wherefore come out from among them; and be separate, says the Lord, and touch not the unclean thing. . . "

So we provided delightful formal banquets with elegant decorations, a delicious four-course meal, a fun program, funny skits, beautiful music, and a short challenging message.

A committee of teenagers helped with the plans, and parents and others made the events happen. These banquets were so popular that we eventually had separate ones for junior high and senior high each spring and fall.

One of the highlights of the evening was crowning the King and Queen and their attendants, who were chosen by their peers. Seniors were eligible for the senior high banquet and royalty at the junior high banquets were chosen from freshmen. Runners up became first and second attendants. Queens were crowned with a sparkly rhinestone tiara and received a presentation bouquet of red roses.

Each year the theme and decorations became more elaborate and elegant.

The theme for the spring 1960 banquets was "Paradise of the Pacific." Norman Nagata, president of the Honolulu YFC board, owned a florist business. He air shipped exotic orchid leis for us to present to the queens and attendants. A live small h plate as a souvenir.

trees were spread throughout the banquet

mirrored ball gave the romantic atmosphere

stars in the low lighting.

among other themes were "Stairway to the Stars," "Moonlight and Roses," "Southern Reflections," "An Evening In Paris," "Piccadilli Square," "Shangri-la,". "Chimes of the Orient," and "Castle of Dreams."

Gorgeous decorations transformed the room. A stairway ascending into oblivion was the focal point of "Stairway to the Stars" with swings made in the shape of a star and sliver of a moon for the royalty to swing in.

A huge English castle with 20-foot tall turrets that reached almost to the ceiling covered the stage—with a moat holding water and goldfish separating it from the audience for the "Castle of Dreams." Storefronts on the street in Paris, including a garden café, pastry shop, perfume shop, etc., formed the backdrop for "Evening in Paris."

## Mothers' Club

"Show us, Lord, how to reach out to the parents," we prayed.

This was 1956. In the thirteen years since we started the ministry, many mothers and some dads had limited involvement. But we knew we needed to reach more parents. Too many kids told us of parents who objected to their new-found faith. Some took their Bible away from them. Others ridiculed them. Some parents disciplined their children by taking away their privilege of going to the Club or Rally.

Other parents cared very much that their children were involved in such a wonderful organization, and they wanted to be involved by helping. So, God gave us the idea of a Mothers' Club. We could do both—reach out to the unsaved parents and involve the Christian parents.

The questions plaguing us were how do we organize and get it started? This is what we did.

From the mothers I knew, I chose one from each school to be the "representative" from their school. These ladies formed the nucleus upon which to build. We met as a committee and discussed our goals and how to attain them.

We decided our Mothers' Club would meet the second Friday of each month for lunch. Our desire was to have speakers who would teach parenting skills—give answers to their problems. We wanted to support each other by sharing ideas.

Mothers' Club would be an outreach to unsaved mothers of teens who had become Christians through our ministry. By reaching out to the mother, we hoped to help the teenager as well.

As with the Directors' School, I planned the menu and carried it to completion with volunteers

My mother had taught me how to cook for crowds. If a favorite recipe, for instance, normally serves eight, divide eight into the number you will be serving and multiply the recipe that many times. It's simple! Knowing that three teaspoons equals a tablespoon and 16 tablespoons equals a cup, etc. made it easy.

When the food was served and the tables cleared, I hurriedly changed my clothes and joined the crowd as a hostess. Then when the guests were gone, I changed back into my working clothes, along with volunteers, and did the dishes.

The programs included an update on the YFC ministry, sharing prayer requests and needs for volunteers, and a message relating to parenting teenagers but always including the gospel message. From this group of 100-130 mothers, we recruited help for all areas of our ministry. Often the ladies would say, "I enjoyed that message so much. I wish my husband could have heard it."

Hearing remarks like this prompted us to dream of having an identical meeting in the evening, so fathers and working mothers could get in on the blessings.

We taught the teenagers that being obedient and respectful

was the best way to win their parents. They should surprise their parents by doing what they should without even being told. We taught that if Christ is real in their lives, it should show in the little things as well as the big.

Because of this outreach, many parents came to know Christ as their Savior. What a joy it was to see whole families become Christians as a result of their teenager's decision and continuing dedication.

## Citywide Hayride

Friday, November 23, 1956, at the KCYFC headquarters 375 teenagers loaded into five busses and seventeen cars and headed to Clinton Miller's farm at Hwy 7 and 10 near Bonner Springs for a hayride. Crisp air and biting wind nipped their cheeks as they mounted wagons and trucks loaded with hay. Shouts of glee and voluminous laughter permeated the quiet countryside. A clear, full moon illuminated the hills and valleys as the tossed hay fluttered aimlessly. The fun continued on the ride back to the YFC headquarters where mothers ladled big pots of steaming chili into bowls.

Club Directors Bob Kraning, Bob Beyler, Bruce Washburn and Jack Palmer pulled off hilarious antics. As was always our custom, the evening ended with a brief clear-cut gospel message—this time by Darrel Handel. When the invitation was given, twelve terrific teenagers prayed to receive Jesus into their hearts. It was a great evening!

A variety of fun activities like this were carried out hundreds of times through the years—always with a gospel message and invitation. God blessed our ministry so that we seldom had an event without leading teenagers to Christ! We were so happy to be working with teenagers. They search for the truth without being skeptics. Our greatest joy was that when a teenager got saved, not only was a soul saved—but also a life!

## Explosion

Saturday, November 23, 1957

"Just as I am without one plea…" The words of the invitation song floated passionately from the lips of the 1,200 young people packed in the Grand Avenue Temple at 9:25 P.M. It had been a glorious Rally that evening. Lots of great music, testimonies, and an inspiring speaker. Al was on the platform just about to close the gospel invitation. Suddenly a frightful explosion shook the building! The stained glass windows radiated the flickering red of fire. Everyone panicked!

In a calm, assuring—but forceful—voice, Al commanded: "Everyone stay right where you are. You'll be all right if you do as I say." He really didn't know what had happened, but he knew a stampede would be disastrous. He told the musicians to keep singing.

Sirens grew louder. Crimson flickering through windows terrified the crowd.

While his brother, Lowell, who was the head usher went to check on the situation, Al continued the invitation.

"If that explosion had been this building and we were all ushered into eternity, would you have been ready? If you haven't received Jesus as your Savior, now is the time. Don't put it off any longer. You never know when it will be too late. God has given you another chance. Come now. Counselors are waiting for you."

Another dozen people joined those already in the prayer room, knowing that they had to make peace with God.

Al continued to calmly order everyone. "Stay right where you are. Everything will be OK." Lowell soon returned, went to the platform and quietly informed Al of the situation. An explosion had destroyed the four-story Sterling Building and seven-story Eight-O-Four Grand Building diagonally across the street. Brick walls had fallen on cars and buses that had brought teens to our Rally. Police requested Al to hold the people until they approved our leaving.

Al announced what buildings had blown up and that the buses and cars parked in that particular lot were demolished, so we would have to find ways home for all who came in those vehicles. When the police gave the signal that we could start vacating the building, Al methodically asked about each area of the city.

"Who came on the Northeast Bus — raise your hands." Then he asked,

"Who drove a car from the Northeast area? We need you to take kids home."

As he connected teens with rides, they were released to go but were told to exit only to the right, away from the explosion.

Al masterfully controlled the crowd. The police commended him later, saying it would have been chaos if those young people had been turned loose.

We praised the Lord that the explosion didn't happen ten minutes later when hundreds of teenagers would have crowded the parking lot loading into the buses! Doubtless many of them would have been killed.

That night after the explosion, John Wilson, a teenager from Bonner Springs, rushed to the prayer room because he knew he was not ready to meet God. There he found new life in Jesus Christ. Through his high school years he continued to be active in YFC and grew spiritually. Eleven years later as a soldier in Vietnam he witnessed to all his buddies. On May 4, 1969 he met Jesus face to face, a war casualty. How glad we were that YFC was there presenting the gospel to teenagers!

### Mayor Bartle's Letter

This letter dated July 19, 1958 was presented to Al along with a key to the city as we completed 15 years of ministry in KCYFC from one of the greatest mayors the city has ever had. He was a champion of Boy Scouts of America and Bartle Hall, the Kansas City Convention Center is named for him.

"When I think of the commanding life of Al Metsker, as he has dedicated his many talents, energy, and money to the work of the Lord, I realize fully the great and matchless contribution he has made to the youth in the Heart of America and throughout our nation and, indeed, the world at large.

Because of his earnestness and zeal in serving the Master he has gone all-out seven days a week as he has dedicated his very being to God's service and for the well-being of youth. Greater Kansas City today is a finer, cleaner, and better city because of his inspiring leadership and the wonderfully fine example which he has set for youth. Many young Kansas Citians have been put on the pathway of life and living which has been constructive because of his patience and his deep devotion to the tasks at hand.

I would certainly toss a healthy and hearty salute to Brother Al. Although he needs not a key to Kansas City, Missouri, whose youth he has served so faithfully and long, yet I hand him herewith a gold key to the hearts of all Kansas Citians who love the Lord and know of the work which he has done."

Faithfully yours,  H. Roe Bartle, Mayor

# CHAPTER 13

# World Mission Trip

O verland Park 'Youth For Christ' Leader Embarks For India Meeting" headlined an article in the *Kansas City Star* on Saturday, December 28, 1958 that stated in part:

> Rev. Al Metsker of 6914 Reeds Road, Overland Park, Kansas, Director of KCYFC left for Madras, India, Friday, December 27, to attend Youth for Christ International's 10th World Congress for Christian Youth.
>
> Following the Congress in Madras, Reverend Metsker will lead the crusade in Bombay.

The leaders of YFCI had begged Al to go every year to the Congress on Evangelism held annually in a different country. But his heart's burden was for the teens of the Mid-Central area. He questioned whether or not he would be used effectively enough to warrant his time away from the KC ministry. Finally, he agreed to go.

God had already given him a burden to minister to the teens of India. KCYFC had adopted Bombay YFC as a sister ministry and for more than a year we had sent a monthly offering to them. This was another of our missionary outreaches.

God had provided a great staff in Kansas City and Al felt comfortable leaving the ministry in the competent care of his staff.

Jack Cousins had been a valued, dedicated, right-hand-man to Al for eight years. His secretary, Joan Keller had played a significant roll in her day to day responsibilities for three years.

Irving Philgreen, whose father had played piano at those earlier rallies, had been Assistant Director for three years. When

Irving was twelve, he had dedicated his life to serve Jesus at one of our Rallies featuring Billy Graham. From that time, he became a "shadow" to Al—always at Al's elbow, ready to do anything he could and learning from Al. They became great buddies. He was a natural leader who was well liked by everyone so became a key person in his YFC club, quizzing and every area of YFC.

While he was still in high school Irving led singing in Al's evangelistic meetings. After high school graduation, he went to Bob Jones University and became KCYFC's unofficial public relations guru recruiting all the sharp, talented guys to join our staff. When Al went to BJU as chapel speaker, Irv encouraged the best students to interview with Al.

Immediately after Irv's graduation from BJU in 1956, we went to Detroit where Al married him to his college sweetheart, Vonnie. We were happy that Irv became Al's Assistant Director.

The weeklong Congress in Madras was held for leaders and teenagers from across India and several other countries. All delegates attended morning and evening sessions and workshops during the day. The forty YFC leaders from America preached and taught. After the Congress was finished, the American leaders divided into teams and fanned out into large cities across India for individual city evangelistic crusades.

YFCI president, Sam Wohlgemuth, and executive director, Ted Engstrom, assured Al that he would be the evangelist for the crusade in Bombay because of his interest in that city. Al was not one to sit around doing nothing, nor was he interested in taking a "pleasure trip." He wanted his time to count for eternity, or he would stay home and work at the job God had given him with KC teens. With promises that he would be busy serving God, he was ready to go. Les Davis, a Kansas City Christian businessman, accompanied him on the whole trip.

Most of the US delegation flew on the same plane—a 707 jet that was fairly new at the time. It was Al's first experience on this big jet and he loved it.

Rome was their first stop after NYC. Al wrote:

> "What an eight hours we spent in Rome! We went down the Appian Way where Paul traveled to get to Rome. We went to the Coliseum where the saints were martyred, St. Peters Cathedral, the Basilica, and Vatican City. We visited the prison where Paul was in chains when he wrote II Timothy. That was about the greatest to me!"

This was the first time Al and I had been separated for more than five days and oh, how terribly our children and I missed him. Martha was 14, Marilyn was 12, and Ronnie was 8. We placed a big map of the world on a wall of our house with a line marking Al's itinerary. Each day we traced his travels praying for each step and imagining what he was doing.

When letters arrived I read them aloud to them—crying all the way through. I couldn't help myself. I was happy for this great opportunity, but I missed him so much.

Their next stop was in Tel-Aviv, Israel, where they saw the Sea of Galilee, Nazareth, Mt. Caramel, and crossed the Jordan River into enemy territory.

The following day he wrote:

> "This has been a fabulous day! This morning we had a little service on Calvary then another at the *empty* tomb! What a thrill! What a blessing to start the year with a meeting at the empty tomb praising our risen Savior."

**From Madras, India - Jan. 1:** I am sitting with Sam Wolgemuth (President of YFCI) during this flight to Madras. He asked me if I would be willing to take a leave of absence from KCYFC, bring my family, and move to one of the big cities of the world to establish a YFC ministry and train native workers—like Joe and Berniece Weatherly have done in Singapore.

I told him that before we were married we told the Lord we were willing to go any place He led us—that if God led that way we would be willing. I told him it would have to be from the Lord and reminded him again the reason this is my first Congress is because I hadn't felt God's leading before. It is a wonderful thing to just be committed to Him!

**Madras - Jan. 4:** A crowd of 4,000 were at the afternoon rally which was translated into three different languages. Tomorrow we will be speaking to Bible Clubbers in eleven languages. About 75% speak English.

This is a fascinating land! People everywhere! Cows are sacred to the Hindus so they roam loose everywhere. Little children pick up their droppings and set them in the sun to dry—then they are used for fuel. Men pull 2-wheeled carts big enough for a horse to pull. There are lots of bicycles and motor scooters. The whole street is a sidewalk. People sleep everywhere—even on the street. We saw a man who had just died on the side of the road and someone stripped off his clothes. Otherwise everyone just walked around him. It breaks your heart!

This land has another side, though. At the meeting the people were clean and well dressed. The men were dressed in white and the women in saris of the brightest colors! What a pretty sight! The mosquitoes are plenteous! We sleep under netting. There is no hot water in the hotel and it is one of the better ones. When you see the food, it's strange how you get over being hungry. I'm glad I brought a few candy bars from NYC.

**Madras - Jan. 5:** Wonderful day! I worked with high schoolers organizing Quizzes. In the morning meeting I led three girls and eighteen boys to Christ. This afternoon I gave my testimony and Sam preached. About 75 more were saved.

I practiced with the Bombay quiz team. They are sharp! I hope we can start Bible Clubs there next week while I'm having my crusade. These people just love us.

**Madras - Jan. 6:** Did I have fun tonight! I went 10 miles to a little village where I had a meeting. I started by giving my testimony to the 400 people. When I told about being thrown from a horse, I asked how many had ridden a horse and only one raised a hand. I asked how many had ridden an oxen and they all raised their hands. So tomorrow when I go back, they are bringing an oxen for me to ride. Ha! When I gave the invitation 24 were saved. The missionaries were thrilled.

I met a brilliant fellow, Victor Monagoram, who wants to come to KC to Director's School in September. Les Davis said he would get another Kansas businessman to help and they would pay his way. Victor will make a great leader. He wants to come back to India and teach others what we teach him in KC.

I've been gone eleven days and still no mail. I think I'll die if I don't hear from you tomorrow!" [I had written every day but mail delivery was slow.]

**Jan. 8** - Yesterday I spoke to the Convention about how to start a YFC ministry. This morning we started out with Quizzes and then I preached at 11:00. Ten came for salvation and 19 for dedication.

The little kids are trained to be beggars. They walk backwards in front of you everywhere you go rubbing their tummy and saying, "No mama. No papa. Very hungry." It is sad. But sometimes they drive you batty. Tonight I beat one to the draw and asked him if he could help me. He reached into his pocket and gave me a handful of coins. I gave them back and all the guys with me were dying laughing at me.

**Madras - Jan 9:** The Quizzes have really gone over big! The kids are now cheering and clapping just like in America. One missionary said she had never heard hearty laughter from India's teens before. A son of the official at the Indian Embassy came forward in one of the meetings along with several teenagers from his neighborhood. He was very pleased! The whole city of Madras is conscious of our Congress here.

The Bombay Quiz team won the national championship—Al's team! Winners just like the KC kids! There were 10,000 people at the final meeting of the Congress.

Tomorrow we will split up to do our crusades in different cities. I'll be going to Bombay. I just got my schedule. Brother!! Twelve meetings lined up for the middle Sunday. I can hardly wait! They tell me that our meetings will be the biggest of all. Pray for me the 13th through 21st in Bombay. [Of course, we prayed every day.]

**Bombay**—Had a reception at YMCA for pastors and youth leaders—52 attended. The Bombay Quiz champions gave testimonies and I spoke about how to start YFC and Bible Clubs. Then I went to speak at the Bombay Youth Council.

I teach a Bible Class every morning at 8:00. They expected only about 6 to show up but the first day there were 23 and the second day 26. I teach a counselors course every evening at 5:00. I've had several special prayer meetings with pastors and others.

Today I took Roy (the missionary) to get a new suit and I gave his wife some money for a new outfit. They need it so badly and they were thrilled!

I spent time at Roy's office to check out his books and records. He didn't have any. I told him I couldn't support a ministry that didn't have good financial records, so I set them up for him. He was so grateful — said no one had ever shown him how. I am determined to get YFC and Bible Clubs set up before I leave and hope to find someone to head it up and help get their support raised.

I spent 2 hours with 37 sharp Christian teenagers who plan to start five Bible Clubs for starters. I taught them how to program, emcee, give a testimony and lead singing. They are fired up! We had a great prayer meeting with them. Roy said he had never been able to get them to pray before. We're going to keep communicating with them from KC giving them ideas.

The sharpest Indian pastor I have met has attached himself to me. Everywhere I go he is there drinking in what I say.

Phil and Louie Palermo were terrific brothers who played the accordion and guitar and sang together as well as being comic entertainers. They were on YFCI staff and were greatly loved everywhere they went. Palermos were also favorites at KCYFC. They were a part of Al's team to Bombay.

I wrote Al about the January 17 Rally here:

"We had 16 kids at our pre-rally party at our house—eight of them new! They are all really sharp kids. Several other clubs had parties and the Rally was jammed! We overflowed 165 into the basement of the auditorium and Bob Page emceed and Don Schmucker led the singing. There were 30 saved—6 of them from the meeting downstairs.

"Oh, honey, how the Lord answered our prayers! Five of the kids at our party were saved! We were so thrilled when we got home we fell on our knees and had a praise meeting!"

I went on to tell him about each of the kids who got saved.

**Jan. 18**: After my 8:30 A.M. meeting nine men came to be saved. While I was leading them to Jesus, the crowd was gathering for the next service. I preached the same message and 150 came to be saved. Thinking they misunderstood, I re-explained to them what they were coming for and gave

them an opportunity to return to their seats. They were all truly seeking Christ so I led them to the Lord just like I would one on one.

**Jan 20:** Last night I preached to a packed house. Thirty-three really sharp folks were saved. After the meeting we went to a YFC Board meeting where I crammed them full of information about how to lead the ministry. They were blessed! By midnight they were all saying 'For the first time we feel we know what we're doing.' Roy is blessed, too! We had a great time of prayer. This afternoon we have a high school assembly.

**Jan. 21:** Man, we had a meeting last night! The place was jammed. People were in the aisles, on the stairs, on the platform and looking in the windows. We put up speakers outside for those who couldn't get in. I preached on 2 Chron. 7:14 and titled it "The New India." There were 37 saved and 10 came for assurance!

I took pledges to support the YFC ministry here and 235 Rupees a month were pledged. Roy and all the pastors are blessed! After the meeting people crowded around me for autographs and many cried because we were leaving. Three girls about 14 came to my flat and gave me a little lamp for a going away gift. One of them was saved two nights ago.

Among the nine men saved Sunday morning was a man who owns a factory and was a heavy drinker. He went to work and told his employees about finding Christ, that he was quitting drinking and gave them all Bibles.

**Jan. 22:** Calcutta would break your heart more than any other big city in India. There are six million people and I think about three million skinny cows. People sleep on the streets in long rows like logs side by side.

**Jan. 23:** Praise the Lord, I'm in Singapore with Joe and Berniece Weatherly! I preached this morning and had 5 saved. In my noon meeting 49 were saved! These kids are sharp as those in US. It's good to see Kee Kok again!

Keo Kok Lew was a sharp young native of Singapore who had spent six months in Kansas City learning from Al and the Club Directors how to do a YFC ministry and then had gone back to Singapore and done the job. During those months in KC he practically became a part of our family—even living at my parents' house part of the time.

> **Jan. 26:** The Saturday night Rally in Singapore was wonderful! There were 1,400—mostly teenagers—in an auditorium like KC's Music Hall. Keo Kok led the singing, Joe emceed, Palermos and Dave Grant did the special music, Ted Engstrom and I brought greetings and T.W. Wilson preached. There were 85 saved.

A debilitating case of the Asian flu seized Al in Singapore that required him to fly directly home—missing Hawaii.

He had been looking forward to being in Hawaii because a KC boy, Jack Hatton, pastored a church there and Al was to preach in his church. It was in Jack and Jeannie's home in Kansas City that we held our first Soul Winners Class back in 1944. So Al's terrific missionary journey ended abruptly with the Asian flu.

We were so glad to have Al home! With our tender loving care in a few days he was good as new and ready to start on his next heavy schedule.

He brought me a sari from India. A sari is the women's dress—a hand-woven, pure silk, brightly colored cloth 44 inches wide and 18 feet long. One end of it is wrapped around your waist and tied. The rest is pleated on your fingers and tucked into the waist to form the skirt and the other end is draped over the shoulder.

The *Kansas City Star* did a follow-up article on his trip including a picture of us trying the sari on me.

## Directors School

Just two weeks after Al returned, fifty young men from across the nation would arrive in Kansas City for Director's School. He had written me: "Honey, could you start lining up homes for the fellows to stay in? Try to get homes where they can take at least two to four men so transportation to the Headquarters won't be so much of a problem."

By the time he arrived home I had places for all the men to stay for their two weeks here. I also had menus planned and volunteers lined up to help me cook.

Being with these guys from across the nation almost around the clock for two weeks, we became very fond of each other. That made the YFCI conventions even more fun because each one was like a reunion. Our children were always around except when they were in school, so they were included in those relationships.

Directors' School was a big drain on our ministry because it totally consumed the time of our whole staff, took over our facilities, and depleted our finances. This was one of our missionary projects because these men would start similar ministries across the country.

## Dormitory

"Great numbers of teenagers are being saved through KCYFC; however, we feel a responsibility to help these new Christians more than can be done in a once-a-week Club and Saturday night Rally," Al proclaimed. "They need to be taught how to pray, how to have a quiet time, and how to cope with the many problems they face daily."

That was his motivation behind wanting to build a small dormitory at the back of our Headquarters lot.

Every spring and fall we had citywide weekend conferences but this would allow small one-school-at-a-time conferences.

So that spring, 1959, he drew plans for a 40'x100' building for these small conferences, and to house men when they came for the two-week Directors' School. Parts of it were contracted and volunteers did the rest.

An entry parlor divided the boys and girls sides. Each side had room to sleep 24 teenagers plus adult leaders. Showers and restrooms were on each side.

The lower level provided a large multi-purpose room, a kitchen and our print shop. The multi-purpose room was used for numerous other events like quizzes, parties, dinners, etc.

### Irv Leaves

All had gone well in the ministry while Al was gone on his trip to India—so well, in fact, that a few months after Al's return Irv Philgreen dropped a bomb.

"It was fun 'acting' Director!" he told Al. "I enjoyed being the #1 man so much I don't know if I'll ever be happy until I head up my own ministry."

We understood. He had the ability—but we felt the pain of loss. So in 1960 Irv and Vonnie stepped through an open door to become the Director of Toledo, Ohio YFC. They were always our very dear friends.

# CHAPTER 14

# Capital Teen Convention

The scene: Kansas City Union Station, second only in size to New York City's Grand Central Station, and in our eyes the most beautiful and exciting train station anywhere.

The time: 6 A.M. a crispy Sunday morning, December 27, 1959.

With snow crunching beneath their feet and the reflection of bright sun rays blinding them, teenagers screamed as they spotted their friends among the crowd. An excited 375 teenagers lugging suitcases hugged their family good-bye. Along with 125 adult chaperones and YFC Staff, they were pushing and shoving their way to the chartered Santa Fe train waiting to chug them off to Washington, D.C. for the YFCI Capital Teen Convention.

Most of the kids had worked hard to raise $95 for the trip plus a little spending money. Verl Thurman, a sales executive and father of two YFC clubbers going on the trip, Verla and Eric, set up a candy distributorship where the kids could earn 35% profit on all the candy they sold. The kids were ready to reap the benefits of all their hard work.

All day Tuesday, December 8, had been set aside for prayer for the convention and people had dropped by our headquarters to pray.

The railway company had not exactly met the standards they promised. Our train cars appeared to be reclaimed World War I relics that bumped along on the tracks with great gusto. The 24-hour trip was exhausting — but unforgettable. The aisles of the trains streamed with kids walking from car to car to visit friends. Freezing gusts of wind blasted you as you moved through the ramshackle passageways between cars. Sleeping time was mostly a disaster. The remote possibility for sleep was to roll up in a blanket sitting propped next to a friend like a can of sardines. The "nice meals" they had promised turned out to be sack lunches we received by bouncing through six or seven cars to retrieve them from the "dining car."

But it was a ball! It could have been the Hilton as far as the kids were concerned. They were having a long party with their friends on their way to Washington, D. C. Upon arrival we boarded buses and checked in at our hotel.

Ten thousand teenagers from 48 states and fourteen foreign countries descended on the Capital for this unprecedented event. We were to be at the Armory by noon where we were served lunch. Imagine feeding 10,000 teenagers. The American Dairy Association delivered 50,000 pints of milk to the armory to serve the teens—the largest single delivery of milk ever made to one place at that time. All our meals were served in the Armory and we were housed in 25 hotels.

"You and Your Country" was the opening theme when U.S Senator Frank Carlson from Kansas, a dear friend of ours, a great Christian and honorary Chairman of the convention, introduced national leaders. President Dwight Eisenhower sent his greetings and Vice-president Richard Nixon made an appearance

A gigantic banner proclaiming: "Teens Telling Teens in this Decade of Destiny" dominated the area above the platform.

We were thrilled when Al was asked to emcee one of the morning sessions. Jack Cousins reported that we had 700 there from our seven-state Mid-Central Area.

Ted Engstrom, president of YFCI at the time, explained: "We brought these teens here to see their American heritage and inspire them to go back to their high school campuses to be better ambassadors for Jesus Christ. We're very optimistic about our teenagers. They're the greatest bunch in the world."

Seminars were held in the mornings after a morning challenge. Teens were awed by the tour of the White House and other historical sites.

Bob Pierce, founder of World Vision, delivered a forceful missionary challenge. The closing rally was a powerful salvation and dedication message by Billy Graham on "You and Your World." Many teenagers made life-changing decisions during the convention.

On our way home, we stopped in Chicago to do a little sightseeing and take a tour of Moody Bible Institute. All returned home exhausted but exuberant!

A normal fun-loving dedicated Christian 15-year-old, Martha had sold enough candy to pay her way. No question, she was off somewhere in one of the coaches surrounded by devoted friends having a great time. We knew everything would be loving, peaceful and tranquil in her presence.

Thirteen-year-old Marilyn was another story. We prayed that in all her antics, she wouldn't get carried away. She constantly created tricks and jokes. Never a dull moment in her presence and her friends just egged her on. She would make sure she got her money's worth of fun.

Our girls never minded us being a part of all the activities because we treated them like any other teenager during YFC activities. Although Ronnie was only nine, he sold his share of candy to earn the trip. He was with us the whole time since he would not have been eligible to go without us. The whole trip was one of those exciting and memorable experiences that could never be duplicated.

## Memorial Hall

"We have a problem. It's a good problem but nevertheless one that needs an answer," Al told the staff and board. "We are outgrowing Grand Avenue Temple. Several Rallies have overflowed into the basement auditorium. How long can we shuffle our performers downstairs after finishing in the main auditorium just to do it all over again?" We had to make a move.

So Saturday night, June 11, 1960, we moved to the 3,300-seat Memorial Hall in downtown Kansas City, Kansas. This move not only gave us a larger auditorium, but also provided a large stage with curtains and special lighting effects so we could do better productions.

Our goal was to have a bus coming from every school to the Rally. Adult sponsors or Club Directors arranged for and sometimes drove the buses—many from area churches.

Competition among schools for Rally attendance added incentive for teens to bring their friends. Students would sign up for their school on a list in the lobby. A feature at every Rally was reading the attendance from the top five schools in Junior and Senior High. Kids strategized how they would stand and cheer for their school if they were listed in the top five.

With this method several things happened.

1. We had the name of everyone from each school so we could keep attendance records for follow-up.

2. It motivated the kids to not miss attending because they wanted their school to win.

3. It also provided another selling point—when teens invited new ones they could say, "Come and help our school win!"

We knew that record keeping was important. When you are working with hundreds of kids it would be easy to forget some. Keeping records reminds you: "Hey, where's Jeff? I haven't seen him for a couple of weeks." Teenagers, just like everyone else, need attention and want to know if they are missed. They know you care if you call and tell them how much you've missed them, ask if there's anything you can do for them and tell them how much you're looking forward to seeing them next time.

From time to time we varied the prize for the winning schools. Sometimes it was a bag of candy bars for them to eat on their way home if they came on a bus. Sometimes we honored a club after they had won four times by doing a special segment spotlighting them during the Rally. Sometimes we had a roving trophy that was given to the club that won. They would have to bring it back the next week to be given to that week's winner. When they won it ten times, it was theirs to keep. Sometimes a representative from the winning school could come to the stage and throw a pie in the face of their Club Director. If they hit a certain high attendance number, they could throw it in Al's face.

Innovative new ideas are vital when working with teens to hold their long-term attention. Funny skits put on by the Club Directors caused hilarious laughter. At times an object fastened under a seat determined who would receive a mystery prize. Special recognition of YFC teens who were star athletes or held top student body or class offices in their schools delivered encouragement and challenge to others. Testimonies from teens about leading someone to Christ were a blessing to all. Others told about papers they had written or speeches given for school that gave a witness. Not only did the teens grow by this experience; they challenged others to do likewise.

We experienced a rather tough financial situation after incurring the added expenses of moving to Memorial Hall. God laid it on Al's heart to challenge the benefactors themselves—the teenagers. He started the Teen Booster Club.

"To be a Teen Booster, you promise by faith to give at least $1 a week to YFC." Al told the kids. "One of the Christian graces is to give of your money to support the work of the Lord. If you are not engaged in a systematic program of giving, you are missing a great blessing. You must not give money to YFC that you should be giving to your church." When they gave their second dollar they received an Amplified New Testament. Within a few weeks, 203 teens had joined and more joined each week. The financial boost was a great blessing but the greatest blessing was that the teens were learning the joy of giving.

Our crowds grew, sometimes reaching 2,500 to 3,000. The weekend of March 3 & 4, 1961 was great! We showed Billy Graham's new film, "Shadow of the Boomerang," at Memorial

Hall. Friday evening 3,200 attended and 3,300 on Saturday, plus another 600 overflowed into a church down the street. A total of 152 people were personally prayed with in our counseling room making salvation decisions. What a great victory!

We had always worked diligently to be friends with pastors. Al assured them, "We are not a church and will *never* be a church. Our purpose is not to take people out of your church but to reach the unchurched and get them involved in your church."

He vowed that we would never schedule anything on Sundays or Wednesdays, the times churches had activities. We had a good relationship with most churches.

The last statement Al made from the stage at the end of every Rally was: "Be in a good Bible-believing, Christ-exalting church tomorrow morning and pray for your pastor." He often added, "and have an unsaved person sitting beside you."

Nearly every Saturday night sometime during the Rally Al would ask: "Hold up your Bible! Everyone who has your Bible with you, raise it high!"

Bibles were thrust into the air all over. He encouraged teens to carry them, read them, memorize them, and live by them.

For quite a few years YFCI published a special edition of Bibles with bright red leather covers. Teenagers worked hard to have a red Bible to carry. In later years after YFCI quit offering them, KCYFC made a special edition of red Bibles.

Al quipped, "All Bibles should be read!" (red)

Over the next five years our Rally home was moved several times—to Grand Avenue Temple, to Memorial Hall, to First Nazarene and to Evangel Temple.

No matter where we met, our spotlight always went with us.

## Len Rodgers & Dick Hatfield

Dick Hatfield, as a teenager in East High School, was an energetic leader and a fireball preacher. After college graduation he became a Club Director but also wrote for the

*Conquest*, our monthly four-page newspaper, and carried total responsibility for our yearbooks, BEAM. In 1961 he became head of the senior high clubs.

Leonard Rodgers took the challenge to oversee clubs in the new junior high schools that were springing up all over the area. He recruited at least one parent from each school to be a Sponsor, relieving the Club Directors of many details. He had phenomenal success and soon the junior high clubs had all the activities of the senior high—only their own.

Leonard had been a valuable Club Director for over five years when God called him to go to Beirut, Lebanon as a missionary. We hated for him to leave but knew he must follow God's leading. For a number of years, his finances were received and receipted at our office—a free service to him. Our ministry helped support him for a number of years and printed a report from him in each of our Conquests so people would know how to pray. In the years that followed, Leonard founded Venture Middle East, a missionary outreach in Lebanon.

Dave Koser attended Directors' School in Kansas City in 1958 and went to Mansfield, Ohio, where he was YFC Director for nearly five years before becoming a Club Director on our staff in 1962.

## Directors' School Move

A strange turn of events happened. After Directors' School had met here for several years, someone from YFCI suggested that Al was getting too much power. "We have little Al Metskers all over the country. If he wants to, he can win an election and do anything he wants."

To us that was ridiculous. Al was not looking for power. He certainly did not want another job. But leaders finally decided that, to keep everyone happy, the school should be moved from

Kansas City. Al was asked to teach in the new location but he felt "all the teeth had been pulled" from the teaching process. Al believed the "hands on" learning – to experience as well as to be taught in a classroom setting – was the winning combination. The new location did not provide that opportunity. So Al put his energies into teaching men for our staff here in Kansas City.

# CHAPTER 15

# Al Named President of KCBC

On Tuesday, January 24, 1961, an announcement was made to the student body of Kansas City Bible College that the Board of Directors had unanimously appointed Al Metsker the new acting president.

Al had been a KCBC board member for about six years. In a meeting the previous day, the board discussed closing the school because of financial and other problems. The thought distressed Al.

"We can't close the school." Al was impassioned. "There has to be an answer."

But the board members were tired of "whipping a dead horse." Al tried to convince them not to give up. Finally someone stated: "Well, Al, if you think it can be saved, *you* become the President and see if you can do it." They decided this was the only way they would keep the school open.

Al didn't *need* another job. He didn't *want* another job. But he felt so definitely that Kansas City should have a Bible College he finally consented to try to "get it back on track" and find a permanent president. He immediately went to work trying to correct the problems, generate income and implement new programs.

All of this he was doing while continuing to lead the huge KCYFC ministry.

When the announcement was made, among the many encouraging letters of congratulations Al received from leaders across the country, was this letter from Billy Graham:

"Just a note of congratulations on your becoming the acting president of the Kansas City Bible College. I hope you keep the post and combine your Youth For Christ activities with this great training center. I believe that you could build this into one of the greatest institutions of its kind in the United States. This would give you a long-range ministry that would be second to none in the country. I have a great burden and vision for Christian education. I don't know anyone better qualified to lead a school like that than you.

I shall never forget when I accepted the presidency of Northwestern Schools that you were one among the first to encourage me. I also remember the students and financial gifts you were able to get for us. Therefore I consider myself in your debt.

I should be most delighted to be of any service to you that I possibly could in this new venture of faith. Your pal, Billy

## Calvary Bible College

Within five months God had helped Al to eliminate the problems and turn around the financial picture. Al had also learned that Midwest Bible Institute in St. Louis was looking for a new campus. KCBC was looking for a new president. So Al contacted President Roger Andrus in St. Louis and initiated talk of merging. A spirit of harmony and cooperation drew both boards together, realizing that each had what the other lacked. It seemed like the perfect marriage.

They decided a fresh start with a new name was best. Calvary Bible College was born in Al's office at KCYFC. Roger Andrus became president and Al was named vice-president. All of this was done with not a penny of remuneration. It was out of the burden of Al's heart. As vice-president, Al was no longer on the board.

We were happy that the school was on solid footing and that Al was free from the added responsibility.

## Lazy-M Ranch

During this time Al started having chest pains. He was hospitalized for a series of tests on his heart at the age of 40. The pressure had been too much.

The doctor told him he simply *had* to do something to relax.

"I don't care if you play golf, go fishing, plant a garden or what," the doctor advised. "You decide. But you must do something to help you relax or you will die of a heart attack."

"The only thing that appeals to me," Al told me after thinking about it for a while, "is to find some ground out in God's open country where I can get away from the phone."

We didn't have any money but we started relaxing occasionally by driving in the country looking for ten acres we could buy. It seemed ten acres weren't being sold.

"I have this beautiful 80 acres I want you to look at near Louisburg," a realtor urged one Sunday afternoon. Louisburg was only 30 minutes from home.

"You're wasting your time," we warned him. "We would never be able to afford that."

"Just let me show you," he insisted.

We went with him. When we walked over the acres we fell in love with it. Big walnut and oak trees. A pretty little creek wound through the hills. Some flat tillable soil. We couldn't resist. This was our answer.

We refinanced our house to make the down payment on what we called "Lazy-M Ranch." At that time Uncle Sam was paying farmers to not grow grains. Wheat had been raised on this land, so we put it in the Feed-Grain Program and planted it with brome grass, which kept the soil from eroding and provided great pasture. Each year Uncle Sam gave us enough to make the payments.

Midnight and Lightning were our first two additions to Lazy-M. Their names fit them perfectly. Both the horses were so full of energy they chomped at the bit to gallop over the countryside when we saddled and jumped on their backs. This made Al relax.

There were no buildings on Lazy-M so we bought a used mobile home and leveled it on a foundation under a big tree way back from the road. A cistern Al buried in the ground provided storage for water we had hauled from Louisburg. Electricity was run to the mobile home so we had all the comforts of home. What a refuge!

We went to Lazy-M for fun and relaxation whenever we could get away for a few hours or overnight. Those were great father/son days.

Al and Ronnie built what we called a barn—a 28'x28'-foot structure with a loft. This is where he parked the old tractor he bought, stored tools, and hid tack.

One winter Al brought our little Allis Chalmers tractor to Overland Park and parked it in our garage where he and Ronnie overhauled the engine. This was a teaching/learning experience for them. When Ronnie was younger, Al had taught him to overhaul a little one-cylinder lawn mower engine.

Having had experience on the farm with stock, one year Al thought he could make extra money with very little effort by grazing a dozen yearling calves. It worked. After letting them graze a year we sold them at a profit. No work but just checking on them weekly.

That seemed so good he decided to do it again—only a little bigger the next year. Did he make a mistake! Unable to find a farmer who wanted to sell yearlings, he went to the stockyards and bought 22 calves that looked like they needed to fatten up. What he didn't know was that they were from the open range in Wyoming—wild as the raging sea and didn't understand fences! Oh, boy! Were they a headache! They constantly jumped fences and ran wild! It was such a relief when we finally caught and sold them that we never tried that again!

But before long we were inviting friends to join our fun. Dick and Sherley Bott had recently moved to Kansas City and put KCCV, a Christian radio station, on the air. They bought several horses and put them at Lazy-M. Their four children were just a little younger than ours and we had great times together.

By now, Martha was 17, Marilyn was 15 and Ronnie was 11. Quite often, they invited their friends to spend the day. Some frequent visitors were Murray and Florine McClain with their children, Linda, 16; Dennis, 14; and Mike who was Ronnie's age. Murray and Florine were long-time YFC Club Sponsors, volunteers, and Murray was a board member. Nearly always included were our 16-year-old nephew, Danny Hocklander, and David Lewis. (A few years later our Marilyn became Mrs. David Lewis and Linda became Mrs. Dan Hocklander.)

Ronnie saved his money from lawn mowing jobs and bought a little black filly that he named Tinker Belle. As time went on, colts came and Al had fun breaking them to ride. The herd of horses was growing.

Soon Al started inviting his young preacher boys—a few at a time—to come to Lazy-M. They alternated preaching a sermon with riding horses. When the weather was nice they preached out under the trees but during bad weather they preached in the loft. If they stayed overnight they slept on sleeping bags in the loft. To them it was a blast!

*Do I remember correctly that we bought this place to get away to relax?*

Al was so motivated he couldn't help mixing ministry with relaxation. Besides, he was having so much fun doing it all—it wasn't work, but play.

Ronnie started attending Milburn Junior High by this time. He had received Jesus as his Savior at age six and had eagerly looked forward to becoming officially involved in the ministry.

On Saturday nights, we drove all over the neighborhood picking up his friends to take them to the Rally. His leadership skills developed as he led the singing and presided over club meetings. More on-stage experience came as he played in a trumpet trio, became a top quizzer, and a member of Dr. Al's Young Preacher's Club. He took first place in the song leading contest two years while in junior high.

Oh! How we enjoyed those great, fun years when our children were teenagers! Our house was constantly filled with our children's friends. They would stop by nearly any time of the day or night.

I was perpetually baking cookies or biscuit cinnamon rolls or brownies or something! Milk disappeared as though being poured through a sieve. When our children's friends came over it was a party for all. We were included. Al could usually beat any of the teenagers at a good game of Ping-Pong. Any number could play "Round Robin" Ping-Pong so everyone could join the fun. Hilarious laughter resulted.

Guys had the most fun, I believe, when they wrestled Al on our living room floor. It got pretty wild! Of course, we girls screamed, which egged them on all the more. Guys love attention—especially from girls when their brawn is concerned. The funny thing is that none of the girls' boyfriends ever beat Al. He was strong! (Now I could speculate that they didn't want to beat him—but it certainly didn't appear that they were giving in!)

We had our share—maybe more than our share—of being TP'ed. Our big trees in front often turned white overnight.

There were lots of jokes and tricks, but these kids were all great, dedicated Christian kids having harmless "fun."

## Headquarters Addition

By 1963, we desperately needed more office space so Al had a plan. We built a 2-floor, 25x50-foot addition onto the north side of our headquarters. The 2,200-square-foot addition provided 13 private offices for the Club Directors, and a large conference room able to hold 70 teenagers for small meetings.

Utilizing volunteer help and donated materials, the cost was estimated to be $10,000. The teenagers set out to raise a "Mile of Dimes" hoping to completely pay for it. They didn't reach their goal but what they did bring in was a big help. Probably the greatest good was their experience of being actively involved in the project.

"The first week of December," Al announced, "is our week of prayer. A room will be set aside for prayer from 9 A.M. to 9 P.M. all week. Come and pray with us. Your faith will be strengthened as you experience answers to prayer."

We were praying especially for the teenagers of Kansas City and for the funds to build the needed office space. God gave us great victories in both areas.

## Martha and Don

In August 1963, Martha went to camp at John Brown for her second year as a counselor.

Don Philgreen had graduated from Moody Bible Institute and Wheaton College. In September he would enter his first year of Medical School at University of Chicago. Home for the summer, he also went to camp as a counselor.

Don and Martha had known each other all of their lives. In fact, they had been out together a few times before. But something was different now.

In spite of their responsibilities at camp that week, they still managed to spend time together. By the end of the week, it was pretty obvious that the love bug had bitten them. After Don left for Chicago, they kept the mailman and the phone lines busy. By the time he came home for Christmas, he was ready to pop the question and we approved of their engagement.

When he finished his first year of Medical School, Al married them on September 4, 1964 in a beautiful ceremony at

Southwest Bible Church. They wrote their own vows and memorized them so they could look into each others eyes and make their pledge to each other. Something unexpected happened when suddenly Don started singing to her "God Gave Me You." Don was a great one for surprises. I'm glad she didn't faint.

If a marriage could survive those first three years, it had to be strong. They lived in a small third floor apartment in the inner-city of Chicago. Their laundry had to be carried three blocks to and from the laundromat and up those stairs. Martha worked at the University of Chicago as secretary. Don studied every night and could not be distracted by her talking, or having on the radio or TV. She wrote lots of letters home and read a lot. But they were extremely happy.

Al continued to be vice-president of Calvary Bible College without the heavy responsibilities. President Andrus' and Al's abilities complimented each other. Al was able to recruit scores of students each year, hire some of the college students to work at YFC, and help with public relations because of his wide variety of contacts.

In 1967, the whole city was excited about the Billy Graham Crusade to be held in the Kansas City Municipal Stadium. (This was before Royals and Arrowhead Stadiums were built.) Al was Chairman of the Youth Committee for the crusade. Billy had been in KC with us for numerous Rallies, but this would be his first citywide crusade here. Nearly all the churches and Christian organizations were cooperating in this great effort.

President Andrus met with Al and dropped a bombshell.

"I have been directed by the board to tell you that you must give up your position on the Billy Graham committee or you are no longer our vice-president." Andrus let him know that he did not particularly agree, but the board had made the decree.

Al was shocked. In the merger of the two schools some board members were super separatists. Because Billy allowed Catholics and main-line church pastors on his platform, they could not cooperate with him.

Al had also received a seven-page letter from Dr. Bob Jones, Sr, President of Bob Jones University, outlining his implacable criticisms of Billy. He also informed Al that he would not be welcome back on the BJU campus if he did not denounce Billy. For a number of years Al had gone to BJU to speak in chapel and interview students to work in YFC.

We were troubled. Could it be true that this great servant of God had indeed changed his message and actions so that God had withdrawn His hand of blessing?

It had been a while since we had personal contact with Billy so we prayed for wisdom and searched to find the truth. We listened intently to Billy's preaching and discovered it had not changed a bit. When he gave the invitation God's hand was obviously still on him.

We read Romans 8:33: "Who will bring any charge against those whom God has chosen? It is God who justifies." Other scriptures spoke to us as well. There was no doubt that God was blessing Billy's ministry. We would be afraid to criticize God's servant. We decided if Billy was doing something against God's will—God would show him. That was not our calling.

We did not back off. We agreed that you don't win people by ostracizing them. We must love and encourage everyone but not compromise our message.

Al knew he *must,* in good conscience, support the great evangelistic effort coming to our dear city. And he *wanted* to be in on the blessing. So he resigned his vice-presidency. The college issued a directive to the students and faculty that they would not be allowed to attend or have any part in the Billy Graham crusade. We hurt for the school. They were the losers.

## Awards

Minneapolis, January, 1962

KCYFC received two awards at the YFCI Midwinter Convention. Al received an award for the "Rally with the Best Promotion" and Jack Cousins received the "Unsung Hero of the Year" award.

Winona Lake, Indiana, July 1963

During the 1963 YFCI Annual Convention, Al was presented the coveted "Director of the Year" award for his 20 years of ministry and leadership in KCYFC. An announcement noted that many men are ministering across the country in YFC who have been trained by Al.

Pittsburgh, Pennsylvania, January 6, 1965

Al Metsker, Director of KCYFC, was presented a service pin and received special recognition at the YFCI Mid-Winter Convention for his length of service in YFC.

"Al has directed the Kansas City ministry for twenty-one and a half years, distinguishing him with the longest length of service of any man in YFC. Al was also re-elected to the YFCI Board of Directors—a position he has held since the inception of YFCI."

Receiving awards is encouraging, but nothing more. All that we accomplished was completely from God's blessing. We worked, but God did it!

# CHAPTER 16

# KCYFC Auditorium Planned

For nearly twenty-two years we had held our weekly Rallies in rented auditoriums. Some of the locations were convenient. Some were not. With all of them we had to move in all of our equipment, props, etc. to set up each week. In some places we were forced to work with union stage hands who sometimes came to work drunk and who certainly didn't care about spiritual things or producing a high-class program. At times it was very difficult. Al dreamed of the day we could have our own auditorium.

"In the nearly 1,200 Saturday night Rallies, we have spent almost enough in rentals to build an auditorium," Al lamented. "We need a permanent, efficient, centrally located auditorium where we can meet regularly. I want a place where we don't have to share it with the devil—but where it can be filled with the Spirit of God and will be conducive to producing a great program to reach teenagers with the gospel."

Al and I visited high school auditoriums all over the city seeking the best ideas—evaluating the pros and cons of different configurations. Soon Al had pictured in his mind exactly how he wanted the auditorium. He wanted a stage with curtains, and lights with all the latest technologies.

He was especially concerned about having steps coming from the balcony. For years he had to deal with buildings in which steps from the balcony led into a foyer. A stairway from the balcony leading straight to the prayer room was his dream. To Al the invitation was the most important part of the Rally. That was when kids found new life in Christ—when their lives were turned around.

He drew a plan with enough rise so those in front would not block a teen's view. He designed the main floor in terraces instead of on a slant so it could double as a banquet hall. He always insisted on round tables for dinners instead of the traditional 8-foot long ones usually associated with church banquets.

"Round tables promote conversation so everyone will have a good time," he insisted. So he drew the risers wide enough to hold 60-inch round tables with guests sitting around them. The padded stackable chairs could be moved where they were needed.

Al took his plans to an architect. When he received the first rendering, he was furious. His balcony stairs had been removed.

"It looked unbalanced," the architect complained. That was true but we weren't looking for balance. The architect didn't understand our reasoning. Instead of Al's intended 12-inch rise, the architect had drawn the balcony with only a 6" rise.

"That is the way all church balconies are," the architect advised.

"I don't care. I want everyone in the balcony to see clearly without dodging heads," Al insisted as he sent the plans back to the drawing board. Al always knew what he wanted and would not settle for less.

Verl Thurman, who had organized the candy sales for the Capital Teen Convention in 1959, insisted we should put in a basement. I don't know why Al hadn't planned on it.

"It'll be the cheapest square footage you can get. You'll need it someday."

Al agreed and a full basement was planned.

### Radio Telethon

In March 1965, Al announced his plans to build our own auditorium. We had been blessed with a gift of $50,000 that he planned to use as the seed for the project. Al was a great motivator and salesman and could communicate the need so people's hearts were stirred. Stating the need with a positive solution was always his winning combination. After talking about the auditorium daily on his radio show, within three weeks $5,000 in small gifts came in the mail. (At this writing that sounds like a small amount compared to today, but it would be about the same as $50,000 with today's inflation.) It was great progress. In three more weeks the fund had risen another $29,000!

Our dear friend, Dick Bott, owner of KCCV Radio, graciously offered us a whole day of free broadcasting on Saturday, May 22, for a radio telethon. What a boost!

We contacted nationally known Christian leaders across the country asking them to tape a message for our telethon urging people to give to build our auditorium.

The day came. It began at 5:30 A.M. when the KCYFC staff and many volunteers knelt together at our headquarters to pray for the well-planned effort to finish raising a quarter of a million dollars to build the auditorium.

At 6 A.M., by remote from our headquarters, Dick signed KCCV on the air telling the audience that the whole day's broadcasting would be given to KCYFC for a telethon.

Al's voice rang out over the airwaves. "This will be Youth For Christ's biggest day so far!"

He announced that ten phone lines were open to receive calls. Within 15 seconds the phones started ringing. Excited friends called to make sacrificial pledges.

Al always approached an issue by being honest and highly informative with the people. Some thought he went into too much detail—but no question was left unanswered. He bared his heart and was faultlessly honest. He informed our friends that over the past several months $102,000 had been raised for the auditorium construction. Our goal for the day was to increase it to $250,000—the amount the architect projected as the total cost.

The phones rang incessantly. Pledges were made. Excitement mounted! Phone operators couldn't get a break. Calculators hummed. As soon as the pledges totaled $1000, a trumpet trio fanfare would blare. Half-dozen fanfares brought an air of excitement. When the trumpets sounded, another thousand dollars had been pledged! Pledges were read over the air. The gifts ranged in size from $1 to $5,000.

Some told their stories. A couple shared that they decided to give what they had saved for a car. A five-year-old girl emptied her piggy bank. A teenage boy was going to mow lawns to earn his pledge. We related all kinds of interesting and heart-tugging stories over the air.

The program involved a wide variety of world-renowned personalities and talent. Every few minutes an endorsement or a song from one of these people provided interesting variety to the program—people like Dr. Theodore Epp from Back to the Bible, US Senator from Kansas Frank Carlson, Dr. John Brown, Dr. R. G. Lee, Dr. Merv Rosell, composer John W. Peterson, Dr. Sam Wolgemuth, Tony Fontane, and many others.

The phones remained jammed for the longest period of time when Tony Fontane came into the studio and sang his greatly-loved "Peace Like a River," and announced that he would talk for a minute to each of the callers in the next hour.

Tony Fontane was a fantastic singer who, before his conversion, had his own network music television show from Hollywood. He and his wife, Kerri, were both movie stars.

He now was a popular Christian recording artist for RCA and traveled in Christian concerts.

Albert Lane, who had been our staff pianist for fourteen years, was in the studio to play whatever was requested on a moment's notice. Albert had come from Banghor, Maine and never lost his strong New England accent of dropping his "Rs." Our audience loved to hear him play and sing a novelty song:

"I'm sending my timba' up to heaven every day,
And I know I'm going thea' some sweet day!. . ."

Dave Rolf, one of our singers, announced he would give an album to the next five callers. The secretaries gave away thirteen before we could stop them. A total of $700 came in from those thirteen calls.

All during the day, the emcees reminded the audience to join YFC that night in a big Victory Rally in Memorial Hall with Suzanne Johnson (former Miss Illinois) and Tony Fontane.

KCCV normally went off the air at 6:30 P.M. However, at 6:30 the phones were jammed, and Dick announced that he would keep the station on the air as long as the phones rang. They did not stop ringing. Al had to get to Memorial Hall to start the Rally so they signed off at 7:16. He knew he couldn't get there on time but rushed out to his car.

To his surprise a police officer, who had earlier phoned in his pledge, was sitting in his patrol car—motor running—ready for the occasion.

"Follow me. I'll get you there!" he shouted to Al.

With siren blaring and red light flashing, he escorted Al to Memorial Hall. Al hurriedly parked at the stage entrance and breathlessly dashed onto the stage. The Rally started on time!

All of this added to the excitement of the more than 3,000 people at the Rally. Suzanne Johnson and Tony Fontane gave outstanding performances, presenting the gospel of Jesus Christ.

At offering time Al announced that $110,000 had been pledged over the phones during the day making our total $212,000. He appealed to the audience to finish the job. The rally offering totaled $18,000 in cash and pledges bringing the total to $230,000—just $20,000 short of the goal.

Albert Lane had accompanied Tony all evening on a concert Steinway grand piano we had rented. Before Albert played a captivating solo during the offering, Al announced:

"We need a grand piano like this one Albert is playing for our new auditorium. It will cost $4,000 to $5,000. I know tonight the Lord will lay it on someone's heart to buy that piano for us. I will stand at the side of the stage during the offering, and I want whoever God is talking to about this to come see me while Albert plays."

This was totally a statement of faith.

A businessman *did* come forward during the offering.

"Al, I want to buy your piano," Wayne proclaimed with a catch in his voice.

We had never met Wayne before, but learned that he owned a grocery store in Mission, Kansas, and had been a Christian only about six months.

When Al announced: "We have our piano!" the spontaneous emotional upheaval from this excited crowd was a rare experience. Pastors in the audience later told Al, "I sat there and wept as I saw God work miracles." and "My faith has been greatly strengthened today."

God seemed to place his smile of approval on the entire day. As Tony Fontane gave the invitation, more than 100 teenagers responded, forty-nine of them for salvation. One of those was 9-year-old Rich Bott, son of Dick and Sherley, who had donated the day of radio. How better could God have rewarded them?!

The staff and board of directors were jubilant. But at the same time they were humbled at the cooperative spirit demonstrated by a city united together to win teenagers to Christ. One of the most inspiring parts of the day was that more than thirty ministers called in their own personal pledges while others led their churches in pledging. Some pastors even called their church members and asked them for personal pledges.

Al summed it up: "This miracle day was a whole lot more than just building an auditorium. It was positive proof that great things are going to be accomplished in the immediate future because of the spirit of Kansas City Christians."

The broadcast day ended with a song that we all felt in our heart, "To God be the Glory, Great things He hath done!"

No one knew that as I worked all day on the telethon I was having terrible cramps in my abdomen. In fact, very few knew I had been suffering with them for several months. Fresh from the excitement of victory, we were plunged into the hardest time Al and I had faced.

# CHAPTER 17

# Cancer

At this point a big change of events came into our lives. "I want you to just lie around and rest for two weeks and see if you feel better," Al instructed as we arrived at our Lazy-M Ranch for a vacation

During all of my 41 years I had been a strong, healthy person who seldom felt pain. But for six months I had felt weak and experienced terrible stomach cramps.

The doctor found nothing in tests he administered so he suspected it was stress and overwork. Muscle relaxants he gave me didn't help. Surely after two weeks with no stress I would be well!

Those two weeks snailed by and I only felt worse.

Al called the doctor: "I want you to put Vidy in the hospital and run every test there is until you find what is wrong."

In the hospital an incessant parade of doctors and lab technicians persistently prodded, thumped, and jabbed needles into my body. Orderlies periodically marched into my room toting a gurney or wheelchair, and whisked me off to another lab for further tests.

During those five days my dismal, lonely room transformed into a happy sunlit garden when Al walked in. His love brought me joy. His colorful detailed account of what God was doing in the outside world uplifted me.

On Saturday afternoon, July 17, 1965. Al was at home preparing for the Rally that evening when the telephone rang.

"This is Dr. Reister, Al." Al listened anxiously. "We have found a malignant tumor in Vidy's colon."

Like an earthquake, everything seemed to collapse around him. His mind rushed back twenty-two years when, just two weeks after our marriage, his dear mother had died of cancer. Flashing before him was the agonizing pain she endured—the family's dreadful anguish from being unable to ease her pain.

"Are you sure?" he pleaded.

"Yes, there's no question about it. It doesn't look good. I give her only about a 5% chance of making it." Dr. Reister continued. "Al, we have to keep her spirits up. Don't tell her it's malignant. We can't let her get discouraged. She needs to fight for her life. Keep a stiff upper lip. Be cheerful and happy when you visit her."

Dropping the phone into its cradle, he fell on his face before God. Weeping uncontrollably—tears puddling before him, he cried out to God. He prayed for strength for himself and healing for me.

Across town in the hospital, I was oblivious to the turmoil he was experiencing. I was giving my testimony to my roommate, Betty, and explaining God's plan of salvation.

As soon as Al could gain control of himself, he rushed to the hospital to see me. I could tell he was troubled, but brushed it off as concern for the Rally program that evening. He cheerfully told me they had found what was causing my pain, and that they would perform surgery in a few days to remove a tumor. I was glad that at last the problem was discovered, that they were going to fix it, and that I could get on with life.

Medical care is approached much differently now. Today everything is explained and options offered. Treatments have changed with the advancement of research and technology. But at that time, several days of bowel preparation were necessary before surgery to prevent infection. I felt no real concern, thinking this was routine. Cancer didn't even enter my mind.

Marilyn pampered me by fixing my hair and nails. Martha flew home from Chicago. All the special attention by my family seemed normal so I had no clue.

By 7 A.M. on July 21, several pastors had already come and prayed with us. My family marched beside me as I was wheeled down the long corridor to surgery. Just before the wide doors of the operating room swung open to engulf me, their kisses and hugs were precious. I assured them, "I have perfect peace."

I lay in semi-consciousness with repulsive tubes protruding from several areas of my body—including a stomach pump connected to a tube down my nose. I knew little of what was going on around me for a number of days.

Although I barely knew they were there, I will forever be grateful to three of our wonderful friends and board members' wives, Ruby Anderson, Alice Hutchison and Lela Trewett, who were registered nurses. They sweetly gave their services to be around-the-clock private nurses.

As I made progress I no longer needed registered nurses, but our good friend, Joyce Hoobery, sat with me. How I appreciated her!

In those days visiting hours at the hospital were very strict. I should have suspected something was amiss when my room filled with gorgeous flowers from friends across the country and stacks of cards came each day. But I wasn't thinking at that point.

Then, one night in my semi-consciousness, I heard someone whisper to a nurse coming on duty, "You know, she had three-fourths of her colon removed." This hit me like a bolt of lightening! They hadn't just removed a tumor as I had thought. They had removed five feet of colon also. Then I knew.

Eating on my brain like termites was the thought, "It was

cancer. It was cancer." That terrifying perception nagged me through the long dark night. I yearned for morning when Al would arrive.

My burning question: "It was cancer, wasn't it?" He answered truthfully.

"Why didn't you tell me?" I pleaded.

"I'm sorry, Sweetheart. The doctor wouldn't let me."

"Now, I know. Tell me about it."

"Your cancer was the size of a grapefruit. They had to remove 2/3 of your colon hoping to get it all. I saw it." The doctor had obliged his usual inquisitive mind and showed him what they had removed, explaining it all to him.

Constantly I prayed. "Please heal me, Dear Lord, if it is Your will." It was hard to pray "Lord, if there is someone else who would make a better mother for our children or a better wife for my dear husband, I'm ready to go home to heaven— but please Lord, if it is Your will, please heal me." I prayed that prayer over and over and over.

Ignorance brings fear. I thought I was dying when a nurse worked feverishly over me to irrigate my stomach pump through that deplorable tube down my nose. Obviously not succeeding, she nervously called another nurse who rushed in. I was frightened by their anxious hushed tones about the pump being stopped up. Repeated occurrences like these made me wonder if this was a serious situation. If they had only explained it to me I would have not been so alarmed.

The noises in my head about drove me crazy. It was like a loud rock band playing "Three Blind Mice." It never stopped! I couldn't stand it! Finally, I asked the nurse:

"What is that awful music?"

She answered so tenderly. "I don't hear anything. Maybe you hear the air conditioner fan." She tried to comfort me.

I kept thinking "The devil is making a bid for my soul." That's all I could figure so I prayed desperately. Now, I wonder if it was a result of all the medications I was receiving.

Nurses frequently trekked into my room, giving me two or

three shots each time. After a while when nurses came to give me a shot, they were startled.

"Oh, I can't find any place to put it. Your bottom looks like a pincushion!" they gasped.

IVs provided my only liquid and nutrients. I had nothing by mouth, not even water. Daily, my doctor started listening with his stethoscope to my abdomen.

"We're trying to hear bowel sounds," he explained. "We can't take your stomach pump out until we know your intestines are working."

Oh, how I wished to get that tube out of my nose. My throat felt like it had been rubbed raw with sandpaper. It was almost impossible for me to even whisper.

I received long-distance calls from the East Coast to the West. Tony and Kerri Fontaine called from Hollywood. Kerri was a cancer survivor, so was a great encouragement to me. You seldom heard of survivors in those days.

Assuring scripture verses were written on most of the hundreds of cards I received but the one that captured my attention most was Jeremiah 32:27: "Behold, I am the Lord, the God of all *flesh*: is anything too hard for me?" I knew there was not anything to hard for Him. What I didn't know for sure was God's will in this situation.

After about three weeks the doctor started injecting daily doses of 5FU cancer drug into my IV. My hair fell out by the handful. Joan Carpenter, a friend who had a beauty shop, brought me a wig to cover my frightfully cold head.

Gradually tubes were removed from my body and at last I got a drink by mouth. My first bite of food in several weeks—rubbery, sugar-free Jell-O™—was better than nothing.

Finally, I could sit on the side of the bed. When they got me on my feet a few days later, I had to learn to walk again. The next morning an orderly lifted me onto a cart and said he was taking me for my first cobalt treatment. I was scheduled for twenty.

When my doctor came I told him, "I just returned from my cobalt treatment."

His face burned red! "You what?" he roared grabbing my chart and dashing to the nurses station. He was irate. He had not ordered them to start yet. I should not have received chemotherapy and radiation at the same time.

Evidently the combination of chemo and radiation at the same time was too much for me. My body swelled all over. I couldn't swallow. I got a terrible earache and headache. My 10-inch incision broke open; bleeding, and laying bare my insides. My body's violent reaction to the treatments took away my healing power. My fever soared. The doctors rushed me to emergency surgery to close my incision again.

Treatments to stop the infection didn't work so Dr. Robert Rogers, an ear specialist, was brought in. I cried when he told me they had to rush me back to surgery. I didn't know if I could endure another surgery.

He warned me, "The infection is almost to your brain. This surgery is necessary to try to save your life." He explained it was like potatoes and gravy. "Potatoes are good without gravy but they are better with gravy. The potatoes are your life and the gravy is your hearing. We want to save your life and we'll try to save your hearing."

With this, they rushed me off to surgery again. I survived the surgery but lost the hearing in my right ear—a constant reminder of my cancer experience. Cobalt treatments were stopped, as was the chemotherapy. It had almost killed me. But we believe God used that mistake to heal me.

Yet another surgery came six months later to have my incision redone because it couldn't heal properly. We praised God when it was all over. I would never choose to go through this experience, but now that it's over, I wouldn't take anything for it.

We don't understand why God allows things to happen in our lives—but we *do* know He has everything under control and has a purpose. Second Corinthians 1:3-4 may be one explanation: "Praise be to the God and Father of our Lord Jesus Christ, the Father of compassion and the God of all comfort, who comforts us in all our troubles, *so that we can comfort those in any trouble with the comfort we ourselves have received from God.*" (emphasis added)

Christians often quote tritely Romans 8:28: "And we know that all things work together for the good to them that love God, to them who are the called according to his purpose." But we quoted it from the depths of our soul.

Yet another traumatizing trial lurked in the shadows.

# CHAPTER 18

# New Auditorium

## Groundbreaking

I will never forget Sunday afternoon, September 29, 1965. It was my first time out of the house since my cancer surgery.

The memorable occasion was the groundbreaking for the new YFC Auditorium. Dr. Theodore Epp, founder of "Back To The Bible," was our special guest speaker. Several hundred people were on hand as members of the board of directors each turned a shovel of dirt. Al climbed onto a backhoe and dug a big shovel full.

In his remarks, Al said: "We are especially grateful to Mayor Joe Dennis and the City Council of Westwood for their splendid cooperation. We particularly appreciate the Mission State Bank for agreeing to loan us the money to finish the building while the pledges are coming in."

The most staggering shock came when the bids were opened. The lowest bidder was nearly $100,000 above the architect's estimated cost. The Board of Directors and Al conferred into the wee hours of the morning seeking God's will. They concluded that the only course left was straight ahead. The exact cost by contract became $464,000. We were short $194,000. One businessman who had already pledged $1,000 heard about our plight and called Al to pledge $2,000 more. We believed God had brought us this far and we knew He would finish the job. We could not limit our Heavenly Father.

God provided ideal weather for construction and progress was actually ahead of schedule. By the time excavation was complete, the concrete piers were in, and the foundation begun, Al had a message for our friends.

"In Joshua 3, the Lord said for the priests to go down to the Jordan River and step into the water and only then would the Lord separate the waters and give them the victorious crossing.

"We stepped into the water when we started construction. Now is when God will speak to our friends to give for our victorious crossing."

Al used creativity to conquer the huge task of raising the additional funds. He challenged teenagers to help raise money. He promised a new red YFC Bible to the top five for that week. Sixty-two took the challenge and raised more than $4,500 that week. The winner, Connie, who had raised $1,188, gave her testimony after receiving her new Bible. She had accepted Jesus as her Savior just four weeks before in her YFC Club at Paseo High. We were thrilled to see how much the kids cared. By this time the $300,000 mark had been hit, so Jack Cousins and Albert Lane helped Al lay the cornerstone on April 10, 1966.

## Board Split

During those months while Al was concerned with my illness and trying to help me, the ministry continued to surge forward. Between taking care of me in the hospital, caring for our family, and raising funds for the auditorium, Al had been swamped. For all of YFCI's twenty years Al had never missed a convention until I lay at death's door in July 1965. Our Club Directors attended the convention without Al and returned energized and excited to try some new programs they had heard about.

When they told Al their plan, he vetoed it. He made it clear that he felt their plan was a step away from his strong conservative stand that was working so well. "If it isn't broken, don't fix it," he proclaimed. But one of the men stood on the Rally platform and announced these new programs. It was a case of blatant insubordination. When the Rally was over, Al relieved that staff member of his position. This was a great guy whom we loved very much. He was a popular leader with a group of loyal supporters. They rebelled.

This staff member went to our board president and complained. The next day the president of the board ordered Al to rehire the Club Director. This was a breach of the constitution that stated the Director answered to the board, and the Director was responsible for all employees. The board had no direct control over the employees. In the chain of command that's the only way it could work. I was still recovering so didn't understand too much at the moment. Maybe, with the pressure he was under, Al did not handle the situation as diplomatically as he should, but he made the right decision. If employees deliberately disobey their employer's orders, that is cause for dismissal.

In our twenty-two years, our board had never been divided. It was now split in half. Some who disagreed had been our very dear friends for years. This hurt us deeply. I don't believe the split was known to the public and the ministry continued as usual.

Al and I prayed and cried a lot together. We prayed desperately that God would bring back unity. We couldn't understand how, instantly, relationships could turn around so completely. We searched our hearts. We prayed. We cried. We prayed some more seeking God's will.

We clung to promises from our God:

* 1 Corinthians 10:13: "No temptation (trial) has seized you except what is common to man. And *God is faithful; he will not let you be tempted (tried) beyond what you can bear.* But when you are tempted (tried), he will also provide a way out so that you can stand up under it." (emphasis added)

* Isaiah 43:2-3: "When you pass through the waters, I will be with you. And when you pass through the rivers, they will not sweep over you. When you walk through the fire, you will not be burned, the flames will not set you ablaze. For I am the Lord, your God, the Holy One of Israel, your Savior."

Downhearted, and wondering if the division would ever be resolved, we considered if we should leave the ministry in Kansas City. How we agonized in prayer asking God to show us the way through the horrible situation. Isaiah 54:17 was a great comfort.

> "No weapon forged against you will prevail, and you will refute every tongue that accuses you. This is the heritage of the servants of the Lord, and this is their vindication from me," declares the Lord.

It seemed that God was confirming that we should stay where we were by His continuing and bountiful blessings. Crowds were large. Scores were being saved. The auditorium fund drive was mounting. Surely God would have halted all of this if He were trying to tell us to move on. Everything seemed right except that the board was split. For a whole year the board continued to meet without making any decisions because votes were divided.

Al was so torn apart at times he could hardly keep his spirits up—but he kept going. He had to make decisions and carry on. We cried and we prayed. Then we prayed and cried some more. Finally, after a year of that heartache, all of the opposing board members resigned in one night. I'm not sure what their thoughts were, but they must have made the decision to resign en masse. What a relief, but also a heartbreak because those men had been our good friends for years.

Why did this happen? Was the devil mad because of our great victories and all the kids who were coming to Christ? I'm sure that's true. I guess we'll never know the reasons for sure while we're here on earth, but God got the victory and from that point the ministry grew by leaps and bounds. We praise God for his goodness to us.

We also praise the Lord that all those who were against us have become our friends again—not as close as they were before, but we still love them.

Ronnie turned sixteen in May. When school was out he started working at YFC full time for the summer. First, he hand stained 256 sheets of 4x8 paneling for the Auditorium walls. He hauled chairs from the factory in the West bottoms to save $1.50 off the price of each chair. He did custodial work or whatever needed to be done.

During YFC Camp at John Brown University in August he made a commitment:

"I felt the dynamic call of God on my life," Ronnie remembers. "That is when I surrendered my life completely to the Lord. The speaker asked us to stand and say, 'Here am I, Lord, send me!' My counselor shared Jeremiah 32:27: 'Behold, I am the Lord, the God of all flesh, Is there anything too hard for me?' That is when things really started happening in my life."

## Tony Fontane

While construction was under way, Tony Fontane returned to our area for a series of concerts. Cuzzy had booked him in a heavy schedule. He toured with Albert Lane and performed to packed auditoriums in Butler, Mo.; Salina, KS.; Wichita, KS.; and Cherryvale, KS.—plus the KCYFC Rally and Mothers' Club and four different Kansas City churches. People made decisions for Christ in every meeting totaling 221 salvation decisions. In the Cherryvale meeting a whole family came for salvation—mother, father and three teenagers.

Tony was excited to see the progress on the auditorium since he had helped raise funds during the radio telethon the year before.

We hoped the Auditorium could be ready by September 1st. At this precise time a special event took place in our family.

## Marilyn and David

In 1956, Clifford Lewis, the young evangelist who had preached when Al and I dedicated our lives to the Lord in 1940, moved to Kansas City. Only by this time he had married and had a daughter, Carolyn, and a son, David.

David attended Milburn Junior High with Martha and Marilyn. He came to our house after school for Club and Quiz practice. Before long Marilyn and David would go to our back yard and spend time together after quiz practice, playing badminton, croquet or swinging.

David had a wonderful home. But, because his Dad was gone most of the time in meetings across the country, he basically lived with his mother, grandmother and sister. Our house was a fun place to be and we had a Daddy who came home for dinner every evening.

By the time Martha and Marilyn were in Shawnee Mission North High School, David had a car and our house was "on his way home" every day. Often he would still be with us when it was dinnertime so I invited him to eat with us. It got to be a joke—he stayed for dinner every night except when we had something he didn't like, then he suddenly had to go home. During this time David became like a second son to us. Al became his surrogate Dad.

David and Marilyn had so much fun together, but through their high school years they agreed that they had to have a date with someone else between each of their dates together so they wouldn't get too serious. This was a good decision but resulted in some jealous moments.

Marilyn was a great quizzer and officer in Club. She excelled in typing and shorthand so during high school she worked part time as secretary to Jack Cousins at YFC.

David had been president of his YFC Club and a star quizzer through all his junior and senior high school years. A great trumpeter, he was Student Band Director in both junior and senior high school, and taught private trumpet lessons to several students throughout high school. In the YFCI national contest, he took first place for song leading and second place in trumpet. He traveled on a YFCI Teen Team to the Orient—Korea, Hong Kong, Philippines, Okinawa, Formosa and Japan—for six months. While a student at Calvary Bible College, he traveled four years with the "Melody Messengers" from the school.

In March 1966, when he was a college junior, David and Marilyn were engaged. Their wedding date was set for September 2. The auditorium was nearing completion and they wanted so much to be married there. They even tried to help get it ready—but it didn't happen.

So their beautiful wedding was at the Open Door Baptist Church and both of their fathers had a part in the ceremony. They also wrote their own vows and memorized them, proclaiming them with feeling to each other.

While in college, David worked part time as a Junior High Club Director. With majors in Music and Christian Education, he graduated in 1967 with highest honors. He could hardly wait to work full time as head of the Junior High Club Department.

## First Rally in YFC Auditorium

The exciting day arrived! September 17, 1966—twelve days less than a year after groundbreaking—the first Rally was held in the new YFC Auditorium.

Nearly 2,000 people jammed the auditorium and several hundred spilled into the parking lot for the opening of the auditorium. Miss America 1966, Debbie Bryant, who had grown up in KCYFC, was our special guest. Debbie graciously spoke to the throngs of teens outside from a makeshift platform.

Albert Lane played the new concert grand piano assisted by teenagers at four other pianos and one at the Hammond organ.

Debbie was welcomed to the stage by 20 young men singing "Here She Comes, Miss America." In her testimony, she said:

"I received Jesus as my personal Savior when I was six years old, but I think any age is the right age to come to the Lord Jesus. The Bible says, "Now is the accepted time, Now is the day of salvation." She went on to say, "Actually, the first beauty contest I ever heard about was recorded in the book of Esther. After a whole year of preparation, Esther was chosen Queen over the 127 representatives of the kingdom's provinces. I believe God has a divine purpose for my life and for your life—and that is service for God."

Al gave a short salvation message following Debbie's talk and forty-one young people received Jesus as their Savior. God did it! That was the reason we were there!

Many years, the girls chosen "Miss America" were outspoken, born-again Christians. So we booked them for our Rallies—Vonda Kay VanDyke, Debbie Barnes, Cheryl Prewitt—so many of them. These and other "Miss Americas" were great attractions and helped us draw many unsaved teenagers and win them to Jesus.

## Dedication

Three months of tremendous Rallies in the new auditorium passed before we held the dedication ceremony. Tony Fontane had been with us all during the auditorium project so it was natural for him to be at the dedication.

Our hearts swelled with praise and pride as our 100-voice teen choir backed Tony on two of his songs. Tony's dedication song was "Bless This House" sung as only he could sing it.

We were thrilled to have Dr. Walter L. Wilson, Al's mentor who led him to Jesus, as the special speaker. Although 85 years old, he charmed the audience with both his unusual wit and blessings from the Word of God.

Three pastors prayed dedicatory prayers: Rev. Ben Hinkson from First Baptist Church Shawnee, Rev. Glenn Lindell from

Hillcrest Covenant and Rev. U. S. Grant from First Assembly of God in Kansas City, Kansas. It was difficult to choose so few pastors to take part because Al was close to many.

The Rally the night before had been exciting and action-packed with 1,800 teenagers jammed into the auditorium. Tony Fontane was the special attraction and was backed by the 100-voice teen choir. Besides singing, he told parts of his life story and about some of his experiences performing for servicemen in Vietnam. At the close of the Rally, 40 teenagers accepted Christ as their personal Savior. God did it!

We constantly praised God for letting us be a part of a ministry in which we had the joy of leading thousands of teens to the Lord. We often talked about how some servants of God go to the mission field and work for years before they see their first convert. How discouraging that would be. I guess God knew our personalities just wouldn't fit where we couldn't see results. I admire those who can.

We knew full well that what we read in 2 Corinthians 3:5 was true of us. ". . . not because we think we can do anything of lasting value by ourselves. Our only *power* and *success* comes from *God*." (emphasis added)

## Rainbow Room

Another of our long-time dreams was about to become a reality.

Teenagers are social characters. They need fun, activity, food, and fellowship. Through all the years of our having Rallies, teenagers had congregated at a drive-in on their way home. Usually the Club Directors and we would join them. Sometimes it was Winsteads; other times it was Roys & Rays; sometimes Valentine Drive-in. At times, the managers at the drive-ins didn't like to see all the teens coming because they stayed so long, didn't buy enough, and made too much noise. They were just having fun and it was great. But we could understand the managers' concerns. Al's dream was to have our own "drive-in" that was large enough to accommodate all who wanted to come—where the kids could spend all the time they wanted and be as noisy as they liked.

Although we had built a basement under the auditorium, it was unfinished except for the kitchen. The President of Mothers' Club at this time, and for quite a few years, was a very creative and energetic friend, Eva Dodd. She had a never-ending storehouse of ideas we implemented to further the work. The Mothers' Club had raised the money to equip and supply the kitchen. Meals for our dinners were prepared there.

The time had come to finish the basement for the kids. A contest generated its name, Rainbow Room—a rainbow was God's promise and it was situated on Rainbow Boulevard—a natural for the name. We started raising money. Soon the ceiling tiles were in place; a cheerful, durable carpet was laid; mirrors adorned the walls and booths and tables were set up. A hamburger grill that could simultaneously cook three-dozen hamburgers and buns was installed. Two large deep fryers, pop machines and an ice cream maker completed the set-up.

Volunteers—parents, Club Sponsors, bus drivers, staff members—prepared and served hamburgers, french fries, onion rings, shakes, sundaes, etc. We did not make money off the food, but just broke even. The object was to provide a place for fun and refreshments. After the Rallies the room was packed. Buses set their departure time so the kids could fellowship before leaving. The teens could have fun there while they waited for those in the prayer room—both seekers and counselors. We encouraged the counselors to bring their new converts to the Rainbow Room, introduce them to several of their friends, and have them give their testimony about receiving Jesus. This helped them learn how to communicate what had just happened and made them grow spiritually.

We tried having live music in the Rainbow Room. It was OK but the kids seemed more interested in just enjoying fellowship. This was a superb time for us and Club Directors to get closer to the kids and to get to know them better. What a great blessing!

## God Supplies

Since the actual cost of building the Auditorium was so much more than the architect's estimate, we were left with a mortgage. Al felt burdened. He hated to pay interest.

Our monthly payments were $5,000 for three years. Al simplified it. Five hundred people giving $10 a month for three years would cover it. That made the debt seem reachable. He recruited people to join the "500 Club." He suggested they not only give $10 a month, but to ask others to give the same—either new donors or others to give above their regular offering. We kept praying and working until 500 people joined the 500 Club. The front page of the Conquest always announced the balance of the mortgage so people would be encouraged as they saw the amount drop.

How does God answer prayer? Oh, I can share so many experiences. Here's one.

Al wrote in 1969:

"Friday, August 29, at 5 P.M. I had a decision to make. I had to deliver our check for $5,000 to the bank. We had only $4,500. I prayed because we had never been late. The Lord seemed to say to go ahead and send it. "Trust Me."

"At 6 P.M. my phone rang. A radio listener of many years whom I had never met said she had a "little" money for YFC but it was cash and she wanted us to come after it before dark. She didn't want it in her home that night. We went to pick it up. It was $500! The exact amount we needed to cover the check!"

Our faith had been tested—and now it was stronger!

# CHAPTER 19

# More Happenings

### Dr. Al

John Brown University, Siloam Springs, Arkansas was the return address on the official looking envelope. Al read the letter from Dr. John Brown, Jr. It said in part:

> "We would like the privilege of bestowing on you an honorary Doctor of Humanities Degree at the John Brown University Commencement on May 21, 1966." We felt honored and humbled.

Dr. L. A. Thomas, Director of Admission at the University, presented Al on that bright and sunny Commencement day:

> "Rev. Al Metsker is the Founder and Director of Kansas City Youth For Christ. We honor him for launching the YFC Bible Club program in Kansas City that is now spread around the world and his pioneering spirit in starting the YFC Bible Quiz Program, Teen Talent Contests, Directors' School, and Young Preacher Boys' Club which are all now a part of the YFCI program."

Dr. John Brown Jr., in bestowing the degree, said:

> "We want to recognize with appreciation your outstanding service to the youth of America. You have been untiring in training youth leaders and young people. We have seen your leadership each summer as you have brought hundreds of teenagers to our campus for camp. You have worked harder and longer than those who have academically earned a doctorate. There are presently over 50 students on the campus

of John Brown University due directly to your influence. It is my joy and privilege to bestow on you this honorary Doctor of Humanities Degree from John Brown University. God bless you."

We had always been called Al and Vidy by the teens we ministered to and their parents—partly because we were not much older than the kids we were working with when we first started and partly because we thought they would feel closer to us. Now, they automatically started calling him "Dr. Al."

## Prayer is the Key

Attempt any of these projects ourselves? No way! We knew God was our Wisdom, our Guide, our Supplier, our Comfort, and our Peace. He was our all! His promise to us:

"Call unto Me and I will answer you, and show you great and mighty things, which you know not" (Jeremiah 33:3) We also knew there was a condition as we read in 1 John 3:22, "And whatsoever we ask, we receive of him, *because we keep his commandments, and do those things that are pleasing in his sight.*" Our hearts had to be right with God—no sin unconfessed. We knew Joshua 1:8: "Do not let this Book of the Law depart from your mouth; *meditate* on it day and night, so that you may be careful to do *everything* written in it. Then you will be *prosperous* and *successful.*" (*emphasis* added)

Living as we are taught throughout God's Word and praying were our two most important duties to be blessed of God. Al was forever scheduling prayer meetings—especially all night prayer meetings.

As we approached our 25th anniversary, he set aside four Friday nights in June for prayer.

They started at 7 P.M. and ran until 7 A.M. Then all who were still there ate breakfast together in the Rainbow Room. Spiritual depth and a close walk with the Lord were the main objectives. Most of the teens and adults had never prayed all night. God met with us and no one was the same at the end of the twelve hours.

169

The rows of chairs were cleared from the main floor of the auditorium and semi-circles were set up to make it cozy for 100-150. At the beginning of each hour a different leader would take five minutes to give scripture and prayer requests. Then we would divide up into groups of four to six, spread out over the area, get on our knees and pray for 50 minutes. At the top of the hour a leader would either play the piano or start singing, which was the call to come together again. Each time we divided into small groups to pray we went with different people. We could have prayed with 50 to 75 different people during the night. Does this ever draw you close together!

You might think you would run out of things to pray about. On the contrary, the more you prayed, the more you thought of to pray about and the more you wanted to pray. These prayer meetings were wonderful blessings. We saw God work miracles.

A year later this was repeated—only on Monday nights— every Monday in July. Through the years at different times we had all nights of prayer. Probably most of the time they were prompted by great needs, burdens or praying for a huge evangelistic effort. Nothing compares to the blessing of praying all night.

## Our Way

"With our own auditorium we are not limited. We can schedule events anytime we desire," Al proclaimed with freedom. So on Friday, April 14, 1967, we had 5:30 and 8:00 showings of a great new dramatic movie, "Worlds Apart" produced by Gospel Films. The next night was our regular Rally. The auditorium was packed for all three events and 71 teenagers received Jesus as Savior.

Karen Lehman, the 24-year-old vivacious star of "Worlds Apart" joined our staff on July 1 as Director of Music and Stage Productions. Besides working for Gospel Films, Karen had worked at HCJB Christian missionary radio in South America doing music and script writing. A natural born comedienne, her rich contralto voice, piano skills and creative writing abilities made her a versatile addition. There was always a party going on wherever Karen was. She worked for us for eight months until she married.

## Dramas

Although I had no formal training, I wrote and directed several musical dramas.

In July 1968, a patriotic musical drama, "That We Might Have Liberty," depicted highlights of our country's history with the gospel woven through.

Again that December we did a Christmas program, "That Joyous Night." The drama and music casts numbered well over a hundred. It was fun doing those productions.

Now that we had our auditorium, we could promote our Mothers' Club without reservation. 450 came to the first Mothers' Club in the new auditorium.

Regular monthly Evangelical Ministers Fellowship luncheons were next on the agenda. These were scheduled the day before the Mothers' Club, so we could take advantage of the auditorium being set up into a banquet hall.

We brought great speakers from outside the city, who would teach, challenge and bless the ministers. From 125 to 350 ministers attended, depending on the speaker. Through this organization, citywide efforts could be launched. Pastors became better acquainted with our ministry and us as well as receiving the benefit of sharing with each other.

Our whole staff mobilized with servants' hearts on those days—greeting, acting host and hostess, serving food, clean-up—wherever there was a need. One instant stands out in my memory. I was serving plates when a pastor from a large church motioned to me as I passed his table. He whispered into my ear, "Vidy, you shouldn't be serving. This is below you."

I was stunned. The reprimand hurt so much I went to the restroom and cried. After reflecting on it, I concluded *"In our beginning days I did anything, for the glory of God, that needed to be done. Nothing was too menial a task. I was willing to be a servant. Now that the ministry had grown and had more resources, am I any less a servant? I must still do what I see that needs to be done."* I understood his point, though, and took it to heart.

## Two Camps

August 1968 was the first time we had separate camps for senior high and junior high at John Brown University. The two speakers were John Ankerberg and Don Engram—both were favorites of Kansas City teens.

Having separate camps worked well. Two camps of a little over 400 each were more manageable than one with 800. Programs could be fashioned for each age group and a smaller crowd gave us an opportunity to get closer to the teens.

In our early days when we rented campgrounds for camp, I was the head cook. However, when we started going to John Brown, I no longer cooked but was usually the head counselor.

The second semester of Ronnie's senior year at Shawnee Mission North, the Club Director for the Old Mission Junior High Club left so Ronnie finished the year as acting Club Director. While attending Calvary Bible College he was a Club Director for the Old Mission Junior High Club and several others.

## Exciting News

"We're coming home!" Don and Martha were excited and so were the rest of us. The news came as Don graduated from University of Chicago Medical School.

"Don has been accepted for his internship at St. Lukes Hospital in Kansas City!" Martha jubilantly wrote. What good news that was for our family. At last we would all be together again.

Ready to be back in the swing of things, shortly after their move back, they became YFC Club Sponsors for Martha's alma mater, Shawnee Mission North.

"We're going to make you grandpa and grandma!" Marilyn made the first announcement. We were delighted! But Al was a typical Dad. "You're too young," he told her. He didn't realize she was the exact age I was when we had our first baby.

In only a matter of days, Martha and Don made the same announcement. We would be double blessed!

Very interesting facts—

*Both were due on October 17—Don's birthday.

*They would be born in the hospital where Don was interning.

*Martha, Marilyn and Don were all three born in that same hospital.

"Wouldn't it be a kick if our first two grandchildren would be born on the same day in the same hospital where one of the daddies is an intern?" we quipped. But it didn't happen.

Marilyn gave birth to a tiny baby girl, Liane, six days before Martha's big boy, Christopher, was born. We were overjoyed with our two darling little grandbabies.

Those were such fun days having two little ones in the family again. But internship lasts only one year—after which Uncle Sam required two years of service from all doctors.

Don served two years in the Public Health Service on an Indian Reservation. So when Christopher was only ten months old, they shoved off to an Indian Reservation near Sacaton, Arizona. They lived in a government compound—6 houses and a small hospital with a fence around them—in the middle of the reservation. It was 25 miles to a grocery store, gas station, or anything! Don delivered lots of little Indian babies and was a family physician. Their daughter, Michelle, was born while they were stationed in Arizona.

We prayed that they would not fall in love with Arizona and settle there. They didn't! Don joined a medical group in Ottawa, Kansas. After those two years, they were back close to home! Again, they immediately started sponsoring the Ottawa YFC Club.

## Dale Evans

Rainbow Boulevard was jammed with cars. Our ten parking lot attendants were going crazy. The Auditorium, the Rainbow Room and the Skylight Room were filled with turmoil as teens tried to find seats even 30 minutes before the scheduled starting time. This was the scene on Saturday, November 22, 1969.

The vivacious movie star, Dale Evans, who had been married to movie star, Roy Rogers for 22 years was our special guest. She was the picture of a happy committed Christian, exultant in her love for Christ.

Hundreds were turned away. YFC music groups filled the stage. Teens were sitting on the floor, on the steps, standing along the walls. A pianist, song leader, and emcee was assigned to the Rainbow Room and Skylight Room. Dale made a personal appearance before each crowd— but loud speakers carried her main testimony to the alternate areas from the Auditorium.

Dale's testimony was clear and to the point. She told her life story from childhood being raised in a Christian home but during her rebellious teen years leaving home for show business. After many years of disappointment an opportunity for a screen test came which led to roles with Roy Rogers — the man she eventually married.

"My teenage son prayed for me and worked on me until I finally went to church with him. The Holy Spirit worked in my heart and I asked the Lord Jesus to forgive me for my sin. He gave me a wonderful new life! Just three months to the day after I was saved, Roy accepted Christ."

Dale held her audience spellbound as her true Christian character sparkled. When the invitation was given, 72 teenagers came to the prayer room and received Jesus as their Savior.

# CHAPTER 20

# Circle-C Ranch

"The money is all pledged to cover the Auditorium mortgage. Now can we sit down and relax?" someone asked Al in September 1969.

"No sir!" Not for a moment," was his response. "As long as the teen population is growing and sin is going rampant across our country, we must double our ability to reach teenagers with the gospel."

Al had another dream. He never ran out of dreams. Our summer camps for the past twenty years had been on the campus of John Brown University. But Dr. Brown had told him in August after our last camp there, "Al, I'm sorry. I hate for you to not bring those hundreds of teens to John Brown each summer—but we are going to start having summer school that will make the campus unavailable. I hope you can find another place."

This was like God saying to Al, "Now is the time for your dream to be fulfilled." For several years Al had been burdened about camp. Our camp attendance had grown so large it was difficult to know the teens personally. Taking 13 busloads of teens and three moving vans of suitcases for the 300-mile trip was exhausting for our staff and used two days of precious time for travel. Al wanted a camp of our own close to Kansas City that could be open all summer, enabling us to do a better job for more teenagers.

We investigated the land bordering our Lazy-M Ranch near Louisburg. No one wanted to sell their land there, so Al and I prayed for God to lead us to the place He had for us for a teen camp. We added a P.S. "And, dear Lord, we would really like for there to be some land for sale across the road from wherever You have for our teen camp if it's Your will." We wanted to personally buy it and build a house near the camp so we could spend as much time as possible at camp. That is exactly what God did.

A realtor showed us a 160-acre farm just 11/2 miles off I-35—35 miles from our Headquarters. Forty acres were in Johnson County and 120 acres were in Miami County. When Al and I walked over the land the first time we just felt God saying, "This is it!" There was no lake but Al could picture in his mind. He could see the lake with cabins lining its shores. A creek ran through the farm with 50 acres of hilly wooded area and plenty of flat land.

We stopped right there with the realtor and prayed. We asked God, if this was His will, to give it to us. Then Al told the realtor to make an offer of $350 an acre for it.

He said, "I wouldn't even disgrace them by offering so little."

"You do it, "Al insisted, "and I'll pray." The realtor finally consented.

Three days later when the realtor called back, Al just had to laugh at his statement. "Well, Reverend, *our* prayers have been answered." He at least acknowledged the prayer.

We learned it had been home to the Seamonds family for years. Mr. Seamonds had died and the children were selling it. They were familiar with our ministry and were thrilled for their farm to become a youth camp.

Here is the miracle—they owned 40 acres just across the road that they also wanted to sell. So Al and I made a down payment on it by borrowing against our home.

Al was long on dreams—but short on money with which to fulfill them. He only had faith. A dear businessman/board member gave the down payment to hold the 160 acres for the Ranch while we started raising needed funds.

Al contacted the Miami County Conservation Agent who met him at the farm to discuss possibilities of a lake being built in the area. He was very helpful and became our buddy helping with layout of roads, sewage lagoon placement, and other things. Al counseled with officials of other camps and their designers. He planned how to build the cabins and the configuration of the land. He was a "DO IT NOW!" person.

The first thing that happened was constructing the dam of the lake so it could be filling when rains came. The curving roads were cut in and graveled.

In January he wrote: "Bulldozers are right now digging basements for the first buildings. How can this be done? John 16:24 says "Hitherto have you asked nothing in my name; ask, and you shall receive..." (John 14:14) "Ask anything in my name, and I will do it." (I John 5:14) "And this is the confidence that we have in Him, that, if we ask anything according to His will, he hears us: and if we know that he hear us, whatsoever we ask, we know that we have the petitions that we desired of Him."

We first dreamed, then prayed, planned and then built.

Al had stipulations. This could *not* be like other rustic church camps with a path to common shower house and bathroom facilities. This would be completely modern with bathrooms and showers in the cabins. Each cabin would have two rooms which would house six teens each, and a counselors' room for two. Curtains would grace the windows and carpet cover floors. The Lodge Building would have five parts—chapel, dining room, kitchen, indoor recreation, and snack shop. It would be carpeted and air-conditioned.

His other stipulation was that it would not be called a camp. He was afraid when teenagers heard the word "camp" they would envision an old, run-down facility. We decided on the name: Circle-C Ranch, which means "Christ the center of your life."

Al challenged teenagers to fill a gallon jug with money— asking people to dump their change into the jug. 372 signed up to take the challenge. They received recognition when they presented their jugs full of money on the Rally stage. The person with the most money got to name a horse.

He motivated adults to volunteer their time to help build.

Teenagers also came and did what they could. Al's goal was to have it ready to open in June.

Ronnie was almost 20 by now, and he did a lot of the plumbing. Someone with "know-how" laid out what he should do and he did it, learning the principles along the way. He also decided the location and configuration of the sidewalks and put in most of the forms.

"I don't really know why I came to see you. I was just driving by and my truck turned in." These words came from a tall, bright, 30-year-old construction contractor when he saw Al at the headquarters building. As he and Al visited a little they both realized God had called Paul Thorup, the son of a minister, to give up his business and become the Ranch Manager of the new YFC Circle-C Ranch.

For several years Paul and his wife, Sharon, had sponsored a YFC Club. They had both gone to camp at JBU as counselors, and Paul had driven a bus. While there, they felt the Lord's call into full-time service, and would not be satisfied until they knew what God had for them. They moved into the little farmhouse on the property and Paul helped with construction. Sharon looked forward to being the head cook.

Isn't it amazing how God provides? But, it shouldn't surprise us if we believe His promises.

Great encouraging letters came to us daily. A few interesting excerpts read:

"I really think you are crazy starting out on another big project but the Lord has a history of using crazy people."

"I never dreamed twenty some years ago when I attended YFC that I would have kids going to YFC Clubs."

"Thank you for starting YFC and for not giving up on us kids when so many others have… ."

"God gave us a buyer for a car that was not even

advertised. So here is the money to help build the Ranch."

"I am past 91 but my heart is still with the youth. I believe your mission among the teens is so important, I'm giving the cash I received for Christmas to help build the Ranch."

"Here is my income tax refund to help build the Ranch."

"Our beautiful Daughter, Rena, was recently killed by a drunken driver. She is in heaven. I'll never forget how she burst into our house in Overland Park when she returned from your camp at John Brown University and said, "Mother, I'm saved! I asked the Lord to save me!" I pray this check in memory of Rena will help other teenagers find Christ."

## God Provided

Al spoke to three Optimist Clubs, Republican Business and Professional Women's Club, Heart of America Conservative Club, and a Kiwanis Club in one month. He shared his burden to help teenagers, the need for financial help and some victorious stories of changed lives. Woven into the stories was a clear gospel presentation. The reception to his message was fantastic.

At a ministers breakfast, a pastor said, "Al, we sent 21 teens to your camp last year. The results have been profound. The kids continue to walk with the Lord. The church voted to make the YFC Ranch our official church camp." Another minister asked for 40 brochures so he could send his teens to camp.

Al announced that we needed a dump truck and then prayed. A dump truck was given.

Contractors started donating their labor.

*A foundation contractor did all the excavation and pouring of footings and foundations for just the cost of the concrete.

*A roofing contractor put on the roofs donating all labor and most of the materials.

*A finishing concrete contractor put in all the basement floors.

*A sheet metal contractor put on all the metal flashing.

*A sewer contractor dug all the ditches for the sewer lines—3000 feet of them.

*One man paid the $12,750 for the lake dam.

*A steel contractor built and donated a dock for the lake.

*Thirty-seven horses were donated—some registered Quarter Horses, a Tennessee Walker, and an American Saddle. We knew we would not have time to spend at Lazy-M so we gave all our horses to Circle-C—Midnight, Lightening, Cindy, Tornado, Princes, and all the others.

"All I want for my birthday is for Dad to go with me to Circle-C to work all day," was 15-year-old Eugene's request. His Dad, Rev. Don Rothfus, Ottawa Wesleyan Church pastor, spent a fabulous day working with his son.

Al had requested a grant from the Kresge Foundation for $50,000 to build the Lodge Building. On May 9 the response arrived. "We are pleased to advise you that the trustees of the Kresge Foundation have approved a grant of $25,000 toward construction of your Lodge Building at your teen Ranch. Payment of the grant is conditioned upon certification by you that the balance of the funds required have been raised in full." This was a great answer to prayer and gave us a real boost. With that promise as an incentive, the money came in quickly.

Al was very much a detail person and he had a reason for every decision. Some principles he espoused about the Ranch were not a choice—but a necessity.

1. **No long lines waiting for anything.** At John Brown University 800-900 stood in a single line for food each meal. This was boring and time consuming.

2. **Food must be good and teen-geared.** We agreed that you could serve food that teens like and still have it nutritious. Because we wanted the kids to have great fellowship, we followed our tradition of buying round tables.

3. **Eliminate all sales resistance.** If the kids don't get enough sleep, they will be tired and cranky. If they don't like the food, they'll complain. If the meeting room is hot and the chairs uncomfortable, you won't

have their attention. That is why Al insisted on having the chapel air-conditioned. He wanted nothing to detract the teens when we were trying to help them grow spiritually.

4. **Specific spiritual goals.** After orientation, first in order was a captivating, clear, and simple presentation of the gospel with an invitation to receive Jesus as Savior. Al's specific prayer and goal was that every teenager who did not know the Lord personally before they came would receive Him as Savior on Monday morning before lunch. This was not by the power of man, but because we asked God, designed the message that way, and expected Him to answer as He promised.

With Jesus in their heart, "a friend who sticks closer than a brother," (Proverbs 18:24), the teens were ready to get their life established on the right road.

Other messages during the week covered the Second Coming of Christ, Burden for the Lost, Living Lives Separated from the World, Dedication to the Lord, Your Prayer Life, Living With and Loving Your Family, How to Make Your Close Relationship with the Lord Last, and the Basic Soul Winning Class.

The Ranchers were taught how to start, or be involved in, a YFC Club in their school. They also learned how to program a meeting, how to be a leader, how to reach out to others. For one session, we separated the girls and guys to talk to them about purity and relationships with the opposite sex.

On the fun side, team competition created enthusiasm. The whole camp was divided into teams. Points were awarded for such things as winning sports events, memorizing scripture verses, a clean cabin, and Bible quizzing—with the most points coming from Scripture memory. Circle-C Ranch opened July 7, 1970 with a capacity crowd of 150 enthusiastic teens. A certain prestige was connected to being at the first week ever!

Teens came for a week, arriving early Monday morning and

leaving on Saturday. A new "batch" arrived every Monday for twelve weeks of the summer—quite a change from two weeks of larger crowds at John Brown University.

David and Ronnie single-handedly ran the entire summer Ranching program the first two years after Circle-C was built. These two young men spent many long hard hours doing everything from running meetings and sports, wake-up call, working with counselors, and overseeing the whole operation except maintenance—and sometimes they even got in on some of that!

The first two weeks were Junior High with Don Engram and Fred Doerge as guest speakers. John Ankerberg was speaker for the following Senior High weeks.

Every teen who had not previously passed the Basic Soul Winning Course was required to take it. Those who were already certified soul winners went to an Advanced Soul Winning Class taught by John Ankerberg and David Lewis, which also became known as the Street Witnessing Course. The first three days the teens learned how to approach a stranger and share Christ with them. On Thursday and Friday those teens were taken to a nearby swimming pool, shopping area or the county fair to witness for a couple of hours. During the four weeks about 15 were led to the Lord by these teens. What a growing experience!

A highlight at the Ranch was the Friday night Cross Service. With the lights dim and all the campers sitting on the soft carpet singing quiet songs of praise, the mood was set for a sweet communion time with the Lord. After a slide and song presentation of the crucifixion, a huge rugged wooden cross was dragged onto the stage. Campers wrote letters to the Lord and told Him the specific decisions they had made. Then kneeling in front of the cross, they symbolically nailed it to the cross with a thumbtack.

We could write a whole series of books about the victories in the lives of teenagers who attended the Ranch—like:

*A 16-year-old boy from a broken home who found Christ

as the answer and then went home and led his family to Jesus.

*A 15-year-old girl who was on drugs, denounced sin and gave her life to the Lord.

*A rebellious young man went home a new person, got his hair cut and came back the next week to help in the kitchen. There he grew spiritually.

*Returning home another teen visited his grandpa in the hospital and, using Scriptures he had learned at the Ranch, led him to Jesus just two days before he died.

"On fire for God" was the best way to describe most of those 700 as they returned home after a week at Circle-C Ranch that first summer!

"I have a client who is interested in your property." A realtor was calling to inquire if we would be interested in selling Lazy-M.

Could that be God taking care of our personal property? Yes. We were offered about five times what we had paid for it ten years earlier. God was proving His promises to give to us as we gave to Him. All these years when we had given 30% of our small salary to the Lord, He was sending in some of the harvest. We sold Lazy-M. This would help us financially in our later years.

On our 40 acres across the road from Circle-C, we built another dam for a 3-acre lake and poured the concrete walls for a walkout basement, with floor-to-ceiling windows along the lakeside. It was not finished at all when we moved in. As we could, we built partitions in the basement making two bedrooms, a bathroom, and kitchen. We lived in the basement like that for four years before building the house on top.

That first summer when John Ankerberg was the speaker most of the summer, he lived in one of our bedrooms. How helpful he was! He was a fantastic speaker and the kids loved him!

Circle-C Ranch added another great dimension to our ministry. Before school started we treated all of our adult Club Sponsors to a complimentary Sponsors' Institute. They arrived after work on Friday evening and stayed until Sunday afternoon. We taught them everything we could about working with teens, and we challenged them spiritually. They got acquainted with each other and shared ideas. Sponsors received information on all the teens from their school who had attended Circle-C that summer so they could disciple them. It was great preparation for the sponsors to start the Clubs off with a bang!

Another benefit of owning the Ranch was the opportunity to host pastors and their wives at Circle-C for a time of relaxation, fellowship and sharing—a much needed R & R.

Al's Young Preachers' Seminar met at Circle-C once or twice a year when young men eagerly drank in all he taught about: how to prepare a message, delivery, gestures, giving a gospel invitation, and how to run a meeting. During these weekends the boys enjoyed no recreation—only learning.

Parents and pastors called to express their appreciation for the growth they saw in their kids. One pastor offered to have one of the young preachers preach one Sunday night a month in his church.

Now that we had Circle-C Ranch, we scheduled more weekend conferences. (We never called them "retreats" because we taught our teens and leaders to "advance" instead of retreat.) As the years went by new names added zing to promotion of these—Bonanzas, Power Charges, whatever fit teenage lingo at the time. No matter the name, the message was always the same—leading the teens into a closer walk with the Lord.

Beginning the 1970-71 school year, David Lewis became Director of the Senior High Clubs and Ronnie Metsker was named Director of Junior High Clubs.

## Ankerberg Crusade

We scheduled an 8-day teen Crusade in our Auditorium with John Ankerberg speaking. His subjects were "Proving the Existence of God," "Ten Reasons Why I Believe the Bible," "Facts of Science and Genesis 1," "Sex, Love and Marriage," and "Drug Scene."

Each of our 78 YFC Clubs compiled a list of 100 friends they hoped to win to Jesus. The entire club prayed for, witnessed to, and invited these 100 friends to the crusade. John spoke at fourteen school assemblies and invited kids to come to the evening meetings. Sponsors arranged for buses to take the teens to our Auditorium. Literally hundreds of prayer meetings were held all over the city. More than 1,200 teens had passed their counseling test during the previous year. At least 300 of these certified counselors were scheduled to be on hand each evening. A special guest or entertainment was booked for each meeting.

Monday night was Queen Night. All high school Homecoming queens received a special invitation. Thirty-nine, formally dressed and with an escort, attended. They were presented to the crowd and received a long-stem rose from 1968 Miss America, Debbie Barnes, who also gave her testimony.

The Friday night special was "The Great Give Away." Volunteers worked for weeks contacting merchants for prizes. Everyone who attended received a prize—some of them special, valuable ones. "Love, American Style" was the message the night John repudiated the moral standards of the era's youth and proclaimed that purity is still in style. This meeting saw the largest crowd of the week, and 168 teens made decisions for Christ that night.

Imagine the thrill of watching rows and rows of teens

talking in the Rainbow Room with one of our YFC trained teen counselors, and seeing them kneel and ask God for forgiveness for their sin and for strength to live for Him twenty-four hours a day. By the end of the crusade, we had recorded 678 making decisions for Christ—549 were salvation decisions and the rest were those who dedicated their lives to live completely for Christ. More than 2,200 teens attended each evening except Tuesday when the city was struck by a blizzard. The largest crowd was 2,700, with the overflow jamming into the Rainbow Room and hearing by loud speaker. This tremendous victory was no coincidence. It was a direct result of much prayer. God did it!

More than thirty bus drivers gave sacrificially of their time each night to see teenagers come to Jesus. Sponsors gave many hours making plans, phone calls, arranging transportation, and Chief Counseling in the prayer room.

## LIFE PLUS

Follow-up of converts had always been important to us but we wanted to be even more effective. We did work on getting new converts involved in their YFC Club, Quizzes, and Rallies. We urged them to attend a Bible-preaching, Christ-exalting church. We tried to send information about the converts to local churches. Nevertheless, our burden was always to do better.

Finally, in 1970, I stayed home from the office for a few days to write a follow-up booklet for teenagers. I wanted it to teach in a captivating and easy to understand way how to grow as a baby Christian. "LIFE—PLUS!" was the title I gave it.

KCYFC published the 54-page book in our print shop and we started giving one to every convert in all of our meetings. Soon churches started asking if they could get a supply to use with their converts. We supplied them for our cost—which was minimal. Other YFC Rallies across the country started asking to use the book and we obliged. Finally, I got a call from Dr. Kenneth Taylor, who translated the Living Bible and was

President of Tyndale House Publishers.

"Your *LIFE—Plus!* book is the best follow-up material I've seen." he said. "I wonder if you would let us publish it?" Of course, I was thrilled because of the possibility that it would be used more widely. So I consented.

"I don't care about royalties," I told him. "I just want it to help baby Christians get started in their new life."

In the agreement, Tyndale was to supply KCYFC with all the copies of the book we needed at cost. Tyndale could otherwise do what they wanted with the book. They gave the book a new cover and new layout design, but didn't change the text. I'm not sure how many books they sold. I was too busy with our ministry here to pay much attention. I do know they did a second printing and raised the price. When they were ready to do a third printing, I felt that the price was climbing so much churches would not be able to afford them for their converts so I asked for the rights back. Upon my request they sent everything to me.

I realize now how naive I was. All I could think of was "ministry." Now I realize many think of "business." After I got the rights back, KCYFC published thousands more over and over. We continued to supply copies of the book for our cost to churches and other youth ministries—whoever wanted them.

### Dave Boyer

The Auditorium was jammed to overflowing with energized teenagers.

Silver-toned tenor Dave Boyer had won the hearts of Kansas City's teens. He had grown up in Pennsylvania in a musical Christian family but left home at the age of fifteen to go "pro." He changed his name to Joey Stevens and at age 17 he was signed to emcee the show at the famous 500 Club in Atlantic City. In this lifestyle he became an alcoholic and druggie. Finally, God got hold of him. He repented and his life turned 180 degrees. He started traveling around the world singing for his Lord and telling others how Christ can change a sin-wrecked life.

We booked him in seventeen high school assemblies in one week, and then had double Rallies on Saturday night—one at 5:30 and the other at 7:30—packing the auditorium both times. Huge crowds came and large numbers of salvation decisions happened every time Dave Boyer performed. For years Dave ministered for us a couple of series each year.

## CHAPTER 21

# New Outreach — Television!

"How can we possibly reach all these people with the gospel?" Al and I were driving through a suburb full of beautiful new homes and we envisioned throngs of people in our area who had not heard the gospel. The burden we felt for such a responsibility caused tears to well up in our eyes.

Suddenly, God spoke to our hearts. "Your access into every home is Television!"

"No, Lord, we can't do that!" we argued. The thought terrified us! But God impressed our hearts that many could be reached only through television.

Scriptures vaulted from our memories. "Whatsoever He says to you, do it." John 2:5

We had tried to always do what God told us. "I can do *all things* through Christ which strengthens me." (emphasis added) We knew this to be true also. The terror in our hearts began to give way to faith. God could do it! Maybe He would use us.

First we prayed. "Teens reaching teens" had been our motto. That's our answer! We could feature sharp Christian teens using their talents to proclaim the gospel into people's homes

One of Al's favorite quotes, "Plan your work—then work your plan," was put into motion. We decided the 30-minute program featuring teenagers would be a mini Rally with music, testimonies and a short message.

Three major hurdles we faced were acquiring television time, a program producer, and funds to pay for it. It seemed like a tall mountain to climb, but God was our strength and source.

Al called on television station managers. His first choice was to have time donated. But found that even to buy time was difficult.

In November 1971, we hired Karen Lehman Wise who had directed our music and drama in 1967. Now the mother of two, she was eager to direct music again. Karen auditioned numerous teenagers for music and drama, from which she organized two main groups of twelve, which we called "Extra Dimension" and "Living Expression." Other groups—quartets, trios and duets—added variety.

Karen planned a theme for each show, chose songs, booked the talent and led repeated rehearsals for all those who were to "perform."

Marilyn designed costumes for each group, however every individual was responsible to pay for his or her own. We were soon ready.

Through much prayer and persistent calling on television station managers, we finally secured a promise of airtime—albeit not what we wanted. We would go on the air with a 30-minute "Christ Unlimited" telecast starting April 15, 1972. The program was scheduled to appear on Channel 41 at 11:30 P.M. on Saturdays, and Channel 4 at 1:00 P.M. on Sundays. Though the times were not great times, it was a beginning, we reasoned.

We knew that a little 30-minute, locally produced program at those times would hardly be noticed. A spectacular event, we reasoned, would draw attention to its beginning. So we planned another Super Rally in the 12,000-seat Municipal Auditorium. This multi-purpose Rally would not only announce the beginning of the television venture, but we would also burn the mortgage on our beautiful Auditorium. What a special night of celebration!

Dale Evans would be the star of the evening. We would also feature our Extra Dimension music group, and other teen talent from our coming Christ Unlimited television show. Teen testimonies were also scheduled.

Our guest speaker was Rex Humbard, from Akron Ohio, known nationally for his weekly "Cathedral of Tomorrow" telecast. At the time Rex appeared on more television stations than any other person.

Al motivated people to rally around the cause—to financially support this big venture. God honored his big faith. He quoted, "With men this is impossible, but with God *all* things are possible." (Matt.19:26 emphasis added)

Preparing for the Super Rally, we hosted a complimentary steak dinner for ministers. One hundred thirty nine attended. After Al revealed the plans for the Super Rally, the ministers filled out a questionnaire indicating areas in which they wanted to participate. Many volunteered to fill their church busses with teenagers and bring them to the Super Rally. Several, answering a question unrelated to the Super Rally, indicated they would bring their whole youth group to Circle-C Ranch for their summer camp because they appreciate the spiritual impact they receive. Some of them personally pledged a monthly gift to KCYFC to help on television expense. Others agreed to put the TV ministry in their church missionary budget. The interest in TV was tremendous.

KCYFC has historically stood by the evangelical ministers and churches. Their appreciation and enthusiasm was evident.

Al wrote in Conquest.

> Every major victory in YFC has been won as we melted our hearts together on our knees. The goals of achievements we have set for ourselves in the immediate future are beyond human strength. But God says, "Call unto me and I will answer you, and show you great and mighty things."
>
> How will we get 12,000 people in the arena April 15? Where will we get enough money to buy TV time?
>
> God made the walls of Jericho fall; He delivered Peter out of prison; our YFC Auditorium was paid for as people prayed for the impossible. If you want to see an exciting miracle happen, come and pray all night. Victory is assured if we unite our hearts in prayer.

So, on March 3 many friends came to pray. Some stayed a while and had to leave, but about 150 people stayed to pray all night and ate breakfast together at 7:A.M. The power of prayer is something you cannot explain—you must experience it.

At one point during the evening, Al told us to pray for ourselves—confess our sins, get our hearts right with God. (This he had learned from Dr. Bob Cook, his mentor) After this session, two young men confessed hard feelings toward each other. They forgave and hugged—uniting with one purpose.

During the first prayer session of the evening David Lewis noticed a junior high boy didn't pray, so asked him if he needed help. He said, "Yes." The result—David led him to Jesus. About 2:00 A.M., a college student who had been on his job as a supermarket security guard, came rushing into the prayer meeting. There had been a hold-up at the store. Thankful to still be alive, he wanted to be saved. During the previous weeks, staff members had been witnessing to and praying for him.

What can be more exciting than to experience answers to prayer!

## Super Rally 1972

God answered prayer! Thousands of cars and more than 200 buses converged on downtown Kansas City on Saturday night, April 15, filled with happy, singing teenagers who were on their way to the KCYFC Super Rally, scheduled to start at 7:30.

Just before 7:30, the KC Fire Marshall closed the doors to the arena. "You already have 15,000 people in here. It's not safe to let in any more." Some of the nearly 3,000 in the arena who stood during the whole two hours said they were happy to stand to be in on the blessing of the Lord. More than 100 ministers were platform guests.

Every event of the program was thrilling. The KCYFC music groups combined to sing a stirring arrangement of "The King is Coming." On the final chorus of the emotionally powerful presentation, the entire audience rose to their feet in honor of the King of Kings.

The President and Chairman of the Board of our bank, along with Al and our Board President, ceremoniously burned the

$150,000 mortgage on the $600,000 KCYFC Auditorium. Dale Evans' singing and testimony glorified Jesus, and Rex Humbard's pointed preaching caused the youthful audience to erupt into applause frequently.

When the invitation was given the aisles were filled. Trained counselors prayed with more than 500 people making life-changing decisions. A whole family came and received Jesus as their Savior.

After the Super Rally, everyone rushed home to watch the initial telecast of "Christ Unlimited" television which we had taped in the Channel 5 studio. Al ended the program by inviting people to call for spiritual help. The phones at our Headquarters, where counselors were waiting, rang. Eight people prayed over the phone with counselors to receive Jesus.

The next week after the telecast, thirteen people were saved. In the first nine weeks a total of 70 had received Jesus into their hearts through phone counseling.

Was it worth it? Yes, it would have been worth it for one soul. And we were just beginning.

## Double Headers

Nearly 1,300 teenagers who spent a week at Circle-C Ranch were all fired up and ready to take their school for Christ.

At the Rallies, teens consistently filled the auditorium to overflowing, so we scheduled two a night—5 P.M. and 7:30 P.M. We hoped the busloads coming from a longer distance like Topeka, St. Joseph and farther would come to the early Rally to relieve the crowd. Then, we reasoned, they could get home earlier, even with their long drive.

The 5:00 Rallies were identical to the 7:30 except the crowds were not quite as large. We continued this for almost a year but discovered a problem. The teenagers wanted to see *all* their friends from across the area. When the crowd was divided, they missed some. So we abandoned the idea and just kept trying to cram in the crowd, sometimes having overflows in the Rainbow Room.

## Behind the Scenes

Saturday mornings, the KCMO-TV studio was bustling with activity. Dozens of sharp, talented teenagers from the KC area were donning costumes and preparing to perform. Union stage crew, sound technicians and camera operators were getting ready. When Al stepped to the middle of the studio and said, "Let's pray," everybody, including technicians, froze as Al asked God to direct and have His will in every area of the taping.

Our teen talent included a variety of music and teen testimonies. We received great satisfaction working closely with all these talented teenagers. They were great kids!

We were extremely thankful for Joe and Joyce Hoobery who for years dedicated themselves to helping with set decorations for all our activities—TV, Rallies, Luncheon and Dinner Clubs, and Banquets. They were creative, resourceful, and skilled—giving many hours each week. Because of their work we had professional looking, sets, for the teens to perform in. Our weekly Christ Unlimited television program continued to flourish. The funds to pay for television were always a challenge, but as in everything in our life, we trusted God and He supplied.

## David Lewis Directs Music

Karen did a great job with programming but home responsibilities once again caused her to leave. So in October 1972, David Lewis became Music and Program Director for both Christ Unlimited TV and the Rallies. Until this appointment David's main responsibility had been as Senior High Club Director. Now he was needed in this position for which he was well qualified.

David produced excellent programs and the music groups he directed were tops. With his leadership, and as a result of listener demand, our music groups recorded an exceptional stereo album, of "Christ Unlimited" music by Capitol Records. We soon had releases for the program on four different stations.

We eventually ventured out of the studio and taped "on location" programs at Circle-C Ranch, Worlds of Fun, and Silver Dollar City in Branson, Missouri.

With David becoming Music Director, Ronnie became Director of the Club Department, adding 55 senior high clubs to the 55 junior high clubs that were already his responsibility.

As we launched our television ministry, we celebrated 21 years of radio. Al had preached daily on an early-morning 15-minute radio program for all those years. This audience was valuable to us because they formed a prayer and financial base. They were like family to us.

Al wrote the following for the January 1 Conquest:

### Al's Editorial
- Daniel resolved to not eat the king's meat
- David resolved to read the Bible and pray every day
- Jacob promised to tithe
- Paul's was a prayer and determination that his generation might be saved.

How did it turn out?
- Daniel became a world influence for God.
- David became a man after God's own heart.
- Jacob was blessed with riches.
- Paul was the greatest preacher and soul-winner of all time.

None of this would have happened without the power and blessing of God. Solomon said, "As long as he sought the Lord, God gave him success." (2 Chron. 26:5) Many people don't make a resolution because they say, "What's the use? I've done it before and it didn't last."

Most people fail because they don't have the right formula. Matthew 6:33 promises: "Seek ye first the kingdom of God and His righteousness and all these things shall be added unto you." The secret is to put God first. I mean ahead of everything. Yes even family and (gulp) yourself. Then watch the excitement.

Resolve to give the first of your time. Take time to read the Word and pray. Commit to a responsibility for the Lord and make sure you do it before you take time for yourself. When you get paid, give the "first fruits of your labors" to God, then live on what is left. You will be amazed how much more the money you have left will buy. You will also be thrilled how much you accomplish for yourself and your family. God says, "Try Me. . ." Do it in His strength. It is His battle. Lean on Him. You can't keep a resolution in your own strength, but you "can do all things through Christ, which strengthens you." Remember, "We are more than conquerors through him who loved us." (1 Kings 8:47)

## Christ Unlimited TV

By the middle of February 1975 our teen program had airings in Los Angeles, San Francisco, and Anaheim, CA; Port Arthur, Beaumont, Port Neches, and Orange, TX; Greenville, SC, Peoria, IL; a cable network covering much of Nebraska and northern Kansas; plus our Kansas City airings. The counselors in the KCYFC office often received long-distance phone calls for counseling during these showings so we had counselors available at the time of all the airings.

At 6:20 on a Wednesday evening the phone rang in Al's office.

"I want to know about Jesus and how to be saved," a young man's voice announced when Al had said "Hello."

Sometimes we received prank calls like this, and Al thought it might be one of those calls, so he started asking questions. Terry told Al he was 17, had quit school, had been to church only a couple of times in his life, had never been to KCYFC or seen "Christ Unlimited."

How did he happen to call? A friend gave him the number. Because Terry had no spiritual background, Al took time to quote much Scripture and explain God's plan of salvation. Terry was seriously seeking and earnestly prayed for Jesus to come into his heart and forgive his sin.

After giving Terry more help on living the Christian life, Al suggested he come to the Rally on Saturday night so he could introduce him to some Christian teens.

"I'll probably bring Dave with me," he responded.

"Who is Dave?" Al asked.

"He's my friend who gave me this number to call. See, he watched 'Christ Unlimited' last night and called in and prayed with someone. He's the one who told me to call."

We praised the Lord when we heard that. What better proof is there of a changed heart than that the person wants to share the experience!

Another day a mother called because she was burdened for her daughter who was hooked on drugs. We encouraged her to bring her daughter to the Rally and then to register her to go to Circle-C Ranch. They came. When the invitation was given, mother and daughter tearfully hurried to the prayer room where they both found peace with God.

A surprising letter came from a pastor.

Dear Al,
 It was like meeting a long-time friend when I turned to Channel 38 here in Cupertino, Calif. and saw you and heard you are still with KCYFC. Your program is great and the kids are beautiful. For years I lived in Kansas City and was at most of the Rallies in Grand Avenue Temple. You brought

a group to the church I pastored in Holden, Mo. nearly thirty years ago. Praise the Lord—you're still at it!

## Goober and Leroy

"Don't let the stars get in your eyes if you've got water on the brain…." sang Goober and Leroy, alias Ronnie and David.

Ronnie and David had a routine of funny songs and jokes for their Goober and Leroy act. Dressed in patched bib overalls with mismatched shirts, crazy ties and shirts; and barefooted, David played a guitar and Ronnie played a "string bass" made from a galvanized washtub with a rope coming from the middle attached to a pole. Plucking the string while tightening or loosening the string made different tones. They were a comical pair impersonating a comedy duo, Homer and Jethro. They usually performed at parties or assemblies but occasionally they appeared at the Rally.

On Nov. 2, 1975, they received a rare opportunity. They provided a two-hour program for the Missouri Educational Secretaries State Convention. The entire crowd of over 500 ladies, which met at the Plaza Inn Hotel, responded hilariously. Besides doing their Goober and Leroy act, Ronnie and David used the same fun, games and music they used in High School Assemblies. Then concluded the program by telling about YFC, its history, reason for existence and goals—emphasizing that Christ was the only answer for the day's youth. (The same is true today!) They asked for support whenever possible. Each teacher was given literature about our ministry to take with them.

Their leader reported that this was the best beginning of a convention they had ever had.

We were thrilled as, through the years, we received hundreds of unusual opportunities like this to share our ministry vision and the gospel with secular organizations and groups.

## Music Groups

"Give a big welcome to our own KCYFC music groups directed by Gordon Chrisman with accompanist and arranger, Mary Buboltz!" was Al's enthusiastic introduction for a dramatic musical at the Rally

The grand curtain opened! The music began! Captivating harmony saturated the auditorium. Extremely talented teenagers performed for the next 90 minutes. A variety of solos, duets, trios, quartets, and larger group songs tied together with powerful drama presented a forceful message.

As the group reassembled for the reprise, the audience jumped to their feet cheering with wild enthusiasm. Later, many teens went to the prayer room to make decisions for Christ. So ended another KCYFC musical!

On average our staff and music groups produced about five dramatic musicals each year. Whether these presentations were lighthearted or stirringly dramatic, they achieved their purpose—to present Jesus Christ as Savior and Lord. They drew big crowds and all ended a super success! We were very proud of our music department!

"I see music as secondary," Music Director Gordon Chrisman emphasized. "First we want our kids to love the Lord with all their hearts. I would rather they be great soul-winners than great singers. I consider the Bible studies with the musicians an important part of our ministry. My goal is for each teen to be grounded in the Word of God with a great relationship with the Lord."

Gordon had been involved in YFC during his teen years at Blue Springs High. Although he earned his degree in instrumental and vocal music education, he wanted to serve the Lord full-time instead of teaching school. While counseling at Circle-C the summer after graduating from college, he told Ronnie about his music degree and that he wanted to serve the Lord.

David Lewis, then YFC Music Director, offered Gordon a position as his assistant while he attended CUBI. David was soon so overloaded with television that Gordon took over the music.

Mary Baker (later, Buboltz) was his close associate. God had brought us Mary Baker, a cute little blond senior at Van Horn High School, shortly after we started our weekly television program. Not only could she sight-read music and play by ear, God had blessed her with perfect pitch and the ability to write arrangements. While still in high school she started attending UMKC Conservatory of Music. Upon graduation from high school she became our full-time accompanist/arranger, but continued her studies at UMKC until she earned her degree.

Gordon and Mary demanded complete attention and perfection from the teenagers—and they received it. For instance, after six hours of rehearsing for a musical, when Gordon said, "We're going through this again," his announcement was not met with reluctant groans, but with compliance. And though they had their light moments—like playing "pass-Gordon's-hat" behind their backs while retaining innocent expressions and earnestly singing—the teens took their music seriously. As Gordon critiqued, the teens listened attentively.

"There's no reason why we can't improve each time, Gang." Gordon admonished "And remember, your stage performance will be no better than your dress rehearsals. If you don't concentrate now you won't concentrate then."

"We set high standards for our teens," Gordon explained. "The more we demand of them, the more they give. These kids live in a glass house. People watch to see if they are real. If they are not living clean, separated lives, they're hurting the Lord's name. It's their ministry, not just a singing group."

Gordon and Mary loved the teens and desired to develop not only their musical potential, but also their Christian lives. In-depth Bible studies and prayer times were a vital part of each weekly 2-hour rehearsal.

Every year about 800 teens auditioned for music groups.

Of those, only 100 were chosen. They had to make strong commitments. Gordon and Mary were experts at taking raw talent and skillfully developing it into a beautiful blend of harmony that often brought chills to the spines and tears to the eyes of the audience.

The two top groups, Extra Dimension and Living Expression, each performed about 30 different numbers during the year, while the other six groups each performed around 15. The teenagers annually performed in 45 television programs, 50 Rallies and at about 15-20 churches. In addition the Living Expression and Extra Dimension took a summer tour, performing in about 20 concerts. All performances focused on leading people to Christ.

Mary created original arrangements on most songs.

Each song was memorized and choreographed to help project the message. The teens' eyes glowed as they looked directly into the eyes of the audience, as if they were communicating with each person individually.

Each group had its own set of matching outfits. Marilyn Lewis designed and shopped for these every year. Usually she bought fabric by the bolt from the warehouse along with all the notions needed and gave instructions with supplies to each girl. She found the suits, slacks, and sweaters or whatever for the guys and made arrangements for them—a huge thankless job. But she did it beautifully. As a result, the teens looked sharp on stage.

# CHAPTER 22

# Thirtieth Anniversary

### Pat Boone Rally

The headline read "39,000 AT RALLY IN NEW ROYALS STADIUM!"

Months before, Al had announced: "This gigantic 30th anniversary celebration of KCYFC will be the biggest adventure in teen evangelism we've had yet!"

Pat Boone, the famous recording artist, movie and television star from Hollywood was scheduled to bring his wife, Shirley, and four lovely teenage daughters to sing and share their testimonies.

Because we felt Pat Boone would reach a tremendous crowd, by faith, we booked our largest meeting place yet—the brand new Royals' baseball stadium. It took vision! It took faith! It took hard work and detailed organization. Prayer was the foundation. It had to be if we expected to see miracles. And we *did* expect miracles!

Al always said, "If it can be done by man, it's not a miracle. Only God does miracles."

And, "If we don't *expect* God to do a miracle, then He won't. We must *believe* that God will *do* it."

For several weeks prayer meetings were held in the KCYFC Auditorium starting at 7 P.M. and lasting into the wee hours of the morning. Al told people, "Come when you can...leave when you must. But come and pray as long as you can." Many came.

In those all-night prayer meetings, it always seemed that by about one or two o'clock we felt the Lord's presence in a special way. What great prayer meetings they were.

People from across the city opened their homes for friends,

family and neighbors to come and pray for the Super Rally. Those prayer meetings were conducted the same way as we conducted all of our prayer meetings.

We prayed and believed that thousands of people would experience God's touch at the Super Rally. So we began to train counselors who could talk and pray with those people. We held numerous counselor-training sessions in different areas—four of them in the KCYFC Auditorium. Several hundred new counselors were trained.

KCYFC teen music groups practiced long hours to be ready with all their music memorized and choreographed. Under Marilyn's leadership mothers and volunteers sewed new, colorful costumes.

We encouraged Churches, YFC Clubs, and other groups to organize delegations to attend. A huge stage was built over second base, which volunteers decorated with patriotic red, white and blue fabric.

Our hearts sank when we heard that rain was predicted for that night. The stadium was not covered and we desperately needed good weather. We started calling on God. We asked everyone else to pray. Surely God wouldn't let us down now. All we could do was trust and go about our business.

We had invited about 200 leaders to have dinner with Pat Boone and us in the Royals Stadium Club before the Rally. As we looked out the Stadium Club windows about 5:00, Al and I couldn't hold back our tears of joy when we saw a caravan of church buses and yellow school buses streaming along I-70 toward the stadium entrance. They were arriving two and a half hours early.

The near capacity crowd flowed into the stadium by the thousands for the 7:30 Rally. Well before the program began the stands were loaded. Many of the teens had arrived in one of the 400 buses which flooded the parking lots. All of this set the stage for the excitement, which was to follow.

The rally was set into motion at 6:45 with pre-rally music

by KCYFC teen music groups.

At 7:30 sharp, the giant 12 1/2 story high scoreboard burst into full glitter as it read "Welcome to KANSAS CITY YOUTH FOR CHRIST SUPER RALLY!" Then in even larger characters, the words "SUPER RALLY" began flashing. Everyone rose to their feet and sang our national anthem as the Shawnee Mission South High School band played, and the Ruskin High School R.O.T.C. color guard paraded.

The YFC music groups presented a medley of patriotic songs. With the patriotic spirit running high among the nearly 40,000 persons, one of the evening's intense moments came. Former Vietnam Prisoners of War (POWs) Captain Ronald Mastin and Captain William Byrns, and disabled veteran retired Marine Lance Corporal Mike Kennedy, came to the platform and gave their testimonies of what the Lord had done in their lives. The entire crowd, as if being lifted by helium, rose in thunderous emotional applause. Each of these men noted how even in moments of deepest despair, they had felt the Lord's comforting presence.

The entire crowd, now in high gear, clapped to the rhythm of the unique arrangement of "This Little Light of Mine" sung by the Come Alive Four quartet made up of Ronnie Metsker, David Lewis, Phil Freeman, and Bob Anderson.

Al's enthusiastic greetings to the great crowd and his spirited introduction of "Pat Boone!" boosted the audience to their feet again. The right field bullpen gate flew open and, to the tune of "April Love," one of Pat's signature songs, out rolled a sparkling new custom convertible carrying the bright yellow-suited Pat Boone. As he circled the field, he held his hand up indicating the "One Way" sign to this giant crowd. When the car passed through the outfield, Pat held up his foot to show his famous trademark white buck shoes. The car stopped near the first base dugout where Pat leaped from the car and went into the stands, shaking hands and greeting many of the people while singing: "Joy to the World." As the crowd in the stands pressed toward him, he jumped to the top of the dugout where he continued to sing and shake hands.

As the song ended, he strolled to the stage over second base. Pat was so moved by the audience reception that his performance was electric. He sang several hits from his golden records of the '50s to show, he explained, "That I am the same guy who made the movies and golden records. The same guy—the only thing that's really changed is something that happened inside of me."

Pat was backed by the Extra Dimension, KCYFC's top teen music group, as he sang selections from the musical "Come Together" including "Clap your hands all you people, Shout unto God with a voice of triumph" taken from Psalm 47.

Ronnie Metsker made announcements about Circle-C Ranch and the Saturday night Rallies, so those who had been attracted to the Rally solely by the prospect of seeing Pat Boone also learned about our ministry. We found that many people who were introduced to YFC through Super Rallies later became very involved in the ministry.

Pat and Shirley Boone were joined by their four charming daughters—Cherry, Lindy, Debby and Laury—performing various types of music followed by each of the girls giving a brief testimony. This was before Debby became famous for "You Light Up My Life."

Cherry, 18: "I really want you to know that I love you people and it's because of Jesus."

Lindy, 17: "If Jesus can love me the way I am, I can't help but love Him back . . ."

Debby, 16: "We really need to share Jesus with every single person that we're with, if not in words, then, just by living lives that show that Jesus lives in us."

Laury, 15, tearfully concluded: "I just praise God right now that He loves me. . . and I pray that He can use me more."

Shirley shared: "All of us have come to such a sweet awareness that we want to be used of God, to share the love that He's given us. We had come to the point where there was nothing left. Pat allowed some things to get in his way and I allowed a lot of things to get in mine. It almost brought a broken home... and we almost missed the opportunity of sharing what life is really about with our children.

"I challenge you to let the love of God come into your lives. Men, humble yourselves before Almighty God—get on your knees and seek how you can be the heads of your homes...wives, humble yourselves and be submissive to your husbands. Learn how to be available to your children, to be an example. Young people, honor your fathers and mothers because there's something so magical that happens when we do that. It brought our family together and I really believe that's the main thing that's going to bring the body of Christ together."

Pat shared: "Every one of us must make a choice. Will I live in the world and for myself alone, or will I put myself totally in the hand of God? You are looking at six people who have decided to follow Jesus." Joining hands, they sang "I Have Decided to Follow Jesus."

As the Boone family softly touched on the final notes of the song, Al stepped to the microphone and briefly shared the simple but certain plan of salvation, and the promises of God from the Bible. Al gave an invitation for people to come forward for counseling and prayer to receive Jesus as Savior, just as he had thousands of times before.

As the first note of the invitation song, "Just As I Am," rang out through the stadium, hundreds of people left their seats and walked to the infield where they met certified KCYFC prayer counselors who showed them in the Bible the way to Jesus.

The remaining thousands in the stands stood prayerfully, and virtually motionless, since it took some people in the upper deck nearly 15 minutes to make their way to the counseling area on the infield. Soon the entire infield was packed shoulder to shoulder and knee to knee as seekers knelt in prayer.

A total of 1,300 people (mostly teens) made decisions for Christ—900 for first time salvation decisions and 400 for dedication.

As the last counselor was ushering his new child of God off the turf, big drops of rain started falling. By the time most of the people had reached their transportation in the parking lot, a deluge of rain poured. Another miracle! God kept the rain away until all those dear people had made their decisions for Christ!

I can't tell you how our hearts overflowed as we praised God for every miracle He performed that night! We knew only God could do this!

Ten days later Pat Boone called Al from Hollywood for a half-hour visit. "I still tingle over that fantastic Super Rally! It thrilled my heart to see such a huge crowd of teenagers. I have never seen such a beautiful sight as 1,300 teenagers kneeling on the turf being led to Jesus by their friends! I am praying that what has happened in Kansas City can send vibrations across the country so that thousands more can be saved. What a tribute to your thirty years of ministry!"

# CHAPTER 23

# Impact Snowballs

The impact of the Super Rally plus the television program produced high attendance at Circle C Ranch. A record 1,350 teens at the Ranch grew in spiritual depth and went home with a burning desire to win their friends to Christ.

Ronnie reported at the end of the summer: "For six years I have been directing clubs at KCYFC and some mighty terrific events have taken place. However, after this summer at the Ranch, I am more optimistic than ever about what God is going to do on our campuses this year. Some happenings over the summer were:

*Over 400 teenagers accepted Christ in 10 weeks at the Ranch.

*Hundreds "sold out" to God to be dynamic witnesses.

*Students from 40 new high schools want to start a club in their schools—besides the 110 already existing clubs."

Al challenged every qualified adult he could find to become a Club Sponsor. "We'll teach you how to work with teenagers. Soon a group of wonderful all-American Christian teenagers will lovingly refer to you as their 'Second Mom and Dad.' What an opportunity for any adult who really cares and loves kids! You'll be so blessed!"

Club Sponsors were great resources for help, love and caring for teenagers. Every August and September we were blessed as they spent a weekend at Circle-C for instruction and challenge. We grew very close to most sponsors. They were like a part of our family.

## Roy Bilyeu

"This is the first year in the last six that school has begun that I am not concerned about lesson plans or student load. This year the plans are on how to reach into all the area schools and the student load is 'out of sight!'" Roy Bilyeu exclaimed in August 1973.

As a teenager active in KCYFC in the '60s, Roy Bilyeu had carried his Bible to high school. He was a star Bible quizzer. He never missed attending the Washington High School Bible Club or the Rally. He dated a girl, Connie, from Washington who received Jesus at a YFC Rally. Their dates consisted mainly of attending KCYFC functions.

During Roy's junior year, however, two tragic events drastically changed his life. First, his brother, who was training to become a naval pilot, was killed while landing from a training flight. While Roy was still suffering intense grief, three months later an auto accident left his father disabled. In a matter of weeks, Roy abruptly became the man of the house with mature responsibilities. These trying times in Roy's life would later enable him to effectively relate to and counsel teens going through trials.

After high school graduation he went to KU. So did Connie. At KU he earned his educational degree in math. And he married Connie. Roy became a math teacher at his alma mater, Washington High, where he sponsored the YFC Club.

In June 1968, I was searching for more counselors for camp at John Brown University. Since Roy was a teacher with summers free, I called him. He and Connie thought it sounded like a fun vacation so they agreed to come. Ten students from Washington attended that year.

"During the Friday evening message," Roy remembers, "Dr. Al was challenging the teenagers to give 100% of their lives to the Lord. I'd been praying for the boys I was counseling when all of a sudden, the Lord started working on *me.* 'Out of the 150 students you had in your classroom,' God seemed to say, 'how many did you share your testimony with? How many of your fellow faculty members heard you confess that Jesus is your Savior?' My heart broke.

"When Dr. Al asked all teenagers who wanted to give their lives totally to the Lord to stand, this counselor was the first to rise.

"That night I vowed, 'Lord here's my life—my job—my family.'" About ten teens from Washington made the same decision.

Roy and those dedicated teens from Washington H.S., had a vision of leading their school to Jesus. God performed exciting miracles in the school. Before long 120 teens were attending YFC Club. Students were receiving the Lord, not only in Club but also in the lunchroom, study halls, at football games, everywhere!

They undertook such feats as an all-school evangelistic crusade, a formal riverboat cruise, taking 150 teens to the Ranch for weekend retreats, and two Bible Quiz teams. Over the next five years Roy was the "in house" evangelist at Washington High. He spent his summers at Circle-C.

Al had invited Roy to raise his support as a missionary to America's teenagers and to join our staff. After teaching geometry six years, God made him bored with it so in 1973, Roy joined our staff full-time as a Club Director to reach teenagers with the gospel. Demonstrating his faith and pioneering spirit, he was the first staff member in the history of KCYFC to raise his complete personal financial support. He likes to reflect on the miraculous ways he learned to rely completely on God for his needs. That was nearly 30 years ago and he is still at it!

## Youth Evangelism Association

Youth leaders representing 16 ministries from fifteen states met in Milwaukee in September 1973, and formed a new organization they named Youth Evangelism Association. YEA was made up of organizations who wanted to help each other project a conservative mass evangelism effort to win teenagers to Christ, teach them how to live dedicated Christian lives and become soul-winners through their clubs at school. Each organization would be completely autonomous without the control of a parent organization.

Al already had almost more on his plate than he could handle—but some in this umbrella organization begged Al to be the president. Anything that would further the cause of Christ among teenagers was his burden so he finally accepted. However, he felt he did not do the position justice. Since his first priority was the KCYFC ministry he simply did not have enough time. George Dooms, Director of Evansville TTT (YFC) was the greatest force behind YEA and served as Vice-President.

Orlando was the sight of the Second YEA Convention in January 1974. The impressive roster of speakers included Dr. Torrey Johnson, Founder and first President of YFCI; Dr. Warren Wiersbe, Senior Pastor of Moody Church and former YFC Director; Dr. Jess Moody, Pastor of First Baptist Church of West Palm Beach; and Dr. Ken Opperman, President of the LeTourneau Foundation and President of Tuccoa Falls Bible College. Besides these great speakers, the convention featured a number of special music artists.

We took a delegation of about 90, including a few staff, board, friends and teens. Bob and Bernie Bland of Teen Missions in Merrit Island, FL were kind enough to host us for this great convention!

In 1976, KCYFC hosted the YEA convention. Al set the pace for the week, urging 160 delegates to dream big dreams. The highlight of this third YEA Convention was when 250 ministers from our Evangelical Ministers' Fellowship joined the convention delegates for a luncheon.

Dr. Jerry Falwell was scheduled to be our guest speaker. We were distressed when his plane was delayed. In fact, we got word that he wouldn't even arrive until after the luncheon was scheduled to be over. However, most of the ministers waited so were treated to a double blessing. While waiting for Falwell to arrive, Dr. Don Engram held the ministers spellbound as he delivered a dynamic message from Joshua 1.

When Dr. Falwell arrived he continued the challenge: "This country is going down and the only answer is a spiritual revolution . . . we've got to be a coalition of God's people in these days or we'll self-destruct . . . I believe we can literally turn this world upside down in the power of the Holy Spirit, with the message of the gospel . . ." More blessings from God were just around the corner.

## CHAPTER 24

# More Events

Our challenge—be creative to find new innovative ways to reach out to the unsaved so they would hear the gospel and have a life-changing experience. The previous May we had held our Pat Boone Super Rally in Royals Stadium with nearly 40,000 attending and 1,300 decisions for Christ. This year we decided to utilize Kansas City's new theme park, Worlds of Fun, on Friday night, May 10, 1974 for what we called a Super Charge—a fun, evangelistic event.

### KCYFC Topples Worlds of Fun Record

It was not a typical night at Worlds of Fun. The crowd was the largest in the amusement park's short history. We had to cut off ticket sales 48 hours early, turning away thousands of people. The park was crammed. Lines waiting for rides were long—but spirits were high and people were happy. While waiting in line, people got acquainted with other Christians. In some lines, Christian teens joined together singing gospel choruses.

Thousands of cars and 321 buses brought the crowd of 16,647. Again, God did the same thing for us as He had done the year before at the Pat Boone Super Rally. Even though it rained that morning and the forecast was 60% chance of rain, the stars shown all evening. As the last bus pulled out of the parking lot, lightening shattered the dark sky! Thunder roared! Rain came down in torrents! But not until our event had finished!

The two most beautiful sights were the backstage of two of Worlds of Fun's indoor theaters, the Tivoli Music Hall and the Moulin Rouge, following each program. Jim Sunderwirth's and

Len Roberts' music filled the Moulin Rouge each hour followed by a short gospel message by Ronnie Metsker and an invitation for people to accept Jesus as Savior. In the Tivoli another music group performed and Al spoke and gave a gospel invitation.

Was it worth it?

To the Sunday School teacher who brought a busload of teenagers, several of whom went home with a new glow of happiness on their faces because they had found Jesus—it was worth it!

To the father standing backstage at the Tivoli watching his teenage son lead a friend to Christ—it was worth it! The son formerly had problems himself, until he surrendered to Jesus.

To the junior high school principal who choked up as he thanked Al for having a Super Charge—it was worth it! He had arranged for three buses to come and he saw some of his kids find the Lord.

To a young couple who had been dating for three years and insisted on being counseled together when they came forward at the Tivoli—it was worth it! They were expecting a baby and neither of their parents wanted them to keep the baby. They found the Lord together.

To the Christian couple whose 8-year-old slightly handicapped son came to be saved—it was worth it! They were overcome with tears of joy!

And, oh, so many more. Yes, it was worth all the hard work!

This was the first of many times that we took over Worlds of Fun—always presenting the gospel and leading scores of teens to Jesus. Whatever it takes we will do!

As the ministry grew, and we utilized more locations in the city, we became acquainted with more of the city's leaders.

A fun experience we had was when Al, Ronnie, Susan Nebel, Ronnie's girlfriend, and I were invited to KC Chief's owner, Lamar Hunt's, suite at Arrowhead Stadium for the Chiefs/Broncos game that fall. I was so nervous I introduced Susan to Lamar Hunt as Ronnie's wife. To make matters worse, they were not even engaged yet and I embarrassed them both. The biggest thrill was to be with the Hunts and others in the suite but the great view of the game and refreshments were an added bonus.

## Circle-C Ranch Open House

Not a day went by without several people saying, "I've been intending to go see Circle-C Ranch, but I just never get there." So we set aside two days to invite our friends to have a tour. It was Memorial Day weekend following our big Worlds of Fun day. On Sunday from 1 P.M. to 6 P.M. and Monday 9 A.M. to 9 P.M., we were on hand to give tours, serve light refreshments and provide entertainment by our music groups.

Groups came from as far as Eldorado Springs, Missouri, 150 miles away. Along with the greater Kansas City guests were visitors from Oklahoma, Arizona, California and Iowa. At times as many as 20 tours were being given at a time. Some people brought picnic lunches for their family. Many rode horses, went canoeing or slid down the giant slide.

Of special interest at the Ranch were memorials for several young fellows whose lives had been specially blessed through the ministry of KCYFC, and had gone on to be with their Savior.

In the lobby of the Chapel were plaques honoring Gary Miller and Billy Runnels. A new sound system was installed in their memory. Billy had accepted Jesus as his Savior in Don and Martha's Ottawa Club only 92 days before he was hit by a train and killed. His parents were so grateful to KCYFC.

*Gary, who was 21 years old, had been active in YFC through his teen years. In recent days since he started a job, he had stopped by our headquarters on his way home from work

216

every Friday. His reason? He was bringing a gift for Circle-C. This Friday was no exception. His gift was $65 that day. He told our bookkeeper he was excited about a trip he would take over the weekend with a buddy because they were going to witness to a friend.

When he kissed and hugged his mother goodbye, he said, "Mom, God has something really great for me!" A few hours later that "really great" something was revealed quickly when a car traveling the wrong way on the highway hit him head on and he met Jesus instantly.

*A flagpole had been erected in memory of Daniel Meinke, the youngest of Rev. and Mrs. Al Meinke's five children. Danny, a 16-year-old junior at Bonner Springs High School, was President of his YFC Club and was involved in all YFC activities. His car stalled on the railroad track on his way home from school. A train struck it and he was killed instantly. All his siblings had been active in KCYFC. One brother, Mark, was a KCYFC Club Director for a while.

*There was a plaque for Randy Woolsey who had been in Ronnie's class at Shawnee Mission North and was often at our house. During camp at John Brown University before his junior year he dedicated his life to the Lord. He played the drums in our musicals; was a Bible quizzer, and spoke at Club—just one of the great guys who was always involved. His parents were sponsors of SMN Club. At the age of 21, he got cancer and God took him home.

God's ways are not our ways. To us these were tragic deaths causing many broken hearts—but we know God is in control. He sees the total picture and we cannot question "why" he allows such events.

Those memorials were reminders of the thousands of teens who found the Lord or dedicated their lives to Christ. They reminded us of the thousands who had learned to study their Bible, memorize the Word of God, have a daily walk with their Lord, live a consistent Christian life, and be a witness to their friends. How thankful we were that KCYFC was there to minister to teenagers before it was too late for them!

Less than a year later, Dana Aldrich, 14, an eighth grade student at Garnett High School, was killed when his tractor slipped on ice and overturned. This popular young man was in football, track, choir and Boy's Glee Club at school as well as being active in KCYFC and church. He had found the Lord two years earlier through the ministry of Circle-C and his church.

Several Garnett teens, shocked by the tragedy, came to Jesus through the witness of Dana's family and friends. His parents, Kenneth and Darlos Aldrich, who were Sponsors of the Garnett YFC Club, established a memorial to send teenagers from Garnett to Circle-C Ranch.

Dana's older brother, Kendall, came to CUBI and serves the Lord in western Kansas reaching teenagers for Christ.

## Christian Movies

From almost the beginning of YFCI, gospel movies were a big draw. Several companies including Gospel Films, Ken Anderson Films, and Billy Graham's World Wide Pictures produced some very effective dramas. A few years later, Russ Doughton's MARK IV Productions released some forceful movies. Because it was easy to get the unsaved to come see a movie, if it presented the gospel clearly, many decisions occurred.

The movies that were especially dynamic were shown several times. Billy Graham's *Oiltown USA*, *Mr. Texas*, and *Shadow of the Boomerang* were some that we showed a number of times.

When MARK IV came out with their graphic prophetic movie, *A Thief In The Night*, it was a smashing success. We probably showed it more than any other movie in our history. Many of our YFC clubs even raised money to rent their school auditoriums and show the film which resulted in many salvation decisions. Every time we showed it, scores of people made decisions for Christ. After having shown it several times before, we scheduled it again for a Rally on September 28, 1974.

Some thought the crowd would be small—that *A Thief in the Night* had been overshown. But the Lord had prompted Al to be prepared for a large crowd. He, by faith, ordered three copies of the film, arranged for three projectors, set up chairs and was ready for the crowd to arrive! He quoted what Jesus said: "According to your faith will it be done to you." (Matthew 9:29)

He believed!

With every seat in the auditorium filled and the floor covered in front of the seats totaling about 2,000, the crowd started overflowing into the Rainbow Room. It was soon packed with 400 people. The Skylight Room was the next overflow area until it was jammed to capacity with another 130 teens.

When the invitation was given 121 received Christ as their Savior and 22 dedicated their lives to the Lord. God always honored Al's undying faith.

## Corrie Ten Boom

The very next Friday and Saturday after showing *A Thief in the Night* we had another overflow crowd. Corrie ten Boom, a victim of the German tyranny of World War II and author of two best-selling books about her life, *The Hiding Place* and *Tramp for the Lord* was our guest speaker. The warmth and love of this unusually captivating person was felt by all. As we heard her tell—in broken English—her experiences as a prisoner in a Nazi concentration camp, her faith came through stronger than the fear, anxiety and hatred you might expect. Bits of humor and stories of miracles were sprinkled through her message as she related the terrible suffering, agony, and shameful experiences. The enthralled crowd reacted from tears of compassion . . . to laughter . . . to applause.

A total of 6,700 people heard her. On Friday and Saturday nights the auditorium, Rainbow Room, and Skylight room were filled. After Corrie made a personal appearance in each place, loud speakers from the auditorium carried her message to the other locations. Several hundred were turned away both nights so we hurriedly scheduled another meeting for Sunday afternoon and 1,200 showed up. Corrie's heart-wrenching stories made all who heard her thankful for the freedom we enjoy in America.

### 1974 Victories

At the end of 1974 we rejoiced as we reflected on what God had done through our ministry during the year:

*Broken record of nearly 17,000 at Worlds of Fun with 147 salvation decisions.

*Started publishing a monthly devotional booklet, "INSPIRATION." It was received in 21,000 homes.

*"Christ Unlimited" television show was being released six times a week—four outside Kansas City. Many counseling calls were received from it each week.

*107 YFC Clubs were meeting weekly with 309 trained sponsors helping.

*6,700 attended meetings with Corrie Ten Boom—44 salvation decisions.

*2,530 attended A Thief in the Night showings with 121 salvation decisions.

*Approximately 3,000 teenagers passed our Soul Winning Class during the year.

*Thirteen music groups involving 150 teenagers performed regularly for the Lord.

*Two hundred young men were in Al's Young Preachers Club.

*A total of 1,718 teens attended Circle-C Ranch during summer—450 salvation decisions.

*An average of 100 each week received Jesus as Savior—a total over 5,000 for the year.

For all this we praised the Lord! It was all His doing! We can be faithful in giving His Word but only the Holy Spirit brings people to God.

# CHAPTER 25

# SOARING SERVICE

The trip to Florida for the YEA Convention was fun but it wasn't long enough." We kept hearing remarks like this. "Let's do it again only stay longer." Normally we didn't do pleasure trips but decided it would be an excellent way to become better acquainted with some of our people. So we scheduled and announced the trip, inviting anyone who desired to join us.

So on January 19, 1975, seventy-five friends were with us on a TWA flight headed for Florida. We planned to have a Sunday morning church service in the air on the way. Al, figuring it never hurts to ask, approached the pilot, and asked if he could use the public address system to have a church service. The pilot said, "In all my 32 years with TWA, we've never allowed anyone to use the PA system for any reason."

But he liked the idea so when we were airborne, he announced, "A delegation of 75 people from Youth For Christ are on board and would like to hold a church service. If anyone objects, please tell the stewardess." No one objected—so we were on!

David Lewis led the whole plane in singing well-known hymns. After David sang a vocal solo, Al announced his sermon, "The Last Flight," and read 1 Thessalonians 4:13-18. The key verse (4:17) says, "Then we which are alive and remain shall be caught up together with them in the clouds, to meet the Lord in the air; and so shall we ever be with the Lord." In his short message, he gave the gospel clearly for the sake of any unsaved people on the plane, and sat down. The reaction from passengers was gratifying.

The stewardess told Al, "I think that was the most

wonderful thing that has ever happened to me on any flight." She then added, "I sure felt guilty pouring alcoholic beverages while you were reading the Bible."

The Captain came back and said, "Doctor, I have been a Captain for ten years and this is a first for me. I loved it. In fact, I can't wait to get home to call my pastor and tell him I was in church today after all—only 38,000 feet above the ground!"

A priest on the flight, who said he was secretary to Pope Paul, came to Al and said he thought the service was wonderful. He then used the PA system to publicly thank Al on behalf of the other passengers. Then he prayed.

What an unusual experience! The trip included three days at Disney World and Epcot Center and a four day cruise. Each morning we had a short Bible lesson led by former YFCI president, Dr. Torrey Johnson. This fun trip was a bonding time when lifelong friendships began.

Besides the weekly Clubs and Rallies and the monthly Quizzes, Luncheon and Dinner Clubs, and Evangelical Ministers Fellowship luncheons, we worked in other special activities.

In March our top music group, Extra Dimension, presented a full-scale dramatic musical, "The Apostle", twice.

In April our Living Expression music group gave two performances of a dramatic musical, "Share." Plus we offered two Power Charges at Circle-C Ranch—junior high and senior high.

In May we held six formal banquets—one for junior highers, one for senior high and four for adults with Dino Kartsonakis, the great gospel pianist and entertainer. All were sell-out crowds.

May 24-25 featured two performances by our Drama Department of a full-length drama "Not Without Honor" directed by our Drama Director, Phil Seaton. Phil had been active in KCYFC as a student at Rosedale High, and after getting his degree in drama at KU, was on our staff for a time producing great dramas.

On May 30-31, Joni Eareckson (Tada) spoke at our Rally and Luncheon and Dinner Clubs. Of this experience, Joni later wrote in her book *Joni* published by Zondervan Publishers.

> I am sitting backstage at a large auditorium in Kansas City. I've been asked to speak to nearly 2000 kids at a Youth for Christ rally tonight. I hear the voice of YFC director Al Metsker introducing me. Suddenly the purpose of my being here is once again brought sharply into focus. The next thirty minutes, I will speak to 2,000 kids, telling them how God transformed an immature and headstrong teenager into a self-reliant young woman who is learning to rejoice in suffering. Hopefully, here—as in other meetings—scores of kids will respond to God.

Her prayer was answered as scores of kids streamed to the prayer room.

The last two weekends of August found several hundred adults—mostly parents of teens—at Circle-C learning how to be YFC Club Sponsors. When Al recruited parents to help as Sponsors, he challenged them, "If you want to be guaranteed having your teenagers live successfully through those dangerous teen years without taking a dip into sin, become a YFC Club Sponsor. We will teach you how to get along with teens, you will be involved in their activities, and you will be blessed by leading many others to Christ."

One couple, seeing the need in their own teenager as well as in others of their area, prayed for someone to help. As God spoke to them, they called our office to see if they were qualified. They were not experienced, but learned at our Sponsors' Institute. They started a Club with a small group but before long it became a large group and teens were coming to Christ each week. Their son became a leader in the Club and the relationship between son and parents grew, too.

Similar stories happened over and over again.

For several years the girls involved in KCYFC had asked, "Why can't we have something for the girls like the Young Preachers' Club for the boys?" Finally, we decided on the name Girls in Royal Leadership and Service—an acrostic for GIRLS. But we nicknamed it Royal Girls. I planned and organized these events.

Our first meeting was at Circle-C Ranch in September. More than 200 girls were inspired, challenged, and taught by nine different speakers. The theme was "Develop Your Gifts." We covered everything from having a moment-by-moment walk with the Lord to poise, make-up and how to dress, to relationships with the opposite sex. The girls were thrilled with what they learned. This became an annual event in our schedule just as the Young Preachers' Club was.

The next weekend the Young Preachers' Club had a great session at Circle-C.

## Worlds of Fun Again?

As I look back I wonder how we did it! We constantly were racing from one special event to another.

We used to say, "If we can just get past this!" My mother replied, "Then it will just be something else. Why don't you slow down?"

We never felt that we were planning too many things. We felt the Lord was leading us and the main purpose for everything we planned was to win teenagers to Christ or to further their spiritual growth.

On October 4, we had our second Worlds of Fun Super Charge with gospel programs in two of the theatres. A total of 110 teens came forward for counseling and asked Jesus to be their Savior on that day at Worlds of Fun—fulfilling the whole purpose of having it.

The very next week we had six formal banquets—five adult and one teen—with The Hawaiians, Mark and Diane Yasuhara. More than 3,000 people attended those delightful occasions. The banquets resulted in several salvation decisions as well as lots of great fellowship.

## No Time to Rest

There was no time to rest. Circle-C Ranch had originally been designed to accommodate 150 teens. The last two summers we had turned away scores of teens because we were filled to capacity. The ministry was growing so fast we knew the next summer would be a disaster if we didn't do something.

Plans were made to build three additional cabins before the next camping season. We would also build another room in the walkout basement of each cabin. With these two modifications, the capacity would be raised to 256 per week—giving a possibility of 2600 teens for the summer.

The increase demanded additions on the dining room, kitchen and recreation facilities. Expansion cost $150,000, even with volunteers doing much of the labor. The construction began in October and—Praise the Lord—it was completed when the campers arrived.

## Wedding Bells

Another special event took place in our family.

On November 14, 1975 Ronnie married Susan Nebel in a beautiful ceremony in the YFC Auditorium. Following the footsteps of his sisters, he married someone he had known all his life, and whose background was deeply entrenched in the ministry of KCYFC. Ronnie and Susan wrote and memorized the vows they pledged to each other.

Susan's parents, Harold and Donna May Nebel, had been active in KCYFC during their teen years. Al had become a second father, of sorts, to Harold since his father had died when Harold was twelve.

When Harold and Donna May were married on January 13, 1956, Ronnie had been the ring bearer in their wedding. Because of her parent's involvement, Susan had been around YFC all her life.

During her teen years, Susan sang in YFC music groups, in a girls' trio, and sang solos on TV and Rallies. She was a leader in her YFC Club, a star quizzer, and had parts in dramas.

"Susan was the 'Exhibit A' teenager," Ronnie proudly exclaims. "She did everything we taught to build a successful YFC Club and proved it worked."

## KCYFC Featured

You couldn't miss seeing it when you opened your paper! There on the front of the Star Magazine in Sunday's *Kansas City Star* was a beautiful photo displaying the radiant, smiling faces of wholesome teenagers clad in vivid costumes. They were the faces of the outstanding teens in our Living Expression and Extra Dimension music groups.

The feature story of the December 7, 1975, Star Magazine spread over six pages and included thirteen pictures. The story was well written, and positive, describing the "thousands of turned on teenagers in our area." We received much favorable response from many of the possible million readers, not only locally but also from across the country where it was received. We couldn't have bought better publicity!

Don Weaver, Editor-Publisher of the Cameron, MO. Citizen Observer wrote an editorial. It said in part:

> I noted, with great interest, the article in the Sunday *Kansas City Star* regarding the area Youth For Christ . . . I have always been enthusiastic about their work. One of the characteristics that makes YFC useful to a community is the fact that it wants the young people active in YFC to also be active in their own church work.
>
> The sad fact is that many churches feel they cannot

support YFC. In the communities in which I have lived, I have found that some of the churches were too small to have an adequate program or they did not have enough participation by their youths to run an effective program. It is my opinion that by supporting YFC we can help our young people be better local church workers. . . and this we need to do—or lose them.

We appreciate editors who realize our outreach to students turns around many lives and brings youth into the local church. Thank you for speaking up!

## CHAPTER 26

# Al's Love–He Teaches Again!

Ten years had scurried by since the YFCI Directors' School had been moved from Kansas City. Al, Ronnie, and David had continued to give on-the-job and individual training to young youth ministers, but Al longed to do more. For longer than three years he had been praying about this burden.

"I want to establish a school where we can train many young men and women to be on the firing line winning teens to Christ," he discussed with Ronnie and David. "There is no college that trains leaders for the specialized ministry we perform."

They agreed it must be done so they designed the plan. Students would attend three hours a day of concentrated Bible study, plus one hour of methods and practical know-how essential for successful youth ministry. Another necessary ingredient was on-the-job training. A session would last twelve months.

Al started searching for a Bible professor. Acquiring a list of candidates from Dallas Theological Seminary and Moody Bible Institute, he searched for someone with proper credentials and years of experience. Several were interviewed by phone. One stood out to him.

"Brother Potratz? This is Al Metsker at Kansas City Youth For Christ." He introduced himself over long distance. At the time Dale was a pastor in Billings, Montana. Al explained to Dale his burden, and how God was leading. He seemed very interested.

Potratz's impressive educational background included graduation from Moody Bible Institute, BA from Taylor University, MA from Wheaton College, and BDiv and MDiv from Northern Baptist Theological Seminary. A pastor for 25 years with a wide range of experience made him a seasoned veteran. Dale and his wife, Carol, had five children, two still at home— Steve a high school junior and 9-year-old Becky.

A visit to Kansas City in which they saw our headquarters and observed the ministry impressed Dale and Carol. A spirit of unity developed between us while they were guests in our home. Evening hours rolled past midnight while we discussed Al's plan. We finally went to bed—confident Dale was to be our Bible professor.

"About 5:00 I awoke —wide-awake," Dale told us later. "The sun was just breaking over the horizon as I looked out the window. Suddenly, the Lord spoke to my heart and said, 'This is it!' I knew this is what God had for us!"

June 2 we started the promotion "CHRIST UNLIMITED BIBLE INSTITUTE BEGINS. CLASSES TO START SEPTEMBER 3, 1975" large headlines in Conquest read.

Al was a good salesman and there was a need for what he offered so it caught fire.

The need of the hour," declared Dr. Al, "is for men and women to be leaders who dare to stand for Christ, live a pure life separated from the world. This institute will be unique because of our ability to 'show and tell'. We will teach only tried and proven methods learned over the past 32 years of ministering to teenagers. Our students will participate immediately in the things they are taught.

Considering that we'd only had three months to get the word out, on September 3, a remarkable class of 35 outstanding students assembled for this exciting adventure.

The size and quality of the student body have surpassed my greatest expectations," affirmed Dr. Al Metsker, President and Founder. "The age, experience and maturity of our students makes us certain our graduates will be in demand and will produce great results.

Look at these interesting statistics about our students:
*Average age was 25.
*Most were college graduates
*Four were high school teachers who gave up teaching to go into ministry.
*Two were communications majors with a first-class license.
*Several were church youth leaders.
*Two were artists who plan to use their talents in specialized ministry.
*One was a registered nurse.

Just as we'd held the Director's School on our location, we held CUBI at the KCYFC headquarters. When CUBI was in session, we set up a classroom in half of the Rainbow Room by using moveable partitions to eliminate distractions. A theological library for students use could be enclosed behind doors when the Rainbow Room was used for other purposes. Rectangle tables provided desk area facing the teacher. Every Friday evening, our maintenance crew converted the area back into the Rainbow Room so was once again ready to be filled with teenagers for Saturday night fun and food. Before Monday morning the space was transformed into a classroom again.

Al required men students to wear shirt, tie, and jacket every morning. In the afternoon study time they could remove the jacket. Girl students were to wear skirts and look neat. When visitors took a tour while class was in session they were very impressed with the students. Their dress enhanced their image. He also would not allow any facial hair. He reasoned that, at that time, beards and sloppy dress were identified with rebellion.

"Your eyes are the main point of communication," Al taught his students. "When you're speaking in front of an audience, maintain eye contact to help your message get through." He felt facial hair often detracted—especially when they stroked it without realizing it. The young men and women were taught to speak or preach in public and he wanted to make sure nothing hindered the communication of God's word. Al wanted our students to be the sharpest looking anywhere. He taught that the way you dress makes a difference in the way you act and the way others treat you.

Dale Potratz was named Dean of the school. He was a colorful teacher with a commanding knowledge of the Bible. Subjects included Bible Survey, Bible Doctrine, Bible Geography and Hermeneutics. Also, a stickler for Bible memory and good preparation for their lessons, students were challenged to memorize scripture and absorb Bible knowledge.

Al was gratified with the opportunity to impart to those young men and women the knowledge he had gained through 33 years in the specialized ministry of youth evangelism. Among the subjects he taught were History of YFC, How to Prepare and Deliver a Message, How to Give a Gospel Invitation, Public Relations, How to Raise Support and Finance a Ministry, Pastoral Relations, Secrets of communicating with teenagers, and much more. CUBI students also learned the minute details of whatever project KCYFC was undergoing at a time.

Some things he preached often and adamantly. In almost a whisper he ordered, "Don't quit!" Then he repeated in his normal voice, "Don't quit!" Next, he would raise the level a notch and continue until he was screaming at the top of his lungs, with every blood vessel on his face about to pop, yelling, "**DON'T QUIT!**" Then he would read Revelation 2:10: "Be faithful even to the point of death, and I will give you the crown of life." He added: "The word 'QUIT' is no longer in your vocabulary."

Another principle he emphasized repeatedly to both his CUBI students and to his Young Preachers Club was that they must take advantage of every opportunity to serve the Lord. First Peter 3:15 instructs: "Always be prepared to give an answer to everyone who asks you to give the reason for the hope that you have." His quote was "**Be ready to preach, pray, sing, or die on a moment's notice.**"

Al was constantly identified with those two principles. Much of his teaching concerned practical living. He taught strong character traits to his students constantly.

Ronnie Metsker taught the Beginning Soul Winning Course, How to Plan and Run a Rally, How to Run Bible Clubs, and other instruction from his vast experiences.

David Lewis taught How to Lead Singing, Basics of Television Production, and other performance skills.

Roy Bilyeu taught How to run a Bible Quiz, Advanced Counseling, How to Raise Missionary Support and other classes.

Well-known preachers and evangelists were occasionally guest speakers.

This was just the beginning of a great training school that continued until after we retired.

About this same time, one of Al's dynamic young preacher boys, Jerry Johnston—a high school junior—was being used mightily of God as he traveled across the country preaching. Having learned from Al, "The Word of God does the work of God," Jerry memorized volumes of scripture often quoting as many as one hundred verses in one sermon. God's hand of blessing was obviously on Jerry and we were proud of him.

### "I Came Back"

We never imagined what the future held for individuals when they walked to our prayer room to receive Jesus as Savior. A sell-out crowd of adults at our January 23, 1976 Dinner Club had been enthralled by Stanley Tam, a businessman from Chicago and author of a book, *God Owns My Business*, as he told his story of how God had blessed him in his business.

When Al gave the invitation a bearded, long-haired young man visiting from out of town came forward for counseling. Mike King led him to Jesus that night, gave him a *Life Plus* book and talked to him about growing in the Lord. They exchanged addresses and the young man left for his home in Minnesota.

Three months later, the same young man, Gordon Buboltz, showed up in our office. He told Al, "God told me to come back here where I could get more spiritual help." What were we to do with him? Al thought of something.

"How would you like to go live at Circle-C and work on the construction? We can give you a place to live and food."

Gordon agreed. He had no idea what he was getting into. He didn't realize that he and the others he would work with would labor twelve-hour days in all kinds of weather. He learned quickly about the dedication of these men—some volunteers and some staff. Soon he fit into the routine and was a great help. Most importantly, our people who worked alongside him were able to minister to him and he grew spiritually with giant steps. By the time camp opened, Gordon was hired to be the head trail bike man. During camp sessions he sat in on all the meetings he could, thereby continuing his spiritual growth. At the end of the summer he became a student in Christ Unlimited Bible Institute. That was in 1976.

That summer at Circle-C it was fascinating to see how he and Mary Baker, accompanist and arranger for our music department, gravitated toward each other. Mary was at the Ranch at least once each week auditioning teens for our music groups. A friendship was budding that would blossom into a beautiful love-relationship. We celebrated their marriage a year later.

Upon graduation from CUBI, Gordon joined our staff. Now, 24 years later, he is Director of Buildings and Grounds which includes all of YFC properties. He chuckles now about his introduction to our ministry working 84 hours a week for only room and board.

God blessed us with myriads of wonderful, dedicated staff members like Gordon over the years.

## CHAPTER 27

# Al's Next Dream—and Distress

"Which one of you guys is going to give us some decent time?" Al chided a group of television station managers. Al and I had been invited to a reception for television personnel at a country club. "If you don't give me better time, I'll just have to build my own station," he continued.

I'm sure they just laughed inside when they heard his remark. But Al was serious.

In the four years we had been producing "Christ Unlimited," our teen evangelistic TV program, we had been bumped from one time slot to another making it difficult to build an audience. And the time slots were never very good—they were the times no one else wanted!

Why did he want good television time? Was it to build a name for himself? Not in the least! His whole burden was to reach out to where the teenagers were. Just as he had wanted to reach into the schools where the teens were back in 1945, now he realized that teens were spending hours in front of the tube.

He remembered what Paul said in 1 Corinthians 9:22: "I am made all things to all men that I might by all means save some."

His whole motivation was to save teenagers!

We had gone to the National Religious Broadcasters Convention for several years because Al had been on radio for twenty-five years, and now on television for four. There were very few all-Christian television stations in the country at the time but the idea was growing. Our friend, Dick Bott, Owner/ President of Bott Broadcasting (KCCV) encouraged us to build a station.

So when we were in Washington, D.C. for NRB in 1976, Al went to the Federal Communications Commission and asked if there was a channel open in Kansas City. There were two—Channel 50 and Channel 62. We chose 50 because it was lower on the dial. The FCC commissioner asked, "What kind of a station are you planning?"

"All Christian!" Al answered.

The commissioner, sticking out his hand said, "Put her there. I'm a Christian and I would love to see you get a Christian station." That remark gave Al the spurt to surge forward.

David Lewis, who was our Music Director, and Andy Wiloughby, whom we hired as a possible TV station manager, worked diligently for months doing interviews, research, and acquiring technical and legal information to prepare for the complicated application to FCC. After the six-inch high stack of papers that made up the application was sent off to Washington, all we could do was pray, pray and wait.

## Blizzard Hampers Triumph

While we were waiting for the FCC to make their decision on giving us the license to put Channel 50 on the air, we planned another Super Rally.

Three years before nearly 40,000 people had come to Royals Stadium to hear Pat Boone. Now it was time to try to fill Arrowhead Stadium—twice as many people. We booked Johnny Cash and planned to help Kansas City celebrate our great nation's bicentennial. The date was set for October 16, 1976. October is normally nice balmy weather in Kansas City.

We started praying for the 80,000 seats to be filled. We wanted to teach and credential 10,000 counselors. We wanted a 5,000 voice choir—1400 buses bringing delegations from all over Missouri and Kansas—1,000 ushers to help with the crowd—500 high school band members to play together. Those were huge dreams—but Al was used to dreaming big.

Other talent would include Paul Anderson, 1956 Olympic weight lifting champion, and Princess Pale Moon, an inspiring

American Indian concert artist.

All the preparations were done. Three different counseling courses were held to accommodate the crowds. Friday, the week before the Super rally, we held a prayer meeting at our Auditorium from 7 P.M. until 1 A.M. Chartered buses were scheduled. Churches arranged delegations. Groups were coming from distances.

Dr. Charles B. Wheeler, Jr., Mayor of Kansas City, Mo. made the following proclamation on October 7:

> WHEREAS, Kansas City Youth For Christ, under the direction of Dr. Al Metsker, has for more than 33 years made an enormous contribution to the spiritual and moral lives of thousands of our young people; and
>
> WHEREAS, God is doing great things in Kansas City as Youth For Christ will be making their first big announcement about the new all-Christian television station they are putting on the air;
>
> NOW, THEREFORE, I, CHARLES B. WHEELER, JR., Mayor of Kansas City, Missouri, do hereby proclaim the week of October 10 through October 16, 1976 as YOUTH FOR CHRIST WEEK in Kansas City, Missouri, and extend my congratulations to Kansas City Youth For Christ on the event of their big Super Rally in Arrowhead Stadium on October 16, 1976.

A 20-foot square stage extended from both 40-yard lines, decorated in red and white and blue. It started out as a beautiful fall day. Gates were to open at 4:30, with pre-rally music provided by Jim Sunderwirth, Ray Hildebrand and Andy Ferrier.

Suddenly, just as people were preparing to leave home, a freak storm walloped the city with gusts of freezing wind. The temperature suddenly dropped 40 degrees to only 30 degrees! The biting wind almost robbed you of your breath. The change was so drastic that it scared people away.

But, despite the record-breaking cold temperatures, about 30,000 brave souls snuggled in winter coats, hats, mittens and wooly blankets to get in on the blessing.

The bone-chilling weather couldn't penetrate the spirits of those attending. With chattering teeth and frosty hands, the crowd clapped and cheered for all the exceptional entertainers as they gave praise to Jesus. What a thrill to see thousands jump to their feet when Johnny and June Cash rode onto the field in a bright yellow convertible! The spontaneous warmth of the crowd nearly moved the Cashes to tears as they circled the field with their forefingers pointed heavenward in the familiar "One Way" sign indicating where the praise indeed belonged.

At the end of the superb evening, Al gave a quick gospel message and invited people to make their way onto the playing field to meet with a counselor who would explain how to become a child of God. About 300 came. The chill was all but forgotten by most as the warmth of God's presence could be seen on the many faces of His new children.

Forgotten—but not by Al. Seldom did he get discouraged. However, this was one time, he had a hard time climbing up out of despair. Normally 30,000 people is a great crowd—but in the 80,000 seat Arrowhead Stadium it looked like a drop in the bucket, especially when we were expecting to fill it.

Yes, this Rally was a great disappointment to Al, but out of it God began a monumental work. We later learned that this was the first contact Mike King, who was a teenager at the time, had with KCYFC. Who could have known that this would be the beginning of one who would, two decades later, become an important leader in this ministry?

Another thing bothering Al was the heavy financial responsibility. If the stadium had been filled with each person paying $2 for a ticket, most expenses would have been met. Al had prayed for an offering to be the kick-off for building the new television station. Now, he had to raise money to make up the deficit of the rally—plus we had no nest egg to start the TV fund drive.

The next day Johnny Cash did a kind act—he called and

offered to give back part of his fee because of the calamity the night before. That was a big help and we praised God for his wonderful spirit.

Al was so physically exhausted and emotionally depleted, we got in the car and drove to a motel in Oklahoma. Sleep. Rest. Reading God's Word and praying. That's what we needed to be refreshed.

Little did we know what would be the next big event in our lives. In fact, his physical condition probably had more to do with his despair than we knew.

### "My Heart is Fixed"

While at the hotel resting, I looked at Al and knew something was wrong.

"What's the matter, honey?" I pled.

"I'm having pains in my chest." he winced.

At first we weren't too concerned because of the stress he had just been through. But the pains persisted, so as soon as we returned home, we went to a cardiologist. A heart catherization revealed one completely blocked artery and two 80% blocked—a potentially lethal situation.

"Take a couple of days to get your house in order, Al," Dr. Padula told him. "When you're ready, we'll do bypass surgery and repair those blockages." That surgery was not as common as today.

"My house **is** in order, Doc. I have peace in my heart because I know where I'll go when I die. I have nothing to make right with anyone. I'm ready!"

"Dr. Padula, tell me everything you're going to do," Al instructed later. His inquisitive mind never was satisfied. He wanted to see the heart/lung machine and learn how it worked and to know exactly what would happen while he was under the anesthetic. The doctor enjoyed his inquisitiveness and took him to see everything—explaining it all to him. Intrigued by all he saw, Al shared in detail what he had learned with everyone who visited him.

Our staff formed a prayer chain and prayed all day for Al during his surgery. Word was received from Campus Crusade, Fellowship of Christian Athletes, Stonecroft Christian Women's Club, Christian Businessmen's Committee, Full Gospel Businessmen and many individuals confirming their commitment to pray for him. Not to mention all the teens from the Rallies, YFC Clubs, and other aspects of our ministry who fervently prayed for the man they'd come to love so dearly!

Al wasn't just an administrator and visionary. He not only preached to the teenagers, but he loved spending time with them at the Rallies, Ranches, and Clubs. Al gravitated towards all the teens—the popular ones, and those who were "misfits," and loved them all. The teenagers sensed his love for their souls, and for them as people. They responded to his warm friendliness and caring heart. And when that caring heart was threatening to end Al's life, they lovingly beseeched God to guide as the surgeons worked on their friend, Dr. Al. On December 7, 1976, when Al was 55 years old, all our family was on hand to pray with him and love him before orderlies took him to surgery. We had assurance in our hearts that everything would be all right—in spite of our deep concern.

We breathed a prayer of thanksgiving when Dr. Padula reported, "All went well. The surgery was successful."

At that time ICU was not the quiet, private room like most hospitals have today. It was a large room with beds lined up like factory work tables—with barely enough room between them for a nurse to walk. Bright lights shone continuously on the patients. And it was noisy! The doctors said Al would be in ICU for five days. I could visit him for only a few minutes once an hour—and that not at all private. He was progressing fine and begged to get out of ICU.

What a blessing God gave him in ICU. At one point seven Christian nurses gathered around him and prayed for him. Finally he was moved to a private room.

"My heart is fixed, O God, my heart is fixed: I will sing and give praise," (Psalm 57:7) was the verse Al quoted to everyone after he was moved to a room.

Desire and motivation plays a large role in recovery. Al was motivated and his progress was excellent. We praised the Lord for his quick recovery. We couldn't hold him down and he was back on the job—too soon, I thought.

Six weeks to the day after his surgery, he preached one of the most powerful and challenging messages of his life at the YEA convention. "Give Yourself Away" was the theme of Al's keynote address to the delegates from 15 states and one foreign country who gathered in the KCYFC Auditorium. "Take your city for Christ, then the city next to you and eventually your whole state," was his challenge. It was hard to believe that it had been less than six weeks since Al's triple-bypass heart surgery. God did it!

The Jesse Oran and Mabel Metsker family about 1940 at their farm near Eureka, Kansas.
*From left:* Alta Mae, Leona, Mother Mabel, Father Oran, Lowell, and Al.

Al and Vidy Metsker—
Married in June 26, 1943.

Teenagers in our "Two Ton Chariot" parade down streets in 1947 advertising Saturday night "Singspiration."

Northeast High School Bible Club teenagers pose beside our red and white "Mobile Chapel" in 1948. Club Director, Jack Hamilton, stands in doorway of bus.

KCYFC Banquet held at Linwood Presbyterian Church in September, 1946. Cliff Barrows leading singing. Billy Graham and Al Metsker on front row. George Philgreen at piano.

Youth For Christ International Board at the first organizing convention at Winona Lake, Indiana, July 1945. *Front from left:* Greg Tingson, Cliff Barrows, T.W. Wilson, Chuck Templeton, Torrey Johnson, Billy Graham, Al Metsker. *Second row from left:* Dick Harvey, Walter Smyth, Wally White, Frank Phillips, Tom Livermore. Third row from left: George Wilson, (two unknown), Ed Darling, Watson Argue

Our Headquarters after the KYFC-TV 50 studio was added in 1978.

Our headquarters in 1966 after two additions - extra offices on the left and 1,600-seat auditorium behind.

Our second headquarters built at Rainbow Blvd, Shawnee Miss Kansas in 1956.

Our first headquarters building—an old mansion at 4500 Walnut in the Country Club Plaza in 1953.

Billy Graham and Al Metsker at the Kansas City Billy Graham Crusade in 1967 when Al was Youth Committee Chairman.

Ronnie, Dr. Torrey Johnson, and Al at a YFCI reunion in 1988.

Our children at Christmas 1950. Martha, 6; Ronnie, 7 months; Marilyn, 4.

*Left:* Daddy Al plays with his little girls, Martha and Marilyn, before they go to bed. 1949.

*Right:* Marilyn, 6; Ronnie, 3; Martha, 8 on Easter Sunday 1953 on their way to Sunday School wearing clothes I made them.

Crowd shot in the Grand Avenue Temple, in September 1945, 1257 in attendance.

Some of us at a restaurant after a Rally in 1948. *From left:* Dr. Walter L. Wilson, Torrey Johnson, Al and Vidy Metsker, Jack Hamilton, Darrel Handel. *Standing:* Darrel Freleigh, Dr. Bob Belton.

Thirtieth anniversary Super Rally in Royals Stadium on May 5, 1973 with Pat Boone. Nearly 40,000 attended. *Below:* The infield at Royals Stadium was shoulder to shoulder people when 1300 came forward during the gospel invitation to make a decision for Christ.

*Below:* Twelve thousand people fill the KC Municipal Auditorium for our Third Anniversary Super Rally in 1946. *Left:* Little 6-year-old "bakers" carried a cake the length of the arena as the crowd sang "Happy Birthday to KCYFC." *From left:* Ted Anderson, Chuck Johnson, Don Philgreen, Paul Bockelman, Billy Keith, and Ronnie Philgreen.

Overflow crowd that was turned away from our Rally with Dr. Charles E. Fuller and Merv Rosell in KC Municipal Auditorium in 1950, Club Director Gene French stands on top steps leading crowd singing gospel songs.

YFCI Board in 1950's. Some of these men started other ministries after they left YFCI. Al was the only one who continued in YFC during his whole life. *Front from left:* Carl Gunderson, Bob Cook (*Kings College*), Ted Engstrom, Billy Graham (*Evangelistic Assn.*), Sam Wolgemuth, Ed Darling, Jack Soneveldt. *Back row from left:* Elliot Stettelebauer, Ben Weiss, Roy McKeown (*World Opportunities*), Frank Phillips, Bob Pierce (*World Vision*), Al Metsker, Floyd Ankerberg, Jacob Stam, Jack Hamilton, Paul Hartford.

Laying cornerstone on auditorium in 1965. *From left:* Jack Cousins, Albert Lane, Al Metsker.

Our Family in 1957, Vidy, Marilyn, Ronnie, Martha and Al.

In KYFC-TV studio after taping "Inside Story." From left: Rob Moritz, Ronnie Metsker, Vidy Metsker, Josh McDowell, and Al Metsker.

Ronnie Metsker, Dr. Bill Bright, Founder of Campus Crusade for Christ and Al Metsker in KYFC-TV studio in 1979.

David Lewis, Chuck Millhuff and Ronnie Metsker cheer as Dr. Al crowned Ivan Walters with his bright red cowboy hat on the "Stampede '82" telethon on KYFC-TV. Ivan gave his sizeable gift but wanted Al's hat.

"Goober and Leroy" alias Ronnie Metsker and David Lewis, 1969, performing their comedy act.

Al, Ronnie and David cheering the total gifts on our "Over the Top" telethon at KYFC-TV 50 in 1980.

Recording a Youth For Christ Hour radio program in 1953. *From left:* Bill Keith, Al Metsker, Albert Lane.

Dr. Al preaching at Circle-C Ranch. He used a corn stalk and a tomato to illustrate his message: "Whatsoever a man sows that shall he also reap." You don't reap a tomato when you sow corn.

Dr. Al at Circle-C Ranch preaching on Luke 9:62. "Jesus replied, 'No one who puts his hand to the plow and looks back is fit for service in the kingdom of God.'"

1966 Shawnee Mission North Quiz Team. *From left:* Dave Cornelius, Ronnie Metsker, Linda Spory, Paula Yeamans and Diane Burns.

Groundbreaking for KCYFC auditorium—September 1965. Ron Pentz, Mayor Joe Dennis, Norm Hutcheson, Don Trewitt, Dean Anderson (with shovel), Bob Pressler, Dick Bott, Murray McClain, Al Metsker, Joe Hoobery.

Al Metsker and Josh McDowell laying stone
at L-Bar-C Ranch, 1981.

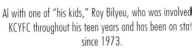

Al with one of "his kids," Roy Bilyeu, who was involved
KCYFC throughout his teen years and has been on sta
since 1973.

Teenagers enjoy the olympic-
size pool at L-Bar-C Ranch.

A few teenagers having a Bible
study on the beautiful campus of
L-Bar-C Ranch.

Dr. Jerry Falwell and Dr. Al Metsker boating on Smith Mountain Lake near Lynchburg, Virginia.

nie and Al took part
Liberty University
duation on May 1,
8. Ronnie received
Bachelor of Science
hurch Ministries de-
e the same day
ncellor Dr. Jerry
vell presented Dr. Al
honorary Doctor of
rs degree.

Grandpa Al and Topher Philgreen as water ski buddies in 1992.

Missouri Attorney General John Ashcroft and Al Metsker following a Dinner Club in the KCYFC Auditorium, 1976. Ashcroft later became Governor of Missouri and U.S. Senator from Missouri.

Al and Ronnie during construction on L-Bar-C Ranch, 1982.

ore than 100 students pray in 1997 at Lee's Summit High School "See You at the Pole." Similar crowds met to pray at the school flag
le at all junior and senior high schools in the Kansas City area and around the country.

Al teaching at Christ Unlimited Bible Institute in 1977.

*Right:* During the 1985 LIGHT House Telethon, Marilyn Lewis was presented a bouquet of roses for her key leadership role in planning and fundraising. *From left:* Willie Williams, Marilyn and David Lewis.

*Left:* David Lewis hosting "Music and You" show on KYFC-TV 50 in 1979.

*Right:* Dr. Al reading his Bible on "Inside Story" on KYFC-TV 50 in 1980.

Al and Vidy Metsker's family in 1982. *Left,* Don and Martha Philgreen with sons Kevin, Jonathan and Timothy *on laps. Behind* Topher and Michelle. *Center back* the Lewis family, Jennifer, Liane, Delinda, Marilyn, Davey, David. *Right* Susan and Ronnie Metsker *holding* Amy. Grandma Vidy *holding* Rusty Metsker and Grandpa Al *holding* Melody Metsker.

Al on backhoe at the groundbreaking for KYFC-TV Studio, 1976.

A common sight, Al and Vidy riding on Al's Honda 100 at L-Bar-C in 1991.

Al preaching at television taping with music groups listening in 1973.

Al and teenagers waving flags at the Saturday night YFC Rally celebrating passage of the Equal Access Act in 1984.

Senator Frank Carlson of Kansas giving autographs to Kansas City teens at Capital Teen Convention in DC in 1959. *From left:* Verla Thurman, Al, Senator Carlson, Jim Nelson.

Richard Bott (right), owner and manager of Radio Station KCCV (Kansas City's Christian Voice) joins Al at the microphone, as Vidy brings in one of the pledges.

Groundbreaking for the Al Metsker Memorial Dining Hall at Circle-C in 1993. *From left with shovels:* Board members Kent Barber, David Heinke, Hal Wood, Bob Schmid, Josiah Smith , John Cowan, Larry O'Donnel, John Cross, and Mike Cummings.

Al Metsker Memorial building at Circle-C Camp, 1995.

*left:* Marilyn Lewis with her daughter, Jennifer and Martha Philgreen.
[J]er was runner-up for Miss Lynchburg 1989.

Grandpa Al with Jonathan Philgreen and Amy Metsker trying out the Go-cart they built together in 1989.

Grandpa Al with two youngest grandchildren, Amy Metsker and Timothy Philgreen at the Kansas flag crossing the Royal Gorge Bridge in Colorado, 1992.

Al and grandson Davey Lewis enjoying strawberry shortcake with homemade ice cream.

Ronnie teaching youth leaders in Cuba during a YouthFront International Training Conference in 2000. Leadership training has also been held in Jamaica, Flovakia, Poland, Hong Kong (with leaders from the Pacific rim), Hungary and Romania (coming from all over eastern Europe). Other confernces soon to come in Berlin and Spain.

Ronnie with some of the 20,000 Bibles YouthFront took to Russia where students on one of our mission trips gave them out in Red Square. 1993.

Chad Stewart and Kevin Knox, high school seniors whose deep burden that every senior hear the gospel before graduating, led a group of seniors to prepare packets that presented Jesus Christ and mailed them to every senior in the eight Johnson County high schools. *Pictured from left:* Ronnie Metsker, Chad Stewart, Kevin Knox and Topher Philgreen. April 1999.

Our grandson, Rusty Metsker, witnessing to students in Jamaica during a mission trip 1996.

Don Philgreen Family in 1997. *From left:* Timothy, Kevin, Dr. Don, Martha, Jonathan, Brian, Michelle and Joshua Gann, April, Topher, Connor and Cameron.

Ronnie Metsker famil[y] Shawnee Mission North H[igh] coming. *From left:* Rusty, Su[e,] Amy, Ronnie and Mel[…], 1999.

David Lewis Family in 1996. *From left:* David II, Liane, Bret and Delinda Phillips, Marilyn and David, Gavin and Jennifer Watson.

Celebrating at the end of a telethon, teenagers sprayed silly string on the heads of Topher Philgreen, Mike King and Ronnie Metsker 1995.

Our great grandchildren: *Above left:* Henry Phillips; *Above right:* Micah Gann, Connor Philgreen, Joshua Gann, Cameron and Chloe Philgreen. *Bottom right:* Grandpa Al with our first great-grandson, Cameron Philgreen, in 1993.

Two Lewis girls graduated together from Liberty University in May 1990. *From left:* Al Metsker, Marilyn, Delinda, Liane, David, Jennifer Lewis and Vidy Metsker.

Vidy, Brian and Michelle Gann, Al in 1991 at Michelle's university graduation.

Vidy with granddaughter, Melody Metsker, at high school graduation, 1995.

In front of Christ's empty tomb in Jerusalem. From left: Mike King, Dr. Al and Eric Rochester. 1985.

Al showing a ceramic eagle we gave to donors who joined our Eagle Club.

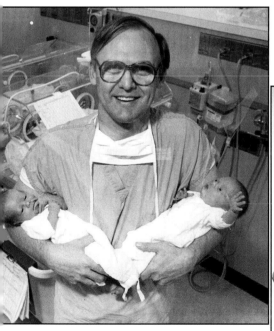

: Don Philgreen with a set of LIGHT House twins he had delivered, 1985

YouthFront Leadership Team who oversee the more than 80 staff. *Front row from left:* Mike King (CEO), Ronnie Metsker (President), Tim Smith (Vice President Public Relations), *Back row from left:* Topher Philgreen (V P Program Events). Eric Rochester (V P Program Ministries International), Erin Toole (Creative Director), Jamie Roach (V P YouthFront Alliance), Jim Baker (CFO), and Gorman Stanley ( Media Director). Three of these leaders received Jesus as Savior in KCYFC ministry. All but two were involved in KCYFC through their high school years. Sept. 2000

Part of the main floor crowd at Impact (formerly called Rally). YouthFront staff member, Josh Shaffer leads the students as they lift their candles high committing to "Light Your World" on their school campuses.

CHAPTER 28

# Motivated Women Work Wonders

I'm fed up to here with the trash that spills into my living room every time the TV is turned on!" Marilyn shuddered as she thrust her hand horizontally to the top of her head.

A shower of words fell. "Amen!" "I agree!" "Me, too!" Say it again!" "Absolutely!"

This was a meeting of our Luncheon and Dinner Club Cabinet in November 1976.

"We women see the need for a positive way to combat the filth that invades our homes via television more than anyone." Again the ladies agreed and determined to do something about it.

Under the direction of the President, Eva Dodd, the Lord gave them a tremendous idea—"Women's March for Christian TV." Their ingenious plan was to find 2,000 women who would raise $1,000 each. A simple way to accomplish this would be to find nine friends beside themselves who would give $10 a month for a year. That seemed reachable for anyone.

Our 30-year-old daughter, Marilyn Lewis, who was a mother of four small children, took the challenge to head up the march. At the Luncheon and Dinner Clubs she told exciting stories of how women working together had saved their country.

She related, "In Brazil in 1963, a Communist takeover was imminent. Women set out to inform the public by buying newspaper and radio ads, staging protests and writing thousands of letters to their Congressmen. They were even willing to risk their lives by covering the airport runway with their bodies to prevent a plane carrying two top Communist organizers from landing. Finally, the men realized that something had to be done and staged a one-day military siege, restoring their country to democracy. But it was the women who really saved the country!"

"There comes a time of desperation—and we have reached it—when you put aside some other things that used to seem important and invest some of your time and talent in an effort to save our children, our city, and our country!" she challenged. "The answer is Jesus! Channel 50 is going to invade our area in our living rooms with quality programming that shows the answer."

"Can we do it?" she continued. "Yes, we can and we must! We are asking Christian women all over the city to stand and fight against the evil influences. Come join the 'March for Christian TV!'" She had her Daddy's motivational skills and nothing would stop her.

Mayor Charles Wheeler invited Marilyn to his news conference and gave this statement:

> I am endorsing YFC's efforts to construct a TV station in Kansas City. I know from having participated in other programs with YFC that this will be good for this community and the viewing area.

Marilyn made appearances on radio shows and spoke at many churches, clubs, and meetings.

Margaret Baldwin was in charge of scheduling bookings in all kinds of clubs, service organizations and civic groups to present the ministry and its needs.

U.S. Senator from Missouri, John Danforth said, "I think this is a great opportunity. The media can be an effective way to proclaim the gospel. I wish your TV station well and hope the people of Kansas City support it."

A new idea was born—ask ladies to have a morning coffee or afternoon tea in their home inviting neighbors and friends and have Marilyn or someone else present the challenge to give to Christian TV. These were a great success.

Jane Park was another enthusiastic booster who spoke at coffees. Jane and her husband, Roy, were YFC Club Sponsors and she was president of the Luncheon and Dinner Club for a year, as well as being an interior decorator and owning a classic antique store. She would later be the hostess of one of our very popular TV shows, "Something Beautiful," for a number of years.

Jim Bates who had connections to get diamonds, and Dale Hedrich who was in the jewelry business made little gold lapel pins the shape of a tower with a small 5 point diamond at the top. These were given as a "thank you" to all who either gave or raised $1000. An additional little ruby stone would be set in a Bible at the base of the tower for each extra $1000.

The first pin was presented to a shy, little, middle-aged lady, Marie Lang, who said, "At first I didn't think I could do it but I was so excited about Christian TV, I decided I could. I presented the idea to my Sunday School Class. After they said they couldn't give, I suggested that I had decided to give up buying a hamburger or something I didn't need to have the money to give. We can always sacrifice something. Several took the challenge and signed up. Then their friends started giving. It was really easy. I have almost $2000 and I'll keep going till I get $5000."

Similar stories abounded. Within a short time we had presented 25 pins.

Soon the "March" expanded to include men and teenagers who wanted to be a part of the mission. Two of Marilyn's daughters, Liane (9) and Jennie Belle (7), asked her for a tower pin.

"You can have one if you raise $1000 for TV-50," she challenged them. They set out to do just that. They wrote up their little speech and started asking their teachers and calling the mothers of their classmates at school until they had raised their $1,000.

Many teenagers wanted in on the action, but some felt $1000 was a little stiff for them, so we fashioned identical little tower pins made from antique brass instead of gold and diamonds. These could be earned by giving or raising $100.

People were so excited about the project they gave sacrificially.

*One young couple gave their extra car for YFC to sell and put the proceeds of $1700 into Channel 50.

*Another couple had a piece of real estate they decided they could do without. They sold it and gave the profit of $3000 to Channel 50.

*A family who had saved for a vacation decided to forego the vacation and put that money on TV-50.

*One person made a sacrificial gift and in a short time God rewarded that one with an unexpected raise that more than made up the difference!

Who received the greatest blessings? Those who gave sacrificially!

## License Granted

After many months of praying and working, in May 1977, the FCC granted our construction permit. By this time God had sent in more than $190,000 in cash plus $130,000 in pledges—an impressive beginning!

## Women in Touch

It was like a pep rally—a spiritual pep rally for women! Marilyn had the idea and she headed it up with the help of many. Coffee and doughnuts were served starting at 8:30 a.m. April 27, 1977 as the women were arriving at the YFC Auditorium. The day would be videotaped so everyone must be in her seat before the taping began at 9:30.

More than 1200 ladies sensed the presence of the Lord as they entered the auditorium for their special day. Jammed into the day were ten exciting musical numbers by YFC music groups spliced between speakers and other activities.

One stimulating speaker was **Hansi**, a former Nazi youth leader who learned the truth and became a child of God and—

by choice—an American. She had been enslaved in a Russian labor camp before escaping to a freedom she had never experienced before coming to America. Her message cemented in everyone's heart a higher regard for our American heritage and made us want to pay whatever cost to keep it from destruction.

I led a prayer time when all the women joined hands and hearts in a powerful believing faith that God was going to do a miracle.

**Irene Conlan**, author of *Women, We Can Do It!* stimulated more courage in the womens' spirits as she related success stories written in her powerful book. Irene had been a nun for nine years, before she left the convent and met a scholarly lawyer, John Conlan, who became her husband and an U.S. Congressman. She led a weekly Bible study for congressional wives in Washington, D.C.

Al, giving up-to-date information on the progress of TV 50, motivated the women to get out there and tell everyone. Without exception all were blessed, challenged and inspired to help see TV-50 become a reality soon. Seventy-six ladies signed up to become a "Marcher," to help raise funds to put TV-50 on the air. Although no offering was taken that day, more than $15,000 was received for TV-50.

The video of the entire day was available for people to use in coffees, churches, or wherever the challenge could be launched.

## Mayor Celebrates Too!

Mayor Wheeler was such a blessing—always giving us a boost. On May 23 he invited Al to his news conference to announce that the FCC had granted our license. Also, we had found and purchased 42 acres where the tower would be built.

Finding the tower sight was no small task because of all the requirements.

(1) It must be a large plot of ground for the safety of surrounding inhabitants.

(2) It must be approved by the FAA declaring it was out of the line of air traffic.

(3) It needed to be a fairly central location.

(4) It had to be affordable.

(5) It had to be approved by the City Zoning Board.

(6) It had to be approved by the FCC.

At one point we thought we had the perfect plot but the FAA said it was too close to air traffic lanes for Richards-Gebar Airport. It seemed there was a restriction on every lot. This made us pray all the harder. God knows how to keep us on our knees. Prayer is the only answer to roadblocks and God is the One who sets things straight. We learned that over and over.

We finally found a plot of ground that fit all the criteria and enough money had come in that we could pay cash—avoiding interest. How we praised the Lord! A tower building company had been contracted to start construction as soon as the land was secured. Huge concrete piers were poured deep into the ground to anchor the pads for the tower and its guy wires. While we were searching diligently for the tower site, Al was designing the TV studio to be built above our office building.

Two years of hard "behind the scenes" battles had been fought and won—seeking the TV license, buying the land, raising money. Now, at last, the drama mounted as heavy machinery arrived at the Headquarters to dig. We were starting to build something the people could see!

On September 17, 1977, several hundred people stood on the front lawn of the Headquarters as David Lewis and Billy Tucker played and sang from the roof of the headquarters building. Al read Scripture. Several leaders prayed and with 20 shovels, everyone helped turn over the first sod. By this time $503,711 (25% of what was needed) had been given or pledged.

## Masses Walk and Jog

When our niece, Joyce Hughes, had asked us to support her for a walk-a-thon a few months earlier, little did we know what an impact it would have on us. But, now the idea hit us. If all those teenagers were raising money to walk for something they knew little about, why shouldn't we challenge the thousands of teens involved in the KCYFC ministry to walk for something they were passionate about?

Ronnie, a meticulous detail man, assumed the huge responsibility of planning and expediting the Walk-a-thon. He developed the systems; trained and organized each of the crew chiefs; and saw it to a successful finish. The date of the 20-mile walk was set for October 8. We prayed that the weather would not be a repeat of the Johnny Cash Super Rally one year before— almost to the day.

A brisk breeze painted rosy cheeks on the 1,009 walkers and joggers for the TV-50 WALK-A-THON . . . But everyone was overjoyed that God had answered our prayers by providing a bright sun shiny day on October 8, 1977.

Upon arrival at the Headquarters the animated participants donned blue "KYFC-TV Channel 50 COME ALIVE, KC" tee shirts and received their red, helium-filled balloons.

Worlds of Fun mascots Dan'L Coon, Sam Panda and Gertrude Gorilla added to the excitement.

The walkers began their trek in groups, and before the first group left, Mayor Charles B. Wheeler of Kansas City gave greetings: "I'm always glad to help Youth For Christ do the great work they are doing with the young people. I'm not walking today but I'm paying! Several of you called me and asked me to sponsor you. I want to meet you before you go."

Ray Hildebrand sang and gave greetings. Johnson County Commissioners Clay Wirt and John Franke were on hand to cheer the walkers on.

Ronnie and his co-workers had designed a scenic 20-mile route through the Country Club Plaza, out beautiful Ward Parkway and Meyer Boulevard and back. The Police Department oversaw our activities.

This was the largest walk-a-thon to be held in Kansas City at this point and 96% made it the whole 20 miles. About 40 people jogged the whole distance and many jogged part of the way.

What a FUN day! Al and I walked the whole 20 miles as did our three children and their spouses, Martha and Don Philgreen, Marilyn and David Lewis and Ronnie and Susan Metsker. (Susan's foot started hurting her terribly but she wasn't a quitter. An examination after she finished revealed a fractured bone.) We were proud of our four oldest grandchildren, Christopher and Liane (10), Michelle (9), and Jennie Belle (8) who walked the whole distance.

*A young mother of three, Cindy Hedrick, jogged 10 miles and walked 10 more bringing in a total of $1500.

*There were a number of whole families who walked together.

*Several small ones, 6 to 10 years old, made it all the way.

*A 61-year-old man jogged nearly all the way.

*A 72-year-old lady finished the course by 4 o'clock and then stayed for the Victory Rally. Bright and early Monday morning she was at the Headquarters with more than $300 she had raised.

More than 300 volunteers worked at the mile markers where they punched tickets and served drinks and snacks, or at the 10-mile marker (the parking lot of Colnial Presbyterian Church) where we cooked hot dogs and hamburgers and served lunch to the walkers. Most of these got sponsors for their hours worked instead of the miles walked. One of those, Mickey Moore raised $826 for what she called her Work-A-Thon.

Many businesses donated food and supplies: Pepsi Cola, Guys Potato Chips, Arlund Mean Company, Clemens and Green food brokers.

The day ended with a Victory Rally in our Auditorium. Although most of the walkers were exhausted, the packed auditorium was electric with excitement. It was unbelievable how the kids in our music groups could look so fresh and perform so beautifully after their 20-mile walk. It was a great Rally. What a day!

Word spread across the country among not-for-profit organizations, and Ronnie was asked to teach how to do a walk-a-thon in fund-raising seminars in other parts of the country.

CHAPTER 29

# FRANTIC JOURNEY

Sandwiched in with all the weekly YFC Clubs and Rallies, the CUBI classes, the TV-50 activities, Bible Quizzes, a Sponsors' Institute and two Power Charges at Circle-C, were two other big events.

I have to admit now that I am reviewing all our activities, I wonder how we possibly made it—and how our staff made it, too! We had such a wonderful, loyal staff most of whom stayed with us for years and years. I almost feel that I should apologize to them now for scheduling so much. But, we all loved it and I never considered—at the time—that we were doing too much.

I must point out again that we never had activities just for an activity's sake. We never did anything without a purpose—and usually that purpose was reaching people with the gospel or helping them grow spiritually.

Two weeks after the walk-a-thon we held six formal banquets in our Auditorium—junior high, senior high and four for adults.

### Cave-In!

I guess we might as well look at what happened during the banquets as comedy and laugh about it! How could anything else so dramatic happen?!

The week of banquets was in progress. Excavation had begun on Thursday in preparation for building the television studio. The studio was being built on top of the office portion of our Headquarters. Because we planned to do productions, our studio would be the largest in the city. Other stations did mostly news.

The hole was 10 feet deep, 20 feet wide and 113 feet long—all across the front of our building. We were planning to build additional offices in the basement which would provide a larger base for our upstairs studio. Then the rains came. Pumps were used to constantly keep the water pumped out. Everything appeared fine. Then, about 7:30 Sunday evening, with a rumbling, noisy fanfare, the front brick and concrete wall of our Headquarters gave away and crumbled into the pit. This was the same rain that caused the tragic flash flood in the Country Club Plaza (just one mile from us) when 25 people died in flood waters.

Our building foreman was summoned to work on the situation and much of the staff came to help salvage office equipment and records. Not one thing was lost other than the wall. Much of the night was spent rearranging offices so business could go on as usual the next day.

"What a tragedy!" someone said. But we chose to believe God when he said: "…we know all things work together for good to them that love God, to them who are the called according to his purpose." (Romans 8:28.) The Master Designer was in control of the project and He knew what was best. Our engineers and architects had laid good plans, but when the existing wall collapsed, new plans were drawn which, in the end, turned out to be better and less expensive.

Besides that, we could not have bought the publicity we received. On the front page of the Monday *Kansas City Times* was a big 8"x5" picture. Several television and radio stations covered the story in the news. One week later all danger of further damages was past, and positive construction was under way.

As quick as we were past the banquets and cave-in, we were in full swing in our next venture—a series of meetings with our good friend Josh McDowell on December 2-3. We kept Josh busy, as usual. His schedule on Friday was:

9:00 A.M. Ministers and their associates and wives and CUBI

251

Students.

12:00 Noon—YFC Luncheon Club

7:00 P.M.—YFC Dinner Club

Saturday—7:30 P.M. KCYFC Rally—Special Teachers' Night. Students were urged to invite their teachers, especially science, history and philosophy teachers. We gave special recognition to all teachers.

Josh's ministry blessed and changed the lives of the capacity crowds the whole weekend.

## Towering High

By April 1st, towering high above ground, the new TV-50 studio addition to the YFC Headquarters nearly concealed from sight the big Auditorium on Rainbow Boulevard. In only two weeks the huge cranes lifted into place the pre-cast concrete slabs forming the floors, roof and side walls of the multi level structure. The 67'x90' studio occupied a large portion of the new building, which also included 21 offices, the control room and equipment area, viewing room, restrooms, large dressing rooms, tape library and prop storage.

Evidence that the people of the Kansas City area were excited about Christian television was proved by the fact that by May first their gifts had topped $1,000,000! We were a little more than half way there financially.

The next milestone we had all been waiting for finally arrived on September 25, 1978. The first section of the 1,125-foot tower was lifted into place. It was fun checking it almost daily as it rose heavenward. At the same time, the transmitter/warehouse building was being constructed near the base of the tower. Volunteer workmen built an apartment in the building for our security man.

God was so good to send us Joe Snelson, a brilliant, talented engineer from California, who was also a dynamic Christian. Joe designed all the technical part of the studio, transmitter, and control room. I cannot begin to express what a tremendous blessing and asset he was. While he was busy building the technical end of the TV control room, he got acquainted with one of our girls who was attending CUBI and they eventually married.

Nine hundred people walked in our second walk-a-thon exactly one year after the first bringing in a total of $142,428.

We set aside November 1 as a special day of prayer for this miracle. All the staff—except one to answer the phone—along with others who joined us, spent from 8 A.M. to 6 .P.M. in prayer. We needed continued miracles and we were going to the source of miracles!

At that time Al's message was:

> **BY FAITH** Noah built the ark. . . . while everyone laughed.
> **BY FAITH** baby Moses was hid by his parents. . . to save his life.
> **BY FAITH** Abraham offered Isaac on the altar. . . but God saved him.
> **BY FAITH** the Israelites walked through the Red Sea on dry land.
> **BY FAITH** Joshua obeyed God . . . and the walls of Jericho fell.

### GOD IS STILL DOING MIRACLES TODAY!
Each step of building TV-50 had been a series of miracles! And will continue to be! The devil does not like it because he knows the degree it will invade his territory. Over 26,000 people have given to make TV-50 a reality. This means at least that many people have prayed for it. It cannot fail.

## On the Air!
For over three years the "prince of power of the air" had been attacking the potential ministry that was about to become a reality, but to no avail. On December 13 at 5:45 P.M., the FCC had given permission to begin broadcasting.

The day: Friday, December 15, 1978
The time: 7:00 P.M. sharp!

Hearts pounded with excitement and apprehension. Everyone was praying. Al anticipated the "go" signal from General Manager David Lewis. Chief Engineer Joe Snelson and his crew alertly monitored a maze of electronic equipment. Satan and his demons trembled.

More than 200 staff, CUBI students and guests gathered in the beautiful production studio. Beginning at 7:00 P.M., they, along with thousands of viewers at home, watched three hours of live music and entertainment. Al began the broadcast with a prayer of thanksgiving and petition for wisdom. He thanked the more than 26,000 friends who had given sacrificially to make TV-50 a reality.

Dignitaries in the studio who were introduced were Dr. and Mrs. Charles Wheeler, Mayor of Kansas City; Larry Winn, U. S. Congressman from Kansas; and Joe Dennis, Mayor of Westwood, KS. the location of KYFC-TV.

Letters of congratulations were acknowledged from U. S. Senators John Danforth (Mo.) and Bob Dole (KS) and U. S. Congressman Richard Bolling (Mo.) God had planted a seed of vision in Al's heart. The need was obvious—an alternative to the vile filth of much secular television. Sharing his burden with everyone he could, Dr. Al saw first a trickle, then a stream, and then a flood of concerned Christians join the campaign to air clean, family viewing. Thousands of people gave their talent, time and money as God laid on their hearts the burden for Christian TV. The going had been tough, the sacrifices great, but the battle had been won! TV-50 was on the air! God did it!

Technical advisors had predicted an approximate 50-mile radius of clear reception from metropolitan Kansas City. But, praise God, He over-rides the "facts" of broadcast engineering! As the evening progressed, the phones began to ring. A call came from Sabetha, KS., 110 miles away, reporting clear reception. Other calls came from Garnett, KS. (100 miles),

St. Joseph, Mo. (75 miles), and many other towns to report they were seeing the results of their prayers and giving. God is good!

## Challenging Productions

On air hours—to begin—were daily from 5:30 A.M. to 10:00 P.M. and 8:00 A.M. to 10:00 P.M. Saturday and Sunday. Unlike radio, television production is very costly and time-consuming. We contracted for all the Christian programs available over the whole country. Unfortunately, not much was being produced. Preaching programs such as Rex Humbard and Jerry Falwell were aired on Sunday. Some children's programs like Kids Jamboree, Captain Hook, and Puppet Tree Gang were available, which was wonderful for that age group. Several other variety, music, or interview shows fit into the schedule.

This was the time for creativity, planning and work. We produced—LIVE—every weekday evening, a music variety program, "Rainbow," using all Kansas City area talent—anything from vocal and instrumental music to drama, puppets and ventriloquists. David, Al and Ronnie were on hand most of the time to help carry the ball.

We were soon producing several other clever music shows. "Majestic Praise" was a trio comprised of Teresa Lowe, Karen Ludwig and Bob Gephart, who'd all grown up in our ministry during their teen years. They produced a very creative music and drama show. "King's IV" was our male quartet with Billy Tucker, Gordon and Jim Chrisman and Rick Knabe, who produced another wonderful creative show. (Darwin Boston and Ron Crooks were part of this quartet at times.)

"Stand Up And Shout It," a Bible Quiz show with Ben Bennett and Michelle Fahrmeier as quizmaster and producer, added interesting variety as it showcased our teen Bible quizzers who had memorized much scripture.

Dr. Dave Breese, our good friend since the beginning days of YFCI, produced "Dave Breese Reports." This weekly analysis of today's news from a Biblical perspective was very popular. Dr. Dale Potratz, Dean of Christ Unlimited Bible Institute, taught a series of instruction on Scripture Memory.

Marilyn Lewis hosted "Vibrations," an investigative reporting program on society's vital issues. Ronnie hosted "To Love and Cherish," a Christian version of the newlywed game that was a fun, entertaining program using local happily married couples.

"Something Beautiful" was a daily hour-long music/interview/variety show that we produced for 15 years. The first eight years, Jane Park was the charming hostess. She did her own producing and recruited volunteers to help with all the details. It was a favorite program that was aired on a number of stations across the country, and received tremendous viewer response. We did appreciate her and all of her hard work and investment financially in this popular program.

The following years, two sisters, Debbie Graham and Donna Wilting, hosted Something Beautiful. All three of these hostess/producers worked many hard hours each week—all at their own expense with no remuneration. What a tremendous asset they were to TV-50! All were greatly loved by the audience. Because Jim Sunderwirth had been a barber before entering full-time music ministry, it provided the springboard for Jim's popular TV show, Sunderwirth Barbershop which we produced for a number of years.

Our Saturday night Youth Rally was videotaped each week and aired several times. An invitation for telephone counseling was always the conclusion and produced good results and many salvation decisions with viewers calling to talk to counselors.

Every broadcast day ended with "Inside Story" done by Dr. Al. A friendly chat with his friends, it was as though he was sitting in their living room having a private conversation with them. Al discussed issues of the day, happenings in the world, events involving teenagers, and anything else on his heart. He reported victories in KCYFC ministry, gave TV-50 news, told about spiritual blessings and decisions for Christ and usually a spiritual challenge. He always ended Inside Story by reading scripture and praying.

On Saturday night after the Rallies, TV cameras were set up in the Rainbow Room under the Auditorium where Ronnie did a spirited Inside Story. This popular show was full of action. In the background was the noise and bustle of hundreds of teenagers who had just attended the Rally. Ronnie usually interviewed some of those kids or had them give a testimony. He gave a live on-location report of the Rally that had just finished.

Later David Lewis did a weekly show, "Music and You," a live call-in requesting songs. David played his trumpet and sang as well as having other guests perform. Talent had to be very versatile and knowledgeable to perform from memory any song that was requested. Viewers loved it.

Ronnie updated our Soul Winning Course calling it Basic Training for Evangelism and developed an advanced course for more experienced counselors. This was taught to teenagers at camp and clubs but he also taught it in a series on TV-50 prior to our big evangelistic thrusts.

An average of 44 hours a week was devoted to local production, resulting in airing over 21 hours. We were amateurs, and I'm sure much of what we did was pretty corny from the industry's eyes—but the many letters we received proved thousands of people who had given to put TV-50 on the air loved it.

Typical letters said:

"We watch TV-50 every night and feel the staff is a part of our family."

"TV-50 gives me so much enjoyment, Christian love, and spiritual uplift every day."

"When I was searching for something decent to watch, I found TV-50. God certainly knows our needs and how to fill them. You have helped me overcome a very difficult time and to heal a hurt by showing me to look to God for His answer.

"The thing I love most, Dr. Al, is your Scripture reading at the close of the day. It is like my Dad having family devotions!"

We were grateful when the producer of "Kid's Jamboree" sought out Al at the NRB convention to say, "When we begin on a new station we usually start getting a few letters after about six weeks. From the first week on TV-50, though, we have been getting an average of over 125 letters a week."

What blessed us most were those who called in for counseling—many for salvation decisions. That was the main purpose in building the station.

## More TV-50 letters

"As I tell my friends about TV-50, I am learning that many people don't know about it yet. I think you should assign a page of the phone book to everyone who would volunteer and we could inform the city of it."

"I'm 89 years old and I used to go to bed at 8 P.M. Now I stay up until you go off the air at 10 o'clock because I get such good spiritual food on TV-50."

"I didn't realize how many GOOD teenagers there are working for the Lord. It gives me new hope for our nation."

"I'm in Lansing prison, but I'm free with Jesus. I love TV-50. I'm glad to see something without violence!"

"We appreciate the way you stick to the Word of God and teach the teenagers to live a separated life from the world. So many have become permissive but God's standards never change."

"We love Channel 50! Things haven't been the same at our house since we started being fed so well spiritually! We have adopted you as 'our second minister.' Thank you and all your family for being devoted to Jesus and bringing His Gospel to so many. Your faces all radiate His love. We love being 'tucked in' each night by your Bible reading and prayer."

"We love to watch good TV without commercials every few minutes and free from violence and risqué inferences."

# CHAPTER 30

# Important Announcement

The announcement in January, 1978 read:
"Dr. Al Metsker recently announced the promotion of Ronnie Metsker to become Associate Executive Director of KCYFC."

Ronnie had been working on staff since he was sixteen, starting at the bottom and having done nearly every job there was. He knew the organization inside and out. In reality, he was actually doing much of the job before it was made official.

What kind of person was Ronnie?

When he was a child he never broke his toys. Even though he enjoyed playing with them, he kept them clean, organized and in good repair. For instance, he liked to keep his little trucks freshly painted. He enjoyed washing and waxing our car and keeping the lawn immaculate. Something about the satisfaction of a job well done made him happier than to play a game of ball—although he played his share of ball.

"From as far back as I can remember," Ronnie said at this time, "Daddy and Mama shared all about the ministry with us kids. We all carried the burden of it together. This was a great learning experience for me. A lot of my decision-making process in my position today goes back to the times when I was eight and nine years old and could barely understand the principles of administration and how things operated—the principles and philosophies I learned from how they operated this ministry."

For some time Ronnie had been handling many details in the ministry like taxes, real estate, property, insurance, legal procedures, and dozens of other behind-the-scene jobs seldom mentioned but very important. He summed it up, "Many times

I see things that need to be done, but there's no one to take care of them, so I take them on."

Ronnie's creative abilities had been utilized as he produced the Rallies, and planned promotional videos, brochures, and strategies.

During those years when David and Ronnie were a team in charge of all the Clubs, Rallies, and Ranches, they worked out new ideas in the club system. They also wrote a YFC Club Manual that was a great tool for volunteers, as well as for people across the country who wanted to reach out to teens in their area.

Ronnie's promotion, of course, left a need in the Club Department. During the previous five years, Roy Bilyeu had become a valuable team member and a dedicated leader with spiritual maturity. He had played a significant role in the development of the Club staff, Ranch programming and established the Northeast Kansas Satellite, which by this time had a full-time director. He was a natural choice to put in charge of the Clubs and deserved the promotion to Director of the Club Department.

### Women Challenged Again!

Numerous requests for another "Women In Touch" day prompted us to schedule another on March 15, 1978. Marilyn was the facilitator.

Two thousand women packed the Youth For Christ auditorium for a provocative day of song, prayer, and motivating messages. Singer Suzanne Johnson, former Miss Illinois in the Miss America Pageant, blessed our hearts with her testimony and songs.

Ann Kiemel, author of several best-selling books, including *I'm Out to Change My World*, and *I Love The Word Impossible* highlighted the day. The master of motivation and positive living, Ann's unique message made you feel you could go out and conquer the world. She made "winning" seem so simple and natural—something that everyone could accomplish.

Exciting musical numbers by the King's IV (KCYFC male quartet) flavored the day. A challenge to count for Christ in today's society by Dr. Al stirred many women to pledge support in the building of KYFC-TV.

The women prayed for their families, their friends, their communities, and for their nation during interspersed prayer times. Those who attended were inspired and motivated to go into their world and serve God boldly.

## Thirty-fifth Anniversary

More than 3,300 people gathered to help celebrate KCYFC 35th anniversary on June 24, 1978. YFC music groups delighted the audience with wonderful pre-rally music. Mark and Diane Yasuhara, "The Hawaiians" who had been KC favorites for years, blessed the crowd by their melodious renditions. As always, Ray Hildebrand, and The King's IV male quartet enchanted the audience. Our special guest, Dr. Jerry Falwell, of the Old Time Gospel Hour from Lynchburg, Va. preached a challenging message.

A couple of letters we received a few days later blessed us.

The 35th Anniversary Rally was a special blessing to us! When the invitation was given from the second balcony, above where we were sitting, ran our 18 year old foster son to accept Christ. No longer does he have the hard, tough look of a street kid, but the soft loving look that only our Savior can give.

I flipped the TV dial and caught your program on Sunday morning while we were in a motel in Ottawa, Kansas on our way to New Mexico. Congratulations on your 35th Anniversary! My, how time flies! I lived in Kansas City in the 1944-47 era. Now, for 22 years, I am Professor and Chairman of the Division of Religion and Philosophy at Olivet Nazarene College in Kankakee, IL. God bless you in all your work for Him!

God is so good! He sends along these letters of encouragement just to keep our spirits up! Knowing first-hand how encouragement lifts spirits, I realize how important it is for me to encourage others in the same way. I pray that God will help me be diligent in this area.

## New Year's Resolution

This is what Al wrote for 1979:

As I contemplate what I want to see accomplished in 1979, I have one chief desire—to be like Him. As Peter wrote in II Peter 1:4, I want to be more of a "partaker of the divine nature." I want others to see Jesus in me. I want my every action to be dictated by God.

To be more Christ-like should be every growing Christian's primary resolution, not just at New Year's, but moment by moment. Dedication to Christ is more than raising one's hand at a gospel meeting, or filling out a piece of paper. Dedication is a totality of self-denial, of "fixing our eyes on Jesus," of complete surrender to God and the increasing of His kingdom.

I love the words of a prayer of Henry Martin: "Lord, let me have no will of my own, or consider my true happiness as depending in the smallest degree on anything that can befall me outwardly, but as consisting altogether in conformity to Thy will."

Beloved, unless your number one desire is to be like Christ, all other resolutions or desires will be doomed to failure. Oh, you may have a measure of success, but unless Jesus is truly first, your efforts will be as a "noisy gong or a clanging cymbal." (I Corinthians. 13:1)

Once we have that first goal nailed down and firmly cemented in place by prayer, we then can set other goals. I am so excited about this new year! TV-50 will grow stronger, programming will continue to improve, and I firmly believe the impact of KYFC-TV will be the most glorious and fruitful happening in the Midwest this century!

But I, like you, can't afford to just sit back and wait. One of the paradoxes of Christianity is that we must plan like Jesus isn't coming back for years, but live like He is coming momentarily!

Plans and goals are vital. People who fail don't plan to fail, they just don't plan. Uncharted goals are never attained. I challenge you to have a plan not only for this year, but also for the next five years! I have one for the next decade!

The first century spread of Christian faith didn't just "happen," it was the result of Spirit-led planning on the part of the early Christians. In order to accomplish great things, God's people today must plan. Do you have a plan? Do you have goals? If not, I earnestly pray and suggest you get some. Don't put it off.

I have numerous goals. Some think it is impossible to meet all these goals. That may be true, but I know that I would not reach one of the goals if I didn't have them thought out and set! Besides, as our living Lord said, "With God all things are possible." (Matt. 19:26) May 1979 be the year that we all reach previously "impossible" plateaus of personal growth and service to our King!

## TV Studio Becomes Party Site

Three years before TV-50 was completed, our projected cost was $2 million to get TV-50 on the air. Inflation and unforeseen costs brought the actual total to $2,460,000. By the time we went on the air on December 15, 1978, God's wonderful people had given $1,822,000 leaving a balance of $638,000. We borrowed $420,000 from the bank, leaving $218,000 in unpaid material and equipment bills. More than 27,000 different people by now had given—many sacrificially—to get us on the air. The programs were being seen as far as 100 miles from Kansas City, and everyone believed having the television station was worth the sacrifices.

But the unpaid bills created an almost unbearable pressure on Al. He didn't mind the long hours of work. The wonderful letters were encouraging and word of spiritual victories in the lives of people gave him great joy—but he needed relief from this awful debt.

So, four months after we went on the air, we scheduled a TV-50 Telethon to run for seven evenings from 5:00 to midnight. Special guests were invited to make a personal appearance, and others from across the country were invited to send a video of their statement. We also had video clips of previous programs. One favorite of the people was bloopers collected during tapings of their favorite shows. These bloopers provided many laughs. Some viewers even requested that a blooper be aired when they gave their gift. Laughter always helps relieve the pressure!

The huge KYFC-TV studio was bustling with excitement each evening as hundreds of friends came by to take part in the telethon. Many had never been in a television studio before, and we invited people to go on camera to present their gift and tell their story if they desired. Some people enjoyed this immensely and their testimonies were great!

Small children brought their piggy banks or emptied their savings accounts. Many friends made sacrificial gifts, whether $5 or $1000. The largest pledge was $25,000. We praised the Lord for every one, from the smallest to the largest. One 11-year-old girl gave the $10 in her savings account. God honored that by helping her win a talent contest the next day, which had a $10 award. Al and I were happy to see people learn the joy of giving, and realize that God promised to multiply our gifts back to us.

Evangelist Chuck Millhuff played a major role as emcee along with Al, David, and Ronnie. As the week went on other staff members: Roy Bilyeu, Mike King, Ben Bennett, Jerry Powell, Rob Moritz, Randy Snavely, Marilyn Lewis, and I also appeared quite often. Willie Williams, owner and manager of radio station KEXS and Associate Director of the "Jolly Sixties" joined the activities several evenings—Willie had a popular program on TV-50. Many pastors appeared on-air voicing their appreciation for TV-50.

The party atmosphere was enhanced by Christian clowns with helium-filled balloons for the children who came. One area was set aside for refreshments furnished by Pepsi-Cola and Guys Potato Chips. We had expected to go off the air at midnight, but the viewers kept ringing the phones calling in pledges. So we went off the air when the phone calls tapered off. Closing time each evening was usually around 2:00 A.M. except for Saturday which started at 9:00 A.M. and went until 5:00 A.M. Sunday morning.

Some people, having given all the money they could, asked God what else they could do. Obeying His leading, they came bringing antiques—dolls, dishes, musical instruments—mink stoles and other things. Businesses started donating goods. Midland Equipment gave a portable TV/Stereo/Clock. So many valuable pieces of merchandise were given that we decided to save them for an auction to be scheduled later.

The entire staff of KCYFC, as well as many wonderful friends who volunteered their time as telephone operators, etc., worked around the clock.

Although the goal of $580,000 for debt retirement and $50,000 a month in pledges for operating expenses was not totally met, the telethon was a great success. It was a *miracle!* By 5:00 A.M. Sunday morning when we went off the air the totals were $414,265 for debt retirement and $6,001 per month operating expenses.

Best of all was the spiritual depth and the great joy people received from giving. Special prayer meetings were held frequently. Some were held on the air, and prayer huddles at the studio were a common sight.

As friends called, they would tell of their spiritual experiences of how God spoke so definitely to them. Some even wept from the sheer joy of being part of a miracle. Many pastors made comments such as "I appreciate the high spiritual plane on which you are conducting this telethon."

The emcees often gave the gospel in a clear, concise manor, inviting viewers who had never received Jesus as their Savior to call in for counseling and prayer. Some called in and were led to Christ. Others called with prayer requests, which were prayed for on air.

A growing closeness in the ever-expanding family of TV-50 involved people from every denomination. We called them "Our TV-50 Family" because we really felt that closeness in our heart. Thousands of people experienced for the first time in their life the thrill of knowing there are lots of God's people out there they never knew before.

## Media Questions Motives

Journalism is known for searching out the negative. After our telethon Steve Nicely, the *Kansas City Star* television reporter, wrote:

> The one worrying thing about the Channel 50 approach was the direct appeals to 'golden agers' who were asked to consign their homes to the station, apparently at some date after the death of the occupants. Asking for gifts of such magnitude brought visions of aging widows being caught up by the enthusiasm of the moment.
>
> Deferred giving of estates to charitable institutions is common, and there is no reason to suspect that YFC would take advantage of anyone. Indeed, contacts with the KYFC staff have produced positive impressions.
>
> At the same time, it is natural to question the motives of those who would ask for a substantial share of the earthly possessions of anyone, particularly the aged.

The reporter then started investigating us. A month later he wrote a follow-up article exonerating us. He reported in part:

> To resolve (my) worry, Channel 50 was asked for a list

of the 20 top telethon contributors. If the donors wished, their names would remain confidential. The non-profit station was under no legal obligation to do so, but the request placed the station on a spot. Many of the contributors gave anonymously and wanted to remain anonymous, but to fail to provide the list would raise more questions, which I probably would have felt obligated to express in print.

The list was provided after much trouble to the station. The situation had to be explained to each donor, who then was asked for permission to be called by the press. Only one person, the largest contributor with a cash pledge of $25,000, refused.

With the list in hand, I was on the spot to call the donors and ask questions that amounted to, "Are you sure you can afford this? Are you sure you are not being taken advantage of?" The answers were cordial, friendly and often inspirational.

Several on the list are employees of the station or the Youth For Christ organization including the woman who made two pledges during the telethon totaling $25,000.

Mrs. Metsker described her as someone "who has been a good giver for a number of years, but nothing like this." She said the gift definitely will not pose a hardship for the donor, a widow who "is not very old" and who had done volunteer work for YFC. "We called the pledges back to make sure they weren't crank calls," Mrs. Metsker said. "It was such a large pledge that I personally called back and asked her. 'Now, are you sure that you can do this? We don't want you to do more than you can do.'

"She said, 'Oh, yes, I can. That's what I want to do.' Then she gave me her testimony and said, 'I did not know the Lord until I was 50 and I have to make up for all that lost time.' She said, 'I'm just so happy to have peace now. I'm alone. My husband is gone. This is what I want to do.'"

The testimony of personal faith was reached. A machine shop operator said, "I just never figured you could outgive the Lord. I've been able to give the first money on just about any project KCYFC ever started. I've given first fruits. I gave when we weren't able and the Lord made us millionaires. There ain't no way you can outgive the Lord. He gave his life and nothing I've given can even compare."

Another explained that the idea of leaving personal property to YFC was a challenge to senior citizens made by other senior citizens who were helping with the telethon. "These people don't have kids to leave it to sometimes," he said. "so what better use than to leave it to a lot of teenagers to enjoy, as well as the general public?"

Mrs. Metsker is a grandmother who fits the image perfectly and is the type of person most would instinctively like and believe. She now works full-time for the organization.

She said some things about the financial facts of life at YFC she did not care to have published unless I thought it necessary. When told of the suspicions that have been voiced to the effect that the Metskers are in religion for the money, she laughed and said, "Well then, I guess it's necessary.

"We pay minimum salary to people who deserve a whole lot more. There are people on our staff, technical people, who are paid more than Al is. It has been six years since he has had an increase in salary. We were both raised during the Depression, when we were strapped for money and that's the way we continue to live.

"I suppose a lot of people can't understand working so hard without monetary gain. We have taken on the added responsibility for producing television and nobody on this staff has received any increase at all. The ones I feel for are those who have families and are having a rough time. I hope someday we can afford to pay them enough to live on.

"Even though Al started this organization 36 years ago, he makes a lower salary now than plumbers and people who work for unions. And we work 18 hours a day six days a week. If somebody would come and follow us around a little while, they'd know we are not in this for money. I would be glad for you to see our books."

Somehow, I don't think that will be necessary.

Maybe it was good that he investigated us. He found we were clean with no motives but to serve the Lord.

# CHAPTER 31

# Crowded Pizza Blast

When the Municipal Auditorium doors opened, teenagers spilled into the arena like leaves being propelled by a mighty wind. More than 10,000 students crammed into every seat available and stood next to the stage in anticipation. The electrifying atmosphere was magnified by the pre-rally music.

At 7:00 P.M. on March 29, 1985, the house lights dimmed. Arc spots followed the teenage singers, the "Extra Dimension" and "Living Expression," as they sprinted from every entrance while singing their powerful arrangement of, "Stand Up America." Thunderous applause followed as the song ended dramatically with the singers waving red and white sparklers. Red and blue spotlights scanned the darkened arena.

That week Jerry Johnston had spoken in 24 area high school assemblies to about 30,000 teenagers. He had told stories of teens addicted to drugs and alcohol. True tales of teenagers committing suicide horrified the students—although many had thought about taking their lives.

Jerry even unveiled the truth of his own experiences—growing up in an affluent home but becoming addicted to drugs and barely being rescued from suicide. "The rest of the story," he had told them, "I will tell on Friday night at the Pizza Blast."

These students were eager to hear more.

Totally absorbed in Jerry's words, the students didn't even notice the enticing aroma of pizza baking. Besides his frightful true stories of teens in trouble, most importantly, Jerry proclaimed how the Lord Jesus Christ had delivered him from hopelessness when he was a teen drug addict. After clearly presenting the gospel of Christ, Jerry asked all who wanted this life-changing experience by receiving Jesus for forgiveness of sin, to stand. Hundreds of teens instantaneously rose to their feet. As he instructed, teenagers poured onto the floor of the arena indicating that they wanted to know Christ as their Savior. Counselors sat down with each one, showed them Scripture and prayed with them.

After most of the counseling was finished, tables were set up to serve the pizza. Ronnie had negotiated with Dominos Pizza to set up temporary kitchens in the Auditorium concourse. Twelve hundred steaming, cheesy pizzas were served fresh from the ovens until the ravenous teenagers had eaten their fill. This was the largest number of pizzas Dominos had ever served in one place.

For at least 951 teens that night, eating pizza was not their first priority. A total of 715 received Jesus as Savior; 166 gained assurance of their salvation; and 70 dedicated their lives to serve God. The event was our plan—but only the Holy Spirit brings about that kind of results! God did it!

Jerry Johnston had grown up in the ministry of KCYFC. As a 13-year-old, immediately after being saved, he came to Circle-C Ranch. There he dedicated his life to Christ and joined Dr. Al's Young Preachers' Club where he learned to preach. Without delay, he started winning many teenagers to the Lord through his dynamic preaching. Following high school he attended Christ Unlimited Bible Institute followed by Liberty University. Now God was using him across the country reaching teenagers with the gospel.

## Another Big Gathering

Seven months later we scheduled another Super Rally in Kansas City's Municipal Auditorium on October 10. On a Thursday night, nearly 8,000 people were inspired by the Spirit-filled singing of Steve Green and stimulating message from God's Word by Dr. Charles Stanley.

A month later, over 7,000 teenagers heard Mike King in twenty-three school assemblies in Joplin, Missouri. On that

Friday evening nearly 3,000 teens ate 289 pizzas. After hearing Mike preach, more than 200 came forward for individual counseling—114 prayed to receive Christ as Savior. God did it!

## Josh McDowell

"I was so ashamed of my dad. On the outside I would laugh about him being the town drunk, but on the inside, I was miserable . . ."

Josh McDowell's testimony, from his heartbreaking childhood to his quest for God, absorbed the overflow crowds at the Luncheon and Dinner Clubs Friday noon and evening. The next day, Saturday, Josh had the rapt attention of more than 500 adults at a seminar in our auditorium. He emphasized, "For more people, it's easier to dissolve a relationship than to resolve a conflict. Our culture has conditioned us for immediate results . . . that if we don't see immediate results, we walk away from the relationship instead of giving it time and effort to develop. It's far more personally rewarding and honoring to God to dissolve the conflict rather than the relationship."

At 7:30 that evening, March 26, 1986, the 1,600-seat auditorium was jammed. Dozens of teens sat on the floor and 300 more watched the program on a giant screen in the TV studio—a total crowd of about 2,000. Josh's message exhorted teenagers to abstain from all sexual relations until marriage. Why?

"For every negative command God gives, there are two positive reasons to protect us and provide for us. You need to save yourself for your mate first of all, because God commands it. . Another reason is it protects you from guilt. . . And because of that abstinence, God will be able to provide you with a maximum marriage. Premarital sex always makes it almost impossible to have the trust necessary for a maximum marriage."

We loved having Josh. He always "hit the ball out of the park"! People loved him because he cared enough to talk to them. Prior to the dinner, Josh always walked around and greeted everyone individually at their tables. But there was something unique about Josh! He wanted to get involved in all areas.

On this trip, he took off his coat and tie and went to the kitchen between the Luncheon and Dinner Clubs. There, he rolled up his sleeves, put on an apron and helped wash dishes in preparation for the evening meal! Tell me, where else do you find someone like that!

During one of his trips here in 1981 when L-Bar-C Ranch was under construction, between meetings, he went with Al and our grandson, Topher Philgreen, and helped them lay stones on the front of a cabin. I believe Josh truly was living out Paul's commitment "become all things to all men so that by all possible means I might save some." (1 Corinthians 9:22)

## Dinner at the Governor's Mansion

Irish political leader Daniel O'Connell, who died in 1847 wrote, "Nothing is politically right when it is morally wrong." In an age when politicians are almost universally and automatically viewed as corrupt opportunists, a vocal Christian public servant is as refreshing as a glass of cool water on a hot day.

That is why we were thrilled to have the engaging duo—John Ashcroft and Max Bacon—share their faith in Christ at our Luncheon and Dinner Clubs and the Rally quite often through the years. These forceful young lawyers in the Missouri state political arena proved that opposing party persuasions could be left aside when they joined to sing and tell the good news of Christ.

Republican Attorney General John Ashcroft, who had been the youngest State Auditor in Missouri's history, belonged to the Assembly of God church. Democrat Magistrate Court Judge Max Bacon was a Baptist. You would expect them to be complete opposites. But their boyhood friendship had continued as their faith in God and dedication to Him bridged all other gaps.

They sang together before a wide variety of audiences as often as their official duties would allow. Their brilliant performances were laced with wit as they shared their Christian testimonies and their commitment to morality in government. Both Ashcroft and Bacon felt that their ministry was important in demonstrating that government and God—Christianity and politics—are compatible. It was gratifying to see two public officials boldly but discretely expressing their Christian testimony and their commitment to morality in government. What great examples of what our government leaders should be!

After two terms as Attorney General, John Ashcroft was elected Governor of Missouri. He didn't change his strong stand. A trademark was that in Christian circles he asked people to commit to pray for him daily—especially grandmas. Maybe that was because he thought grandmas had more time to keep the commitment.

In 1986 we received a cream colored executive envelope from the Executive Office, State of Missouri, Jefferson City. We had received letters before from John Ashcroft but this was a special letter from Missouri's first lady, Janet Ashcroft.

It contained an invitation for Al and me to join them for dinner at the Governors Mansion. Peter Marshall, Jr. would be the guest of honor as he was to speak the next morning at the Governor's prayer breakfast.

Feeling honored to be invited, we drove to Jefferson City that afternoon. Governor and Mrs. Ashcroft greeted us warmly at the entrance of the Governor's Mansion, and we joined the other guests sipping hot spiced cider topped with a dollop of butter. The 30 guests were ushered into the formal dining room. I was impressed that the Ashcrofts included their children in the dinner. After a pleasant meal Governor Ashcroft invited us all to the huge foyer where he handed out hymn books to each of us and sauntered to the piano. He played the piano and led in his booming voice as all joined the sing-along. I could hardly hold back the tears at the thought. The Governor of Missouri was playing and singing well-known gospel hymns with his guests in the Governor's Mansion! We thought, "There *is* still hope for our country if this can happen."

The next morning we attended the Governor's Prayer Breakfast along with hundreds of others and Peter Marshall, Jr's message was clear and challenging.

Since that time, he has become U.S. Senator John Ashcroft. I am proud of him and pray for this great man of God nearly every day.

# CHAPTER 32

# Fire!

"Wake up! Get out! Fire!"
The terrified teen banged the door with both hands, shrieking fiercely: "Fire! Fire!"

He knew girls were sleeping inside

Having awakened early, Rodney Day, a teenager from Bonner Springs, had dressed and was jogging past the Lodge when it seemed the whole front of the building exploded toward him. The clatter of shattered glass catapulted him to action. He dashed to the other side of the building where thirteen teenage girls and one girl Club Director, Michelle Fahrmeier, were sleeping in the lower level. Pulling a robe around her, Michelle fearfully flung open the door and herded 13 girls out in a flash.

It was 5:45 A.M. Saturday, May 18. Forty workers—staff and volunteer teenagers—had come the night before so they could get an early start on a day of final touch-up the week before the opening of the 1979 summer season at Circle C Ranch.

Because of Rodney's quick thinking, every one of the girls escaped, leaving all their belongings behind.

A piercing siren shocked Al and me from a sound sleep in our home across the road.

Startled, we jumped up and looked out the window. Smoke billowed skyward in the direction of the Ranch! Throwing on some clothes, we raced to the car and sped the half mile to the Ranch

Before long the flames, which enveloped the entire building, were shooting 100 feet into the air. Volunteer firefighters were helpless. The heat was so intense that the fiberglass paddleboats melted in our lake. Nothing was saved. The fire inspector had been there the day before and everything had checked out with his approval.

276

Stench from the burning building engulfed us. Our hearts broke as we watched the beautiful Lodge consumed in flames. People were our first concern. After being assured that everyone was accounted for and safe, we all were overcome with emotion.

This was eight days before the first day of camp. Sixteen hundred teens were already registered to come. It was our largest early enrollment to date. In Staff Meeting on Thursday, Roy Bilyeu, head of the Club Department, in admonition to pray had said, "The devil is going to attack us on every front to keep lives from being changed this summer. Pray!" We had no inkling this would be Satan's plan of attack.

When the fire died down and the initial shock was over, Dr. Al, Ronnie, Roy, the other Club Directors and the Ranch Manager dried their tears, prayed and thanked God for His blessing that no lives had been lost. Then they asked for guidance and immediately started the rebuilding plans.

The building was leveled. Live coals were thick on the basement floor. First, Al called the insurance adjuster to ask permission to start clean up and rebuilding. David brought a television camera from TV-50 and recorded a news message from Al. He hustled it to the station for breaking news. It was important to make our friends aware of what had happened. Al announced, "We must rebuild and it must be done in eight days because that is when camp starts. Don't say it's impossible. We serve a God of miracles. This will be a miracle."

## The Miracle Begins

Within a couple of hours, a friend who heard the news arrived with a high-loader and started shoveling out debris. Al made phone calls to strategic people. An engineer examined the foundation walls for strength and approved them as safe to build on.

Al announced on TV-50 that we needed volunteer help—carpenters, plumbers, and electricians—anyone who could help. Scores of people rushed to the rescue donating materials, equipment, and labor. A steel man donated the steel I-beams and delivered them later that day.

Another gave the steel support posts. A plumbing firm donated all the plumbing supplies. Another contractor arranged for 20 tons of air conditioning. A builder sent his rough-in crew to work for two days. Electricians, plumbers, welders and others donated their time.

A whole crew of men and their wives from the Mennonite Church in Harrisonville, Mo. came as an organized army. The wives prepared and served food for the workers. Everyone worked around the clock. Many stayed for several days, taking out just a little time now and then for rest.

"Overwhelming and heartwarming" does not begin to describe the way God's people lovingly came to the rescue and the way He united the army of workers! What a testimony to all of Kansas City! We knew God surely had great victories in store for the summer.

The Circle-C Ranch opened on schedule! Because many friends worked unselfishly around the clock for seven days, and God worked many miracles, 250 enthusiastic junior highers descended on the Ranch at the appointed time. Last minute laying of carpet, connecting the kitchen equipment, and stocking the snack shop were being completed as the first campers arrived early on Monday morning.

Before the noon meal of that very morning, 34 of those teens responded to the gospel message and received Jesus as their Savior—like a reward for those who had worked so hard. God did it!

All who experienced this rebuilding unanimously agreed that our new structure should be called the "Miracle Lodge." No longer was it the beautiful, stately building of the past— but it was compact and serviceable. The wall next to the lake was still all glass but the dining room and chapel were both crammed into what had been the indoor game room. Yes, it was more crowded, but we survived.

Almost 3,000 teens spent a week at Circle-C that summer. Nearly every one went home a changed person.

One pastor sent 31 teenagers, 13 of which received Jesus as Savior. Several dedicated their lives to God and seven joined Dr. Al's Young Preachers' Club.

Although everything was more crowded than usual, the summer was great. But changes were needed before the next summer. The decision was made to build a new Chapel that would also house the Ranch office and some staff housing. The Miracle Lodge would continue to be used for dining room, kitchen, snack shop and indoor recreation – and it was built so solidly that it's still used now, more than 20 years later!

## Sky Drop

Our goal was to have new fun activities at the Ranch each year. One summer a Sky Diving Club used a field about three miles away for their parachute landings. We asked them to come do a few jumps onto our sports field. Of course, they were thrilled to have an audience. So at a certain time each week, skydiving onto our field was an exciting event for our campers. After they were down, the kids could talk to the divers and ask questions.

For several years we did another fun thing. Our friend, Claude Jenks, from Olathe had his own plane, which he volunteered to use to enhance the teens' week at the Ranch. Early in the week, volunteers made objects to be dropped from the plane. We wrote little notes—some with scripture verses or good sayings and some that were a coupon for free ice cream, candy bar, popcorn, or a drink from the snack shop. Some notes gave special privileges or awarded extra points to the teen receiver's team score. We fastened them with a little 1-inch rock and a bright crepe paper streamer so they could be seen as they floated from the plane. At an assigned time each week, Claude flew over and dropped these from the plane onto the sports field where the teens were watching for their "prize." That was just a little fun point in the week.

For the summer of 1980 we decided we needed to tap into a new craze—water slides. All around the country people were standing in long lines and paying $2.50 for 30 minutes of this fun. If we offered it free with the week of camp, our reasoning was, it would draw many new teens who didn't know the Lord

This dream dictated our next big activity—a Walk-a-thon to raise the funds. This time we would walk the country roads around Circle-C Ranch for 20 miles. Lunch would be served at the Circle-C dining room.

Prizes were offered so everyone could be a winner. Prizes, according to the amount the walker raised, were a free Power Charge at Circle-C, a free day at Silver Dollar City, or a free week at Circle C. Ranch

When the day came, 700 walked and raised $90,568—a great success!

As soon as the money was received, construction could begin.

## CONQUEST Expands

At the same time we were expanding Circle-C, another expansion was taking place.

*Conquest*, an 11"x17", four page, two-color newsletter had been our communication device for 20 years. Marilyn had been the editor for a number of years. By 1975, I had taken over the whole operation of our graphics and print shop. Working with the great talented crew was such a joy. This dream was mine. I wanted to enlarge the *Conquest* into a magazine.

Reports of victories. Recounting of blessings. Information on coming events. Stories of people. Testimonies. Editorials on issues. All of these needed to be funneled to our "KCYFC family."

It was impossible to get all the information we needed to convey in such a small publication. *Conquest* magazine became a reality and was mailed to 48,000 homes in February 1980!

The first seven editions were 32 pages, 5x8 inches.

For several years we had produced *Inspiration*, a daily devotional book, which had gone to more than 35,000 each month. Now, *Inspiration* was included in *Conquest* magazine, making the two into one publication. Our staff primarily did the writing and all the editing, with dozens of talented, godly friends writing the devotionals for us. The graphics, plate-making and printing were all completed in our own print shop.

We weren't satisfied until we could produce beautiful four-color publications. So we raised the money and bought a new 2-color, 36-inch Heidelberg press to meet our needs. Starting in September 1980, *Conquest* displayed beautiful 4-color pictures and was enlarged to 48 pages on glossy paper. By this time our mailing list had grown to 65,000.

In the January issue I started my monthly column "Heart to Heart with Vidy." Al's column, "Inside Story," had been a regular since we started the magazine.

I was the editor with all the publication personnel working under me. We had a great team and loved to plan and produce our publications together. Eventually, for a time the *Conquest* mailing list expanded with the free publication going into 123,000 homes.

# CHAPTER 33

# Explosive Evangelism

We constantly asked God to plant new ideas for evangelism in our hearts and minds. The tool of television provided great possibilities. We wanted to present explosive evangelism on TV.

Because the film, *A Thief in the Night,* had been such an evangelistic success in rallies and clubs, we believed this powerful, prophetic film would attract unchurched people. So we devised a plan whereby all Christians who were interested could be involved.

Al outlined and communicated what people could do to reach their friends for Christ.

1. PRAY. Prayer is the key to success. Without it there will be no lasting results.
2. TELL YOUR FRIENDS TO WATCH. You are responsible to see that your friends hear the gospel.
3. ORGANIZE A TV PARTY IN YOUR HOME. A dinner party or just refreshments will be an incentive to get friends to come and watch. This is a good way to get the gospel message to someone who is hard to reach.
4. VOLUNTEER TO DO TELEPHONE COUNSELING. If you know how to use the Bible and lead someone to the Lord, call our office and volunteer your services.
5. GET YOUR CHURCH INVOLVED. Make sure the proper announcements are made and organization done to get everyone in your church excited about this unusual evangelistic outreach. It could easily help your church to grow dramatically.
6. HAND OUT POSTERS AND FLIERS. Attractive posters are available to put up in churches, schools, stores or anywhere

people will see them. Fliers are available for handouts or church bulletin inserts.

We wanted a record of where all the home parties would be, so we urged people to call and register their party. The evening of the showing, we encouraged people to call and report any decisions made at their party. These could be tallied and announced on TV.

The scheduled time arrived—Thursday, February 21, 1980. In the KYFC-TV studio, officials from Mark IV Films and KCYFC huddled in prayer.

"Dear God, lead thousands of unsaved people to turn on their television sets to TV-50 right now. Holy Spirit, as they watch *A Thief in the Night,* touch their hearts. Convict them of sin. Help them to understand the message of the film. Dear Lord, give a great harvest of souls tonight as people turn to Jesus as Savior," we fervently prayed.

At 7:00 P.M. the film started airing. To prepare for the event, weeks ahead of time we'd aired a video of Ronnie teaching our Basic Counseling Course four times so people could learn from TV. Many had written or called for the notes and exam.

Parties in homes or churches were in progress all over the city. Several large businesses supported the effort by allowing their phones to be used for counseling. More than 60 telephone lines were manned by counselors ready to take calls. Now everything was in the Lord's hands. We were waiting for the Spirit of God to convict viewers of sin and convince them to be saved.

When the film concluded at 8:10, Al gave the invitation. All phone lines were jammed with counseling calls and remained that way for five hours. There was no let up through the second showing at 8:30 and the third at 10:30. Instead, calls started coming with such requests as, "My husband gets home from work at midnight. Can't you show it again? I want him to see this movie."

The Mark IV officials were so inspired, they agreed we must show it again while the Spirit was working so mightily–and at no extra charge! So it was shown a fourth time. Counseling calls continued past 1:00 A.M.

Calls came from people aged 5 to 84. Several times a call came from one member of a family who, after praying to receive Jesus, passed the phone on to another member who did the same. During some of those calls, the phone was passed along until the whole family had prayed with a counselor, one after another.

At midnight a call came from a man who said, "My whole family wanted to be saved but we kept getting a busy signal. It was time for our children to go to bed so I just gathered them all around the dining room table and we all prayed for Jesus to forgive us and save us. I'm calling to make sure we did it right."

Reports came from those having parties in their homes and YFC Clubs who had met to watch. They each reported from one to eight being saved. One called and said, "I won four out of four. Everyone who came to my party got saved!"

A pastor, who had invited people into his home, called. "I just led three teenagers to the Lord from this one family," he exclaimed joyfully.

Bales Baptist Church was in the middle of an evangelistic crusade, so they rented a giant screen and showed the film from TV-50. Nine received Jesus there.

A lady called to tell us that her husband, for whom she had been praying for 20 years, watched the film and was saved.

Crews of volunteers sent a letter and our *LIFE Plus* follow-up book to each convert that night and we started efforts to get each caller involved in a good church.

Calls continued to come for several days from people under conviction who wanted to talk to a counselor. Our records show the final total was 724 people who repented and asked Jesus to save them. That doesn't include those who called with other spiritual needs. What a great night of evangelism! This was reaping a harvest from those long hours of working to build TV-50, and from the investment of sacrificial gifts.

To our knowledge, this had never been done anywhere before. Even to this day, I have never heard of such an undertaking. What a blessing it was for thousands of people!

## Victory Report

Al's custom was to total up the victories at the end of each year as a report to our friends. Following are the victories he listed for 1980.

*Over 6,000 recorded salvation decisions in YFC Clubs, Rallies, Ranch and TV.

*198 YFC Clubs now meeting weekly. This included our Associate Ministries.

*2,000 ladies attended Women in Touch Day.

*Burned mortgage for television station.

*Bought and paid for new printing press.

*Dr. Al was appointed to the Board of National Religious Broadcasters.

*Total attendance at Rallies in 1980 more than 100,000.

*Associate Ministries (formerly known as Satellites) now operating in seven states.

*Hundreds of teens memorizing God's word in our Quiz Program—36 schools participating.

*New television version of Bible Quiz, "Stand Up and Shout it!"

*Our four staff evangelists are being used greatly of God across the country.

*Graduated 50 in fourth class of CUBI.

*KYFC-TV aired total coverage of "Washington For Jesus," a huge gathering of Christians from across America.

*Taped and aired all of "National Affairs Briefing" in Dallas, a Christian political forum.

*Miracle of America" seminar held in TV studio, videotaped and aired.

*Creation/Evolution Debate" videotaped before live audience and aired.

*More than 12,250 adults attended Luncheon and Dinner Clubs and Banquets.

*Wrote, printed, and mailed more than 660,000 *Conquest* and *Inspiration*.

*Hundreds learned to be soul-winners through our Basic Counseling Course taught on TV-50 and at Circle-C Ranch.

*Bought and paid for all equipment for TV Mobile Production Unit.

*Total of 1,036 recorded salvation decisions during "A Thief In The Night" showings on TV-50.

*Built and paid for new chapel and 500-foot waterslide at Circle-C Ranch.

*Record 2,976 teenagers spent a week at Circle-C during summer—586 salvation decisions.

*Highly successful Young Preachers' Club, Royal Girls Seminar and three Sponsors' Institutes at Circle-C Ranch.

*Produced more television programs than any other Christian station in America—22 regular programs originate in our studio. TO GOD BE THE GLORY!

### Award of Merit

The announcement read:

> The winner of the National Religious Broadcasters Award of Merit for television station operation and programming was KYFC-TV, Channel 50 in Kansas City, Missouri. Owned and operated by Kansas City Youth For Christ, KYFC-TV emphasizes service to the entire family.
>
> This coveted award was presented to the station's founder and president, Dr. Al Metsker, at the annual Federal Communications Commission Luncheon on Tuesday, February 9, 1982, at the Sheraton Washington Hotel in Washington, D.C. before an audience of 3,500.
>
> KYFC-TV began broadcasting December 15, 1978. Funded entirely by donations, the independent,

non-commercial, Christian station now airs programming 93 hours a week, offering 65 programs and daily 24-hour counseling service.

David Lewis, General Manager, oversees all the station's operations, programming and personnel.

In his acceptance speech, Al challenged the other Christian television and radio station owners and producers to reach out to the young people.

"Our teenagers are our future America. We must pull out all the stops and do everything possible to win our young people to Christ and establish them in a godly life."

No matter what means we used—television, radio, camps, Worlds of Fun events—our focus remained to win teenagers to Christ.

## Evangelism Live

The showings of *A Thief in the Night* on TV-50 had been so successful we decided it was time for another similar outreach. We scheduled five nights of prime time for showing Mark IV's series of prophetic films February 22 through April 26, 1983. Each film would be shown twice, with a live call-in invitation at the end of each showing—just as we had done before. Our plans and promotions were the same as when we showed *A Thief in the Night*.

This outreach was equally as blessed by God. As many as 169 telephone lines—more than for the previous showings—were kept busy on the evenings of the showings with counseling calls. Some calls were tremendously encouraging, exciting, and unusual. We realized that each one was a miracle, which caused the angels in heaven to rejoice.

After the February 22 showings of *A Thief In The Night,* 302 asked Jesus into their hearts.

The Oak Park YFC Club hosted a film party attended by 32 teens. Four of those young men asked Christ into their hearts.

Our daughter, Marilyn sponsored the Old Mission Junior

High YFC Club. She invited sixth graders who would be coming to Old Mission the next year to join their club for a film party at their home. After the film showing, sixteen of the seventeen sixth-graders received Jesus as their Savior.

At the same time our other daughter, Martha, was in her home in Ottawa, Kans. with her family watching the film. The message of the film so touched her 5-year-old son, Jonathan. He told his mama he wanted to ask Jesus into his heart. She took him into her bedroom where she read Scripture verses and made sure he understood the gospel completely. He prayed and became a child of God. That was a special personal blessing for us.

An excited father called. "I just led my two sons to Jesus! Praise the Lord! Thank you for airing *A Thief in the Night!*"

A 36-year-old man with terminal cancer called and received Jesus. A friend across town in another hospital did the same and then called him to tell him. They rejoiced together over the phone that both had been saved.

An older couple—he was 78 and she was 75—both received Jesus as Savior after watching the films.

"I'm 82 years old," a little quivering voice revealed. "I want to pray with someone." After the counselor led her to Jesus, she asked. "Why hasn't anyone told me before that Jesus died for me? I'm glad you have the television station so I could know Jesus before it is too late." That statement exactly expressed Al's and my question when we heard the gospel the first time as teenagers. How important it is that we be faithful to tell others about Jesus!

March 1 *A Distant Thunder* was shown and 398 people asked Jesus into their hearts.

A weeping man sobbed in pain: "My wife died two weeks ago. I don't have a reason to live. I just can't handle it. I was ready to take a bottle of pills so I wouldn't have to face it but this movie caught my attention. Can you help me? Do you think there is hope for me?" Of course, Jesus was the answer—

and the man found Him that night.

The barely distinguishable words of a foreign exchange student from Germany asked: "I never heard this before but I want to know if Jesus can save me?" She was a little more difficult to communicate with—but before she hung up the phone, she knew for sure that she was on her way to heaven.

Three high school boys watched together and all called to receive Jesus into their hearts.

*Image of the Beast* was shown on March 10. A total of 251 salvation decisions were recorded by the counselors

A mother called and was led to Jesus by a counselor. We taught our counselors to instruct new Christians to start reading their Bible, to pray, to find a good church to get involved in, and to tell someone right away about their decision. So when she got off the phone she told her 14-year-old son what she had done. He called that same night and was saved.

"I want to be saved!" a man confessed to the counselor. After the counselor had completed the counseling and praying, the man said: "Last week you showed a movie and my wife called and got saved. She has been so happy and told me she has been praying for me, so I knew I needed to call, too. Now we both are saved!"

In one family a mother, a 9-year-old daughter and twin boys all gave their hearts to Jesus. A 66-year-old lady was led to the Lord by a counselor. She then handed the phone to her 70-year-old husband who also prayed for Jesus to come into his heart and forgive him.

"My deaf-mute father-in-law just asked Jesus into his life after watching the film," joyfully reported one lady.

April 25 and 26 were the showings of *The Prodigal Planet*, Part 1 and Part 2. Another 313 made salvation decisions after those showings.

"I'm a salesman just going through the city but I happened onto this station in my hotel room," a man's voice proclaimed. "I see myself in that movie and I'm calling because I want to pray with someone." The counselor understood and again clearly explained the way of salvation to him. He was eager to pray for forgiveness of sin.

After listening only to Al giving the invitation, a man called and told the counselor: "I just switched on the TV when I got home and see this man telling us to call and talk to someone. I don't know what it's about. What is it?" This was a different kind of call because he hadn't even seen the film. He was just touched by the gospel as Al gave it simply and clearly during the invitation for people to call. The Holy Spirit worked in his heart and the counselor led him to Jesus.

"My husband and I are both on the phone," shared a sweet voice. "We both want God to forgive our sin so we can go to heaven."

We realize that many times people come to Jesus first of all because they want to go to heaven when they die. But when He saves them, the radiant, satisfying joy that fills their hearts is the beginning of a growing love relationship with Him.

Numerous calls resulted in both husband and wife being led to the Lord at the same time on extension phones.

A total of 1,264 people were personally counseled and received Jesus as Savior as a result of the five film showings. Another 732 called to make other personal commitments to God. All of this was evidence of the Holy Spirit working in lives as we had prayed. Our expenses for the showings were $10,000—an average of less than $8 for each of those who became born-again Christians. What a great victory!

As time went by, we scheduled several more of these evangelistic outreaches and each time God blessed with equally tremendous results.

Reflecting, Al made a comment, "I never know whether to chuckle or be aggravated when someone says, 'Only Christians watch TV-50.' I know how wrong they are! Everywhere I go strangers recognize me and tell me they watch Channel 50—Jewish, Catholic, Presbyterians, Methodists, Baptists, atheists. People who don't claim to be Christians—gas station attendants, bank employees, store clerks, lawyers, business owners—several times a day it happens to me. We are reaching people who would never go to church. Praise the Lord for this outreach!"

## Year of the Bible

President Ronald Reagan's Proclamation making 1983 "Year of the Bible" provided the motivation for us to stage a Bible Reading Marathon on TV-50.

We invited all the ministers of the city to participate in reading through the Bible in one week on television. They responded enthusiastically. The reading continued from 10:30 A.M. to 10:30 P.M. Monday through Friday, October 3-7, 1983. We researched how much could be read in ten minutes and assigned that much to be read, scheduling the ministers in ten minute segments. They started with Genesis 1:1 and ended with the last verse of Revelation

Volunteers Earlene McGinnis and Dean Curteman were on duty most of the twelve hours each day to greet the ministers, confirm name spellings, and position them for their reading. Other volunteers worked shorter hours, and all were blessed by meeting so many ministers.

Without a break in the continuity, each pastor started reading immediately where the last had finished. No introduction was made but when a new minister started reading, his name appeared on the screen, along with his position and church. A picture of his church was chromakeyed behind the minister while he read. Some ministers wanted to read a second time if we needed them. A few stood by in case a scheduled reader failed to arrive on time.

We encouraged viewers to arrange their schedule so they could watch the whole reading. Certificates were awarded to all who wrote stating the number of hours they listened to the Bible being read. All agreed the Spirit of God was in our midst during the Bible Reading Marathon and it was an unforgettable experience.

# CHAPTER 34

# Overflow Demands Growth

At Circle-C Ranch there's a disaster coming!" Al wrote in the July 1981 *Conquest*. "No, not broken bones, not concussions, not drownings. Praise God, He has kept us from those. It's not physical or property damage. Of the 2,976 teens who attended Circle-C, 576 of them accepted Christ as their Savior.

"The disaster is that we turned hundreds away—and next year we'll turn away even more who need the spiritual growth Circle-C offers."

## Second Ranch Needed

The thought of rejecting hundreds of teenagers because there was no room distressed us. So we prayed: "Dear Lord, lead us to the land You have for a second Ranch." We were actually thinking another 160 acres like Circle-C, but God had bigger plans. He led us to a 600-acre ranch 17 miles south of Louisburg, Kansas, near LaCygne, with one mile frontage on US 69 Highway. The land also offered a beautiful 15-acre lake stocked with fish, 175 acres of lush timberland, and the rest in rolling hills and grassy plains. It was ideal.

Our dear friend and long-time board member, Gene Land, was with Al this time when he stopped on the land and prayed, claiming it for God. The picture was clear in Al's mind from the beginning! He could see where each building and activity would be. God had blessed Gene and Dot because, even when they were a struggling new business, they gave heavily to the Lord. Now, God had enabled Gene and Dot to give the first substantial gift for starting each new project of KCYFC—the Auditorium, Circle-C Ranch, Channel 50 television, and now the second Ranch.

On Monday morning, July 27, Al appeared at a meeting of the Linn County Commissioners on behalf of Ranch II.

When Al walked into the room filled with eight county officials, they stood and said, "Welcome to Linn County!" The chairman related that he watched TV-50 every night. Another shared that his two teenagers had spent a week at the Circle-C Ranch that summer.

"First, we want to convey to you that we think this is the best thing that has happened to Linn County," they said. "We appreciate the good work you do with teenagers. We have just finished building a $450,000 jail."

They expressed their feeling that if that money could have gone into building a Ranch to help the teens, there would not be as much need for the jail.

Bob Haupt, one of the commissioners, said, "My sons and I own an earth-moving company and we have decided to bring our bulldozers and give you two weeks." Wow! What a gigantic blessing and answer to prayer!

When it came time to buy the building permit, Bob whipped out his checkbook and wrote a check. "Here," he said, "I want to personally pay for your construction permit."

Al had a hard time believing what was happening!

On July 29, 1981, Al's 60th birthday, KCYFC made the down payment on this land that would become L-Bar C Ranch—meaning "Life With Christ." We couldn't waste any time starting the building process because we wanted to open the next ranch season—in only ten months! We felt the urgency to reach the hundreds of teens who would be turned away from Circle-C the next summer. We simply *had* to have it done!

Planning alone was mind-boggling. It would be like building a small city. Roads had to be built. Electricity had to be brought in. A water purification plant constructed. A 48x96-foot building would include the Chapel, offices, and infirmary. A 40x60-foot structure would house the Dining Hall, kitchen and laundry. We would build a 32'x32' Snack Shop. We needed a building for the trail bikes and maintenance. Building twenty-two cabins alone, each to house 16 campers plus two cabin leaders, would be a huge project—not including the other buildings.

For fun activities we needed a game room, Olympic-size swimming pool, a 500-foot water slide, dock on the lake for water activities, and a sports field. Humanly speaking, the task seemed impossible. But again, God reminded us that He specializes in impossibilities.

## L-Bar-C Ground Breaking

By noon cars, being guided by a brightly dressed clown, started rolling down the long gravel road to the future building site of L-Bar-C. People kept coming . . . and coming . . . AND COMING! By 3:30, when the groundbreaking ceremonies began, more than 1,200 excited people were on hand to celebrate That Sunday afternoon, August 23, was perfect—slightly overcast with a gentle breeze keeping it from being too hot.

Ronda Staton of nearby Pleasanton, Kans., coordinated the preparation of sandwiches and desserts donated by over 100 area residents and stores. She and her crew did a commendable job of making sure the crowd was served. The Pepsi Cola company generously donated soda pop for the occasion. The delicious ham and tomato sandwiches, and slices of homemade pies and cakes were sold for only 25 cents a piece. More than $800 collected from the food sales was given to further the construction of L-Bar-C. Ronda, who is the daughter of Commissioner John Rees, explained, "As a Home EC teacher, I have served dinners to as many as 300 before, but never 1,200!" She and her helpers added greatly to the party atmosphere.

We had set up a stage covered with flowers under American and Christian flags blowing in the breeze.

Goosebumps covered my arms as 1,200 strong, vibrant voices rang out under towering trees the familiar words to

"Amazing Grace" led by David Lewis.

With pride and respect, the audience quickly rose to their feet as our Extra Dimension and Living Expression music groups heartfully sang their A Capella arrangement of "The Star Spangled Banner."

Al had asked people to buy an acre of the land for $1,000. We needed 600 of these donors. Part of the ceremony included presenting a certificate (deed for their acre) to those who had donated $1,000. Some shared a few words: "I am not wealthy but only trying to be a blessing as the Lord has blessed me!" one declared.

Others joyfully confided where they wanted their acre to be: "In the bottom of the lake where the big fish are!" said one man. "Where the dining room is with great food!" laughed another. "Where the chapel will be built and thousands of teenagers will get saved." another announced.

The commissioners shared their hearts:

Bob Haupt, who had paid for the building permit, said: "I have done all the clearing on this land for the last 30 years for several previous owners. Over the years each owner had, for various reasons, instructed me not to touch the site where the L-Bar-C buildings are to be constructed. I believe that God was saving this land for YFC. To me it was the Lord working 25 years in advance, setting up a place for a YFC Ranch. It shows me how God works for our children."

Commission Chairman John Rees said, "I thank God we've got people like Dr. Al. He came into our County Commission meeting and didn't say he was going to do a five-year study about building a Ranch. He said, 'We're going to build a YFC Ranch' and Dr. Al has enough faith in God and enough backbone about him to do it!" When the crowd finished cheering these remarks, Rees emphatically added, "You know, we all have so many worldly goods. But worldly goods don't amount to a plug nickel next to our young people. When the Lord Jesus returns, I want Him to see a YFC Ranch right here going strong!"

Commissioner Ron Ware capped the commissioners' remarks by saying, "I sent my teenagers to Circle-C and they had a real good time. It was a great learning experience for them. I know the value of the YFC Ranch."

Prayers of dedication, were followed by our guests turning shovels of dirt. That ended the program. But the fun was far from being over!

Like a little boy showing off a new toy, Dr. Al climbed into the driver's seat of the John Deere to lead one of the hay wagon tours of the ranch land. Over roads that had just been cut the day before, riders surveyed the 175 acres of towering sycamore, oak and walnut trees. As they gazed through timber-lined paths, some spotted an occasional deer hopping through the woods while they got a glimpse of where the buildings would be built.

What a happy day! Now the work begins!

## Enthusiastic Walkers

Despite the chill of the blustery morning, enthusiastic crowds began arriving at the YFC Headquarters before 7 A.M. After prayer and final instructions 900 walkers wearing L-Bar-C T-shirts and carrying red helium-filled balloons trooped down Ward Parkway. Even falling rain didn't dampen their spirits. Amid laughter, some donned garbage bags as rain apparel and continued their journey.

"That gutsiness is the personality of KCYFC people," Al cheered.

The successful day was capped with a spectacular Rally. Despite stiff and sore muscles of those in the audience, the night was filled with standing ovations. Several teenagers received awards for raising the most money, and 17 were honored for raising more than $1,000 for construction of L-Bar-C Ranch. The total raised from the Walk-A-Thon was $175,000—breaking all previous Walk-A-Thon records.

## Killing Year of Contruction

Ronnie and Al, envisioning the finished product, carefully took advantage of the natural terrain and saving the stately trees staked out the main buildings. Their master plan was to build everything large enough to hold 352 campers a week. Temporarily, staff would be housed in some of the cabins until staff quarters could be built. They had to stake out the roads, water lines, and the sewage disposal system and lines. The men also needed to decide on placement of the bike barn and maintenance shop, as well as the horse corral location.

Having run a camp for eleven years, Al and Ronnie knew what worked well and what needed improvement at Circle-C, so they made the adjustments accordingly on the plans for the new Ranch. For instance, they put a lavatory in each of the cabin rooms.

The incredible progress in the first 30 days after the groundbreaking included: excavation for 22 cabins; footings poured on 18 cabins; foundations poured for 12 cabins; land cleared and leveled for chapel, dining hall, snack shop, and game room.

The concrete companies Al contacted insisted the distance was too far to transport ready-mix. However, one arranged for us to purchase two concrete trucks, giving us the option to sell them back when we were finished with them. This called for a batching plant, so Al designed and supervised its construction. We had to stockpile sand, crushed rock, cement and other component parts. With this method, concrete would cost us $17 a yard instead of the normal $45.50. We needed more than 4,000 yards.

Already God had done several miracles. It was a miracle that we received the $100,000 needed to make the first land payment. Miracles happened daily as God provided—whether by cash or donated machinery, equipment, labor and supplies which saved thousands of dollars.

One day a fuel truck rolled into the Ranch. The driver wanted to fill our diesel tank. When our foreman, Fred Gibler, asked the price, the driver, who happened to be the owner of the company, said that the Lord laid it on his heart to give L-Bar-C $1,000 worth of fuel!

As construction progressed, a drywall contractor donated his whole crew for three days. An electrical contractor handled all the electrical installations on a volunteer basis and supervised volunteers.

Without a doubt, this was the hardest year of our lives. Imagine living the following daily schedule for ten months. That is what Al did.

9 A.M.– Work in office in Kansas City.

10 A.M.– Teach Methods Class in CUBI at Headquarters.

11 A.M. – Answer questions of other employees and miscellaneous planning, phone calls, etc.

12 noon – Do a live 30-minute "Inside Story" program on television.

1 p.m. – Drive to L-Bar-C absorbing lunch on the way. Work and supervise workers all afternoon and evening—many times until midnight. Drive home and drop into bed until the next morning when it started all over again.

On top of all this were special activities like the Walk-a-thon, Telethon, Luncheon and Dinner Clubs, Formal banquets, and a 2-day Josh McDowell Seminar.

A Bank President who watched TV-50 was fascinated by the stories Al told on Inside Story about the construction, so he decided to drive to L-Bar-C to see if he really would find Al doing construction. Sure enough, Al was in a trench working when he caught, out of the corner of his eye, the sight of some suit pantlegs standing there. He looked up and the man introduced himself. He confided that he wanted to see for himself if this was true. In the end this banker gave several thousand dollars toward the project.

Besides all of my regular work and covering some of Al's, I researched and purchased all of the kitchen and snack shop equipment and supplies.

Our oldest grandson, Christopher (Topher) Philgreen, was 13 years old at the time and lived in Ottawa, Kansas, 45 miles away. He prevailed on his mother, our Martha, to drive him to L-Bar-C every Friday after school. He worked with Grandpa Al doing construction Friday evening and all day Saturday, stopping just in time to clean up and get to the Rally. During those long months Topher learned how to run big equipment, batch concrete, do electrical and plumbing, hang sheet rock, lay stones and just about everything about construction. He and his grandpa became very close and the things he learned from Grandpa Al have been invaluable to him, even now as he still reaches teenagers through this ministry.

Al arranged for a big van to carry volunteers who didn't want to drive the distance from the headquarters every day. Eighty-year-old Bert Chastain built all the trusses for the cabins. A retired plumber installed or supervised the plumbing. A retired carpenter hung all the doors. Some Saturdays as many as 100 volunteers converged on the Ranch. Women volunteered to cook and brought food.

Lee and Earlene McGinnis parked their motor home on the site and settled in for the duration. When camp opened, they stayed and helped wherever they were needed the whole summer. For several years they moved in when it was time for camp to open. What a blessing they were!

Several people who were by Al's side during the construction described a scene that took place many times during those months. Dead tired, sloshing through ankle deep mud, and climbing the hills—sometimes with tears streaming down his cheeks—he sang in his gravelly voice:

> It will be worth it all when we see Jesus.
> Life's trials will seem so small when we see Him!

We worked such long, hard hours we had little time to communicate and got so tired physically, it was like a year

299

dropped out of our lives. I truly believe this year of indescribably hard work eventually led to Al's greatly damaged heart. He worked too hard. He loved everything he did. He loved to do construction and to teach others how. He loved all the volunteer workers at the Ranch. He praised God for the miracles—which were many!

David Lewis, as General Manager of TV-50, was already working long, hard hours keeping KYFC-TV in top shape. He carried extra responsibilities at the office during these trying months and helped at L-Bar-C when he could.

Ronnie, along with his responsibilities as Director of the Club Department, designed and built the water purification plant, as well as supervising much of the volunteer work. When all the buildings were near completion, Ronnie laid out the sidewalks with the most direct route connecting buildings, but with curves for beauty—more than a half mile of them.

Besides doing so much of the work himself, Al also carried the heavy burden of raising the money to pay for it. Over $1 million was raised and total construction finished in ten months! One fund raising approach was a telethon.

## Stampede Telethon

From the opening prayer at 1:30 Sunday afternoon, February 21 to the closing prayer at 5:00 A.M. the following Sunday morning, the telethon was a rush of excitement, blessings and victories.

Karol Kell Eastman, the artist who was our publications production manager fabricated an authentic-looking set depicting an old-time Western town. Dale Evans was a special guest. The emcees wore cowboy hats and a couple of our horses from Circle-C were on the set.

Much of the time, all 18 phones were busy with volunteers taking pledges. Many callers shared how the ministry of KCYFC and TV-50 had blessed them. Others reported that they, their family, or friends had been saved through the ministry of YFC.

Some told us how they had made life-changing decisions at Circle-C Ranch. Still others reflected on how they met their sweethearts at KCYFC activities. Several mentioned that they were new to the ministry, while others bragged that they had been with KCYFC since its beginning 39 years earlier.

One couple was preparing to go to bed on the last night, but decided to get dressed and come to the TV-50 studio to experience the end of the excitement. Before they left the studio that night they gave another $12,000. Scores called saying the telethon was so exciting they couldn't leave their set all week.

One businessman offered to match each $25 pledge given by a teenager to make it a total of $50. Of the 40 new horses needed for L-Bar-C Ranch, eleven were donated during the telethon. The exciting stories are too numerous to tell. But, the final total pledged by our faithful friends was $836,215. To our precious Savior be all the glory! God did it!

## L-Bar-C Ranch Opens on Schedule

A miracle! Yes, it had to be a miracle! The whole "city" of L-Bar-C was built and mostly paid for in ten months! The only debt was to finish paying for a little more than half of the 600 acres.

It was a historic day—June 7, 1982! L-Bar-C Ranch opened as scheduled!

Despite weeks of rainy weather, which produced ankle-deep gummy mud, the construction crew and hundreds of faithful volunteers worked nearly around the clock the final few days before the teenagers were to arrive.

The Chapel carpet was laid on Saturday, two days before opening. At the same time a large crew of volunteers poured 2,200 feet of 10-foot wide sidewalks connecting the main buildings, swimming pool, and waterslide. In the cabins, the water and lights were turned on and the curtains hung only hours before the first teenagers arrived. It never would have happened without the dedicated staff and volunteers. They deserved a big salute!

## Some Results of the Summer

*4,421 people spent a week at Circle-C and L-Bar-C Ranches—a 36% increase over the previous year.

*553 adults donated a week to counsel at one of the Ranches.

*There were 793 first-time salvation decisions.

*Approximately 325 who attended passed the basic counseling course.

*396 young men joined Dr. Al's Young Preachers' Club.

*1,368 young ladies signed up for the Girls in Royal Leadership and Service.

*315 adults attended a week at L-Bar-C Ranch.

## Was It Worth It?

As we approached the end of the summer, Al asked himself if all the work and pressure of the past year were worth it. His answer:

"As I stood there and saw the happy faces of teenagers coming from the prayer room, I *knew* it was worth it! They react differently—some with tears of repentance and others filled with excitement of lifted burdens—but they are all happy to have sins forgiven and eternal life through faith in Jesus."

There are many thrilling stories, but I must share just one. Doug had gotten saved a few months earlier at a Power Charge at Circle-C. At the Ranch that summer he took and passed the Basic Counseling Course. He was ready to lead his friends to the Lord. Arriving home from the Ranch he learned his unsaved grandfather was in the hospital. With his Bible in hand, Doug went to visit him. What a joy when he led his 92-year-old grandfather to the Lord!

## An Unbelievable Gift of Love

It still brings tears to my eyes. Even though at this writing it was 18 years ago, I still can't understand it.

In the middle of the summer, we had a staff retreat at L-Bar-C to give the KCYFC employees a week of physical rest and relaxation, as well as enjoying fellowship together and spiritual refreshment. It was a wonderful week with our good buddy, Del Fehsenfeld, Founder and Director of Life Action Ministries, as our speaker. Del had grown up in our ministry as a teenager in KC. God had blessed him and made him a great leader known worldwide. We were proud of him.

On the last day, without our knowing it, our staff took up a collection to send Al and me to Hawaii for a week of rest after having worked so hard that year. We were shocked! And humbled!

Our first reaction was: "You all worked hard, too! You deserve this!" We felt badly accepting the gift from them. But then we realized they gave out of love. We could not reject their love. What a great gift—they sacrificed for us! Nothing can compare with that. How much we loved and appreciated them—more than we could tell! Nobody had a better staff than we did!

We had never been to Hawaii. So when we went, we just relaxed, rested and got re-acquainted. A wonderful gift!

# CHAPTER 35

# National Religious Broadcasters

### Ronald Reagan's Speech

In February, 1984, we took thirteen of our leaders to Washington, D.C. for the NRB Convention. One of the highlights was a dynamic speech by President Ronald Reagan on January 30. He started by saying:

> I was pleased last year to proclaim 1983 the Year of the Bible, but you know a group called the ACLU severely criticized me for doing that. Well, I wear their indictment like a badge of honor.

This statement caused uproarious applause! Our hearts swelled within us that we had a president who fearlessly stood for righteousness.

> My experience in this office I hold has only deepened the belief I've held for many years: within the covers of that single Book are all the answers to all the problems that face us today, if we'd only read and believe.

President Reagan condemned abortion, discrimination of black Americans, pornography, family violence, sexual abuse. He continued:

> Another important responsibility is to prepare our children for the challenges of life. "Train up a child in the way he should go," Solomon wrote, "and when he is old he will not depart from it."
> God's source of all knowledge should never have been expelled from our children's classrooms. The great majority

of our people support voluntary prayer in schools . . . If we could get God and discipline back in our schools, maybe we could get drugs and violence out. We need a new Amendment to restore the rights that were taken from us.

Government bureaucracy spends billions for problems related to drugs, alcoholism, and disease. How much of that money could we save, how much better off might Americans be if all of us tried a little harder to live by the Ten Commandments and the golden rule? Millions of laws have been written and yet, all those millions of laws have not improved on the Ten Commandments one bit.

Reagan's excellent speech motivated us all to work harder to keep our nation great! Then we heard Franky Schaeffer, son of the famous philosopher, Francis Schaeffer, decry the stigma of abortion on our country. Jerry Falwell told how his Save-a-Baby ministry was doing something positive about the abortion issue. We had already been concerned with other issues but strangely the abortion issue had escaped our attention.

At the same time Reagan's new book was released, *Abortion and the Conscience of the Nation* (Thomas Nelson Publishers) The first U. S. President to write and publish a book while in office, Ronald Reagan made an all-out effort to inform the public of the enormity of the situation by forthrightly addressing this volatile issue—abortion. The book so impressed us; we ordered a supply and gave it as a gift to all who requested it with an offering of any size.

I believe most Americans, just as we up to this point, were unaware of the abortions that were occurring—having slept through the Roe vs. Wade decision. During the trip home on the bus, all thirteen of us joined hands and covenanted with the Lord that we were going to do something positive as well as preach against abortion.

Believing that prevention is better than cure, we had for 41 years been working diligently to reach teenagers before they messed up their lives. Now we realized we needed to help put back together the lives of those who had been missed.

## Positive Solution

Our daughter, Marilyn, felt a personal burden, so she set out to champion the cause.

"We will light a candle instead of merely cursing the darkness," she announced.

The candle would be in the form of a home where we could help the girls deliver their babies and turn their lives around. So Marilyn determined to find what property God had for us. The Lord led her to the Benedictine Convent, a Kansas City landmark at Meyer Boulevard and the Paseo. By this time only a few nuns lived in the 94,000 square foot monument. They wanted to sell it and move to a smaller facility. It seemed the perfect answer. One million dollars was the price finally agreed upon. Although the convent was basically in good condition much renovation was necessary to make it ready to house pregnant girls.

Probably a dozen of our staff, including Marilyn and David Lewis, Al and me, and Roy Bilyeu, met with Ronnie in his office one day to brainstorm a name. We finally decided on LIGHT House, an acrostic for Life Is Given Hope for Tomorrow.

## Bobbing Red Balloons

November 9, 1984 had been a delightful day with temperatures in the 70s. But by the next morning winter had arrived. An hour before people were to arrive for the 10-mile trek to raise money for the LIGHT House, Kansas City faced blizzard conditions. Gusty winds and wet, blowing snow compounded the coldness of the 30-degree temperatures. Amazingly, 3,309 people determined that no matter how adverse the circumstances—sleet, snow, wind or cold—they were going to help the LIGHT House become a reality.

Bright red balloons bobbed against the fall backdrop as the bundled-up walkers presented a colorful, continuous procession along the five-mile route from KCYFC to the LIGHT House. The fascinating montage of people crossed all denominational, racial, social and all other imaginable barriers. They came in all ages, shapes and sizes, from a 2-month-old baby to an 84-year-old saint, from two blind people, and one in a wheelchair, to a man with an artificial leg. Families walked together with parents pushing strollers or carrying their younger children. Churches, led by their pastors, walked together as well as Sunday school classes, YFC Clubs, service organizations, pro-life groups and church youth groups. They shivered, sang, shared, quoted scriptures and compared blisters as they walked. Though temperatures were frigid, spirits soared, for these walkers were determined. They had a cause, a mission to complete, and nothing was going to stop them.

"I'm walking because I'm sorry I had an abortion eleven years ago." one lady lamented.

"My daughter wants children but can't have them. Instead of killing her child, I hope some woman will give her baby for adoption so girls like mine can have a family," reflected another.

Homemade signs proclaimed "USA—Unity Stops Abortion" and "Abortion is Dead Wrong!" A sign on a 4-year-old girl's stroller read "Today is my birthday. Thanks, Mom!"

A poster on a carriage with a now-healthy 8-month-old baby proclaimed "I thank God I didn't abort my premature 2 lb. 11 oz. baby!"

Some walkers pushed empty strollers illustrating aborted babies while others carried life-sized baby dolls. Though opinions were strong, the walkers were neither judgmental nor hostile but were filled with compassion.

"I saw the film, 'Assignment Life' in my church and learned what abortion is all about," shared a teenage girl. "It showed babies being killed and presented both sides of the issue. I never realized what it was all about before." Her statement summed up the opinion of many who had never before been informed, and were shocked to learn of the holocaust taking place in our country.

Once the walkers reached the halfway point at the LIGHT House, they received a respite from the cold as they toured the beautiful building and ate lunch. Several tours were given simultaneously while volunteers hurriedly served hot dog and sloppy joe sandwiches. By the end of the day, volunteers had served 3,600 hot dogs, 350 pounds of hamburger made into sloppy joes, thousands of buns and pickles, 15 bushels of apples, 480 pounds of potato chips and 6,000 soft drinks.

Some were interviewed for TV-50. Many caught the excitement generated by the presence of reporters from major television stations and the *Kansas City Star*. After a tour and lunch, the walkers returned along the same route to the KCYFC Auditorium for a Walk-A-Thon Victory Rally.

### LIGHT House Telethon

At noon the next day, Sunday, November 11, 1985, Al gave his opening statement and prayer for the LIGHT House Telethon. Unlike other telethons, the tote board read $475,123 when we started, the result of the fundraising efforts of 3,309 people who had walked 10 miles the day before. This project captured the hearts of all ages, and the 30 phones were never still. Little children brought the entire contents of their piggy banks "to save babies." Teenagers gave sacrificially. Families decided to give in lieu of Christmas gifts. The telethon was filled with highlights.

On Monday afternoon Dr. Jerry Falwell spent an hour in the TV studio proclaiming the need for the support of the LIGHT House. He urged people to call in their pledges. Dr. Falwell had been a long time friend of KCYFC, having attended some rallies while he was a college student in Springfield, Missouri. On Thursday, Ronnie Metsker and Mike King were among a group who met in Washington, D.C. at a White House Conference on Alternatives to Abortion. Interviews were videotaped with officials there to be used on the telethon. Ronnie had the opportunity to distribute literature and tell about KCYFC's LIGHT House project.

Dino, the great piano virtuoso, came to the studio on Sunday afternoon to give his support Willie Williams, host of "Southern and Country Gospel Music," was once again a vital part each evening. Warren Black presented a $2,000 matching gift from the 700 Club Operation Blessing. TV-50 personalities, Jane Park, Jim Sunderwirth, and others appeared. Many area pastors affirmed their support on camera and many churches pledged cash gifts.

Evelyn Glancy, a 77-year-old nun from the Benedictine Convent in Atchison, Kansas, phoned and talked to Marilyn.

"I've called all over the country getting pledges." she reported. "I have a pledge of $1,321 from 21 people!" She was happy, and so were we.

When we began on the last day, Sunday, November 18, we still needed $169,000 to reach our goal. Except for a miracle, achieving this amount seemed impossible. But the phones rang incessantly. The people of Kansas City and surrounding areas—as far away as Topeka and Ottawa, Kans. and St. Joseph, Sedalia and Osceola, Mo.—were excited about the LIGHT House. By 9:45 P.M. our goal was reached—hours ahead of our anticipated telethon end! In fact, before we could let people know, the total had gone to $1.224,151. Celebration erupted! Balloons and confetti flittered from everywhere. The studio audience and staff triumphantly waved American flags. We prayed and thanked God for the victory.

But the phones would not stop ringing. Others wanted to be in on the blessing. So quickly, while a musical number was on, Al, Ronnie, Marilyn and David discussed the situation.

"We can't turn people away!" they agreed. "But we must be honest. We have reached our goal for the building."

"Operating expenses. Let's continue with monthly pledges," someone suggested.

So Dr. Al announced that we would now accept pledges for monthly giving for operational expenses. A total of $2,860 per month was pledged. Our projected monthly budget was $100,000 so that was a modest beginning. I'm sure some fund raisers would have kept the money coming in but we had always been honest and could never deceive our friends.

An interesting sidelight was the story of some of our volunteers. A few weeks prior during the showing of a Saturday afternoon "K.C On Track"—a live show produced totally by teenagers—a 14-year-old boy called and received Jesus as Savior. He was so excited he came to the Rally that night. He immediately became an open, radiant witness. As a result, two weeks later his mother called for counseling after watching TV-50 and she, too, received Jesus into her heart. The following Saturday, mother, son and two younger sisters came to the Rally. The older sister went forward at the invitation and was saved. The telethon started a few days later and mother and son spent nearly every evening at the telethon answering phones. One night the boy gave his testimony on TV. The younger sister called and got saved. Daddy was watching. He even came to the studio once, but it was a few days later before he finally prayed to receive Jesus. The whole family became new Christians within about six weeks.

## Refurbishing

"I have a fun project for you," Marilyn challenged Sunday school classes, churches, groups or individuals everywhere. "We need every room to be adopted." The idea was that all the bedrooms needed to be furnished and decorated individually to make them "homey" instead of like an institution. The response was amazing. Before long, all 75 rooms were assigned and people were busy getting them ready. Oh, the joy they received from their project! Each room had it's own personality but all were beautifully decorated.

Additional volunteers helped prepare areas such as the dining room, parlor, sitting areas, library and classrooms. Soon, the whole building was alive and vibrant.

## LIGHT House Staff

God put together the LIGHT House staff. Each person had his or her field of expertise as well as their own unique story of how God had led in their lives.

Dr. Donald Philgreen, as a teenager thought God had called him to use medicine as a means of service—maybe on the mission field. At this point he had been a certified Family Practice Physician in Ottawa, Kansas for 15 years. His rapidly growing practice included women coming from towns miles away to deliver their babies. He had been Ransom Memorial Hospital Chief of Staff, Chief of Obstetrics, Chief of Emergency Services, had delivered over 1,200 babies and had been President of the Franklin County Medical Society.

In October, Dr. Philgreen flew with several KCYFC staff members to Lynchburg, Va. and Birmingham, Ala. on a fact-finding trip to prepare for the opening of the LIGHT House. He did not know at that time that the Lord would lead him to join the staff.

"As I have become more and more involved in this project, the importance of what is going on here has literally consumed me," Dr. Philgreen confessed. "There is no more vital area where I can personally be involved in the Christian and pro-life movement. I know this is where God wants me and I am very excited about it."

Don and his wife, Martha (Metsker), and their five children left his medical practice, their beautiful home, their retirement benefits, an active ministry in Ottawa Bible Church, and all the teenagers to whom they had ministered through the YFC Club to join this new ministry.

"That's why this was such a hard decision—the hardest I ever made in my life. But I want to be here. I must be here. I find it hard to believe that this is happening to me," Dr. Philgreen explained. He was the first medical doctor to be employed in this capacity at a facility like this.

A contract was signed with Research Medical Center to deliver the LIGHT House babies in their hospital. The contract included delivery services in a state of the art facility, as well as providing us with a wonderful new staff member.

Jo Anne O'Dwyer became coordinator of nursing services at the LIGHT House. She had worked at Research Medical Center for more than nine years—the last four as assistant head nurse in labor and delivery with primary responsibilities in clinical supervision and continuing education. God had been preparing her for the LIGHT House! Jo Anne had been the first nurse at Circle-C Ranch 15 years before and had been associated with KCYFC all her life—her father being a board member. She worked full time at the LIGHT House, but was paid by the hospital. Does that sound like a coincidence? No way! God did it

"I feel like this is a dream that the Lord has prepared for me and prepared me for," Jo Anne explained. "I want to be able to share the gift of eternal life with the girls."

Our Adoption Director, Liz Hutcheson, had been custom made for the LIGHT House. With a degree in religious education, Liz had worked for the Missouri Division of Family Services for 15 years during which she had placed over 700 children in homes across the state. She was highly respected by judges.

"My desire," said Liz, "is to see that the adoption part of the program becomes a 'class' organization."

Chris Iliff was our invaluable volunteer attorney. His pro-life stance and legal expertise helped produce a cohesive program that met the needs in the community and satisfied the legal requirements of the state. Chris explained why he became involved with the LIGHT House: "First, God has convicted me that we must not sit idly by and allow the practice of abortion to continue without providing truly Christian alternatives. Second, I believe every attorney has an obligation to become involved with and support civic activities that benefit the community." This was his choice.

There were many valuable "full-time" volunteers such as Dean Curteman who worked almost day and night to coordinate our volunteer efforts, greet the public, counsel on the phone and much more. Kathy Kirk, a talented interior decorator, gave many hours and items to produce a classy atmosphere. Lowell and Darline Metsker and Ed and Myrtle Skurdal, were unpaid full-time workers. And there were many more.

## Girls Arrive

By April girls were coming for pregnancy tests and counseling. During her first visit, each girl watched a video on abortion. Most had not understood what it was all about. When they knew, nearly 100% opted against abortion, for many there were great hurdles to clear.

The staff was excited the day the first resident arrived. They had been praying for her for months. Now they could put their arms around her and share the love of Jesus. She was lonely, afraid of the unknown, 16 years old, four months pregnant and feeling lousy. As Marilyn was taking her to her room they were greeted by Kay McGuff who gave her a big welcome hug. Kay had been volunteering for weeks making sure each room was inviting.

As they entered her room, her expression changed from fear to wonder. Frilly white priscilla curtains framed the window overlooking the courtyard. A fluffy decorator comforter on the bed complimented the soft burgundy carpet. She had her medical exam and conference with the doctor and nurse. The love and understanding shown by the staff overwhelmed her.

Most days brought new girls, each with her own heartbreaking story. Many came from abusive homes. Tami, 14, (not her real name) came as a ward of the court. Even though she was rebellious toward her family, she longed to see them. When her mother refused to come see her, our housemother, Lynda Tate, took her for a visit. Preparing her for the encounter, Lynda advised, "Tami, it's up to you. You must be sweet and loving to your mother if you want her to be loving to you." She talked to her about forgiveness and the Lord. Upon arrival a shouting match ensued, but before the evening was over, Lynda was able to get them to sit down and talk sensibly and had an opportunity to present the gospel.

Lynda's reaction: "When I first decided to work at the LIGHT House, I was interested in saving babies. Then I realized that helping the girls was just as important. Now I understand that we will be ministering to whole families."

At least ten heart-gripping stories could be told about every day at the LIGHT House. That is a book in itself.

## First Baby

The timing was novel. Eight months earlier, 3,309 people had walked to raise funds to pay for the LIGHT House. An incentive for those people was a ticket to a Royal's game on July 1 for all who raised at least $100. More than 2,000 YFCers from the walk-a-thon were sitting in Royal's Stadium together when Dr. Donald Philgreen's pager informed him that the first baby was on the way. When Dr. Philgreen left the stadium word swept like wildfire as anticipation excited the crowd. The beautiful 9-pound, 8-ounce baby girl was born early the next morning.

The nuns formerly rang the bell in the Convent bell tower when there was a death. We decided the bells would be tolled for each birth. At noon following that first birth, the staff and others gathered for the bell ringing and dedication. After the chimes pealed their joyful melody for all to hear, LIGHT House Chaplain Bill Baum, Counselor Robert Zornes, and TV-50 General Manager David Lewis (Marilyn's husband) prayed a dedicatory prayer. Tears and thankful hearts permeated the atmosphere at that time.

After that first "bell ringing" the group went to Research Hospital where they held a press conference to announce the birth of the first baby. WDAF-TV, KYFC-TV, and other members of the media covered the event. Dr. Philgreen and Marilyn Lewis scrubbed, put on hospital gowns, and carried the precious little one into the press conference.

We had been so disturbed by the fact that when that baby's mother realized that she was pregnant, she had gone to their family physician. He confirmed her suspicions—she was pregnant. The family doctor did not ask the young, scared, pregnant girl if she had talked with her family about this. He did not ask her what she wanted to do. He only handed her the name and address of an abortion clinic. We were thankful that she learned about the LIGHT House and saved her baby.

During the first years of the LIGHT House about half of the girls opted for adoption. Through much anguish, they decided it would be better for the baby; the birth mother could get her life back on track; and the adoptive parents could have their dreams fulfilled. The special "adoption room" was an emotional place—full of tears and joy!

## Dedication

Celebration of Life was what we called the two-day dedication activities for the LIGHT House. On Saturday, May 17, 1986, about 2,000 people toured the LIGHT House facilities and many attended one or more of the three individual dedication ceremonies—Crown of Life Chapel (the magnificent main chapel), the Tree of Life Chapel (a smaller chapel where the LIGHT House chapel services were held), and the beautiful Memorial Garden (created in memory of the millions of unborn babies who had lost their lives to abortion). The next day, Sunday afternoon at 2:30, three thousand people applauded, cheered and even cried as they enjoyed the stirring program. The setting for the dedication service was on the back lawn where a stage had been set up and beautifully decorated with white trellises and live ferns. With the girls dressed in pink or blue dresses and the guys in gray suits, the Extra Dimension and Living Expression music groups caused hearts to swell with thanksgiving to God for all He had done.

The roster of celebrities on hand for the occasion was impressive. Governor John Ashcroft and his wife, Janet, were guests, along with Attorney General Bill Webster and his wife, Susan. Governor Ashcroft gave accolades to Marilyn, Ronnie and Al and all the thousands who had given and worked to make this become a reality. He proclaimed:

> I believe abortion is one of the greatest evils that ever crossed the face of any nation—let alone America. We Christians need to do more than just say, "That's wrong". We have an opportunity to do what's right. This LIGHT House is a light of opportunity . . . a light of inspiration . . . a light of participation. It gives us all the opportunity to be the hand of God extended to someone in need.

Marilyn shared: "It humbles me that God has chosen me to be a part of this—but we must always remember that it is not one person. It is all of us working together that makes this possible."

She introduced some who had played significant roles in helping the LIGHT House become a reality—three of whom were nuns who had lived there and had given their wholehearted support. The crowd laughed when Marilyn said to them: "As soon as you left after turning the keys over to us, I put on my roller skates and skated through the Convent. It was so large and I wanted to see it in five minutes. I didn't know if you'd appreciate that or not!"

Marilyn introduced Kenyan Anderson who had delivered one of the first LIGHT House babies.

"I became pro-life when I could feel that baby moving around in my body. While at the LIGHT House I came to know Jesus Christ as my personal Savior and now He's the Lord of my life." As she shared so dramatically the emotions she had experienced through her pregnancy—finally deciding against abortion and the difficult decision to place her baby for adoption, the audience was in tears. Oh the pain of sin.

We were thrilled that Josh and Dottie McDowell could be there, and Josh, as usual, gave dynamic, challenging, and encouraging words.

First comes concern. I've learned in the life of Jesus, there's another step that leads to action and that is compassion. One thing I have seen in those involved in KCYFC and the LIGHT House is not just concern, but compassion. They have stretched their arms around Kansas City and said to the teenagers, "We care!" I thank God for that.

Dr. Jerry Falwell, who had largely been our inspiration for starting the LIGHT House as he challenged others to do what he had already done in Lynchburg, Va., spoke.

We are addressing America's national sin. When I was in school there were not pregnant girls—not because we were better. We were taught better. It had nothing to do with religion but with what is right and wrong. Even non-Christian parents and teachers taught morals . . . We are doing what is right. We have the responsibility to pray . . . I congratulate you and cheer you on.

When the weekend was over, more than 5,000 people had toured the LIGHT House and had been encouraged and challenged.

# CHAPTER 36

# Retirement

"The past year has been a very difficult decision time for me," Al wrote in the January 1987 *Conquest* magazine. "I found myself struggling physically to keep up with my rigorous schedule of events and responsibilities as the Executive Director of this ever-expanding ministry."

Al had developed allergies that produced a constant cough. I gave him allergy shots every week. Some of his medication made him so drowsy; he could suddenly drop off to sleep even in an important meeting. Besides this extremely embarrassing condition, his heart was very weak.

"I'd rather burn out than rust out," he had always declared. He also had to face his well-known statement: "Don't Quit!" But he had told Ronnie several months before, "Maybe it would be a good idea for me to slow down. Then I could be your advisor and helper for years to come as opposed to trying to maintain this horrendous pace, go out in one big poof, and be of no value to anybody."

With the Board of Director's blessing, he named Ronnie to be Executive Director.

When Al made this announcement, he added,

> From the time Ronnie was born, he was on the front row of the Youth For Christ Rallies. He's always been involved and I taught him everything I know.
>
> I remember the night he came to me with tears of joy and said, "Daddy, I've dedicated my life to Jesus. I'm going into the ministry full time."
>
> He went through his "boot camp" with flying colors and completed all his background work. He worked up to

become a Club Director, later Director of the Club Department and now Executive Director.

It gives me great pleasure to turn the top leadership position over to Ronnie Metsker's able leadership. He's been through all of the storms and challenges—the good days and the hard days—and has done very well.

His leadership is sharp and visionary. He has the gutsiness to step out by faith and tackle big challenges—including the challenge to reach 28.5 million American teenagers for Christ.

When asked, "Are you retiring?" Al replied. "Absolutely not! In addition to being Ronnie's advisor and counselor, and a member of the Board of Directors, I will continue to be heavily involved in CUBI, TV-50, preaching and many other dreams that have not yet been fulfilled. My title is now Founder of Kansas City Youth for Christ."

## Second Generation

Ronnie had a vision and plan for the future of the ministry. He noted: "Proverbs 29:18 has been a favorite verse that Dr. Al has used through the years. 'Where there is no vision the people perish.'"

Vision is so important. Our vision must have a focus, a common goal at which we are aiming.

The vision God gave my parents 43 years ago was that teenagers can be taught biblical truths that will stabilize them through those rough teen years without messing up their lives in sin. That vision has proven true for the past four decades.

We at KCYFC have a tremendous heritage. That original vision has grown from Saturday night Rallies to local Bible Clubs which spread across the nation. Bible quizzing was another facet that originated here, followed by the preachers' club and talent contests which encouraged teens to use their talent for the Lord.

That vision increased to add Super Rallies and the Ranches, as well as 30 years of daily radio and then a full-power television station.

Well over a quarter of a million people have accepted Christ as a result of KCYFC. Men and women who came from our ministry are now great leaders all across the nation.

Those who are experts in the field have told us that we are the largest local youth ministry in the world. They are awestruck and say there is nothing like this anywhere around the world.

Ronnie continued by pointing out that the future could not be based on the past:

The Royals will not win their 1987 ballgames by saying, "We were the world champs in 1985." They must keep their minds off the past and look to the present and the future to become champions again.

We can't live in former victories. Philippians 3:13-14 declares, "Brethren, I count not myself to have apprehended: but this one thing I do, forgetting those things which are behind and reaching forth unto those things which are before, I press toward the mark for the prize of the high calling of God in Christ Jesus."

The vision of Kansas City Youth For Christ is: "To further the kingdom of God in all age groups, specializing in evangelism and growth to teenagers initially in the greater Kansas City area and ultimately to the entire United States of America."

We will continue a commitment to that vision, but we will also have a commitment to excellence. We cannot be satisfied with status quo. We must not be satisfied with our past performance. We must demand excellence from ourselves.

We cannot lose the heart for God and the heart for evangelism. We cannot lose our first love.

Exhausted and in desperate need of a break, Al and I journeyed across the country in our motor home. But it was hard after 43 years of constant, self-imposed pressure, for Al to give up. His daily routine was to call Ronnie at the office for long chats. The transition was difficult—probably as trying for Ronnie and his co-workers as it was for us.

Ronnie embraced new methods of management surrounding himself with a team. They hired consultants. We had worked as a team—evidenced by the fact that many of our co-workers had been with us for 20 years or longer—but Al was still the entrepreneurial personality who ultimately called the shots.

At the precise time Al and I retired, national headlines emblazoned the news of the financial indiscretions of Jim and Tammy Bakker, leaders of a Christian television empire. Then, almost immediately, to compound the embarrassment for Christians, the scandal of televangelist Jimmy Swaggert's immorality blared from the news media.

These two incidents made the Christian public question whether they could trust *any* ministry. With turmoil in their souls, many stopped giving. All Christian organizations and many churches complained of suffering a significant drop in gift income. KCYFC was no exception.

Neither the Bakker nor Swaggart television programs were aired on our television station, so we had no connection to them but people were still squeamish about giving. We had always been transparent—open and honest with our finances. People trusted us.

At the same time as these uncontrollable events in the nation, Ronnie and the new Leadership Team were also making changes to several KCYFC programs to bring them to be more relevant to the youth culture. In some cases it was the name of a program, in others the change was in the program format, and in still other cases they eliminated programs that no longer drew students. I agreed that many of the changes were needed, however, there were some donors whose hearts were touched by those program in the past, who were attached to the names, and who were confused by the changes.

Some who had been long-time friends and good supporters not only stopped giving, but also talked critically to others, making things more difficult. Add all these factors together, and income dropped dramatically. What the staff really needed was prayer—not criticism.

In our hearts, we knew victory would eventually come because the staff was walking with God, praying for guidance, and earnestly wanting to do God's will.

Through this heart-wrenching transition time, they suffered painful birth pangs and trials similar to what we had encountered in our beginning days. We realized we could not impart to them what God wanted them to experience. God has a way of building us into the people He wants us to be only through trying experiences.

> These trials are only to test your faith, to see whether or not it is strong and pure. It is being tested as fire tests gold and purifies it—and your faith is far more precious to God than mere gold; so if your faith remains strong after being tried in the test tube of fiery trials, it will bring you much praise and glory and honor on the day of His return. I Peter 1:8 (TLB)

I believe God took Ronnie and the new Leadership Team through unbelievable trials during this time to prepare them for even bigger things He had for them in the future.

## Cancer Again

At the same time trauma struck us again. When my doctor checked a lump in my abdomen he found I had an ovarian cyst. Because of my cancer history he ordered a CAT scan that revealed unexpected results—cancer in my kidney. Urgent surgery by a team, a gynecologist and an urologist, removed my kidney and did a hysterectomy. The good news was that the cancer was contained in the kidney so they got it *all* and I did not need chemotherapy. My doctor said that if it weren't for the cyst, the cancer would not have been detected until it was too late.

God's promise to me seemed to be "This sickness will not end in death. No, it is for God's glory so that God's Son may be glorified through it." (John 11:4) Again, God was good!

## CHAPTER 37

# Al's Final Days

Al's heart continued to weaken. A few days before Thanks giving 1992, Al started having congestive heart failure. On December 23, my birthday, he received a pacemaker. During this hospital stay, Al came very close to death several times. Our whole family was thrilled when Grandpa Al could finally be home to celebrate Christmas on January 10.

A few days later when Ronnie asked Al to be on the telethon, I was amazed when he agreed. Appearing thin and drawn, he spoke with zeal that night on the telethon—a special anointing from God.

Over the next four months he was in and out of the hospital. He witnessed to and prayed with many people with whom he had contact about his or her relationship to Christ.

One day when he was home from the hospital Al came into the kitchen where I was cooking dinner. Wrapping his arms around me, as was his regular habit, he held me tightly and whispered in my ear.

"I'm ready to go to heaven but I can't stand the thought of leaving you."

We stood there for some time holding each other snugly—crying together.

Another time he said, "I'd really like to have more input into our grandchildren's lives." I wished that for him, too. He was an exceptionally good grandpa – a natural born teacher and an excellent example. When I hear that statement ringing in my ear, it challenges me to try to have more input into our grandchildren.

About that time in early 1993, KCYFC leaders, and hundreds of KC church youth leaders, joined a national evangelistic outreach, "See You at The Party" to be held on March 6. In preparation for the nationwide "Party", students in hundreds of youth groups and YFC Clubs attended a five-week course teaching them how to win their friends to Christ. They were required to read a book, *Under Siege,* by Josh McDowell and Chuck Klein. (Word Publishing)

Ronnie, always trying to keep us informed of exciting happenings in the ministry, gave us this book. Al and I read it on one of our last trips. This compelling novel for teens communicated Bible truths, combining exciting adventures with practical application. The story was about what real life teenagers faced, and how they could reach a lost world through prayer and the power of the Holy Spirit. As we read the book, we both broke down and cried several times as once again our hearts were broken for lost teenagers. We began to get excited and started earnestly praying for the upcoming event.

On March 6, as weak as he was, Al insisted on going to "See You at The Party," a youth concert with Petra, a popular Christian band, and Josh McDowell via satellite in Bartle Hall. I can still see Al sitting on the third row among 12,000 teenagers. He had stuffed tissues in his ears to deafen the thundering sound. As the concert ended, he was overjoyed to watch more than 800 teens come to Jesus for salvation. To cap off the night, Rusty, Ronnie's only son came and introduced his friend, who had just received Jesus, to his Grandpa. This was the first person that Rusty personally had led to the Lord, right there in the chairs of Bartle Hall. How blessed we were!

Afterward, Al walked all over Bartle Hall hugging and loving all the KCYFC staff. He considered them "his kids." Like old times, Al didn't want to leave. He brought out some sandwiches I had made and offered them to the guys who were busy tearing down the stage. This was a huge affirmation to the staff of his support. To this day, the staff still fondly remembers that night and Al's actions.

Al was grateful that the TV station he had founded

fourteen years earlier originated the telecast of the "Anchor Party" that was simulcast across America connecting similar concerts in many major cities. During this effort in partnership with Josh McDowell, more than 89,000 teenagers gave their hearts to Jesus that night across the North American Continent. Nothing gave Al more joy than these victories.

God, in his loving kindness, sent us special blessings during the last couple of months. Many friends from our past dropped by for visits, called or wrote encouraging letters.

"Al? Cuzzy here. I'm in town for a couple of days and Grant and I want to take you to lunch."

"Sounds great!"

Jack Cousins and "General" U. S. Grant had been good buddies with Al for almost fifty years but seldom got to "chew the fat" in recent years. Over lunch they reminisced about God's blessings through the years and the miracles they had witnessed. What a blessed time they had!

In early May, against his better judgement, Dr. Becker reluctantly allowed me to drive Al to Ft. Worth to visit our daughter and son-in-law, Marilyn and David Lewis, and our granddaughter, Liane. While there, Al insisted on treating us to some of his famous charcoal broiled steaks.

One evening he called our grandson, Davey (what we called him from his childhood) Lewis, at Texas A&M and asked him to sing "When They Ring Those Golden Bells" at his funeral. He wanted him to sing it with power just as the late opera singer, Bill Carle, sang it. Two days later our visit ended abruptly when Al became very ill. Several times during our drive back to Kansas City I had to stop along the highway because he was violently ill. When we arrived in Kansas City he was admitted to the hospital.

His last five days in the hospital were a gift from God as he responded well to new medication. He rejoiced, "I feel like a man again!"

Sunday evening, May 23, Dr. Don, Martha and their son,

Jonathan, visited at the hospital. Attached to his IV tube, Al sat on the edge of his chair and taught Jonathan how to preach in preparation for his mission trip to Russia with KCYFC Student Missions. Grandpa Al demonstrated voice projection, gestures and facial expression. He even threw in a few tips on preaching with an interrupter. He never stopped teaching!

Being unable to sleep that night, he searched his room for something to write on, finally settling on a piece of cardboard he found in the wastebasket. He wrote a simple gospel message for Jonathan to preach in Russia. (We later framed that message as a precious keepsake.)

Monday, Frank Horseman, our L-Bar-C Ranch Manager, visited Al in the hospital. Al told him, "I'm embarrassed with the dining hall and snack shop at Circle-C Ranch. When we built it after the fire, it was good for a year—but it's been fourteen years." He proceeded to describe to Frank, in detail, the new dining hall/snack shop he wanted built at Circle-C Ranch. He was still dreaming about unfinished items on his agenda.

Back in February, our children had told us they were planning a 50th Wedding Anniversary Celebration for us. But Al didn't want it to be a "boring reception with white cake and punch."

Ronnie said, "Well, Daddy, what *would* you like?"

"Nachos, popcorn, cotton candy, and Dr. Pepper!" he quickly replied.

We exploded with laughter. Our family always had such a good time together!

Being the practical one, I said, "What would people think?"

Our kids replied, "You've done unconventional things all your life. No one would be surprised. Anyway, it doesn't matter. It's *your* party! You can do what you want!"

We had a hilarious time planning how we would tie a helium-filled balloon on each guest's wrist as they arrived creating a *real* party atmosphere with balloons bobbing up and down as guests moved around.

As the time approached, our children assembled pictures from our childhood through our fifty years—both personal and ministry—to display with captions. The celebration was to be Sunday afternoon on Memorial Day weekend.

On Tuesday Al told Dr. Becker, "It is really important for me to be at our 50th anniversary celebration on Sunday afternoon! You're going to let me out of here to go, aren't you?"

Dr. Becker promised, "I'll have you there even if you have to go with your IV."

But, God had other plans. Wednesday afternoon, May 26, 1993, our TV-50 Chief Engineer Ron Rockrohr, stopped briefly at the hospital for a visit. Before leaving he prayed and told us "good-bye."

A few moments later Al collapsed and was gone.

Jesus tenderly scooped him up in his loving arms, and delivered him safely into the glorious presence of his Heavenly Father. I can imagine his heart bursting with joy as he heard the great choirs singing praise to God! His eyes must have been blinded by the divine brilliance of heaven! His welcome celebration was more majestic than we could imagine here on earth!

Suddenly, our fifty years together melted into memories. Regardless of the suffering or distress of his illness, never could I have been prepared for his death. Only our loving Heavenly Father can give peace and assurance at such a time. Neither do I know how I could have made it without our dear family. What would I do without them?

Sunday afternoon, at the exact time our anniversary celebration was to have been, we had Al's ultimate celebration on earth. Because the entire service was broadcast live over his "pride and joy," KYFC TV-50, thousands were able to rejoice with the great crowd of friends who came to the KCYFC Auditorium. Telephone prayer counselors prayed with those who called.

Al had planned most of his home-going celebration. And a "celebration" it was! Laughter and standing ovations punctuated his sweet memorial. Ronnie was host. David Lewis played his trumpet and led the audience in singing some of Al's favorite hymns. Our daughter, Marilyn, masterfully and enthusiastically quoted II Corinthians 4.

Eighty-seven-year-old Albert Lane, who had worked twenty-five years with Al, received a standing ovation after playing and singing "The Timber Song" which Al had loved so dearly.

Most men of Al's stature would have imported some of his "well-known" friends from across the country for such an occasion but Al chose some of his "Timothys." Just before Dr. Don closed the service by singing "Find Us Faithful," Jerry Johnston, one of Al's "young preacher boys" who had become a nationally known evangelist and author, challenged the audience to take Dr. Al's place as God's servant. When the invitation was given, the front of the auditorium was filled with people accepting the challenge.

The celebration was aired two more times on TV-50 at the request of many who had been out of town over that Memorial Day weekend. Many ordered video copies of the service.

We lived together fifty years as devoted companions, amorous lovers, and faithful co-laborers for Christ. Al was an incredible husband, father and grandfather. Many times each day he told me how much he loved me. He was totally dedicated to God. He was passionately committed to his calling—winning teens for Christ. His walk with the Lord was real—his faith contagious. One of the things I miss most is hearing him pray.

In my loss, I felt compelled to see that Al's last dream was fulfilled so I told Ronnie, "We must build the Dining Hall/Snack Shop at Circle-C." He and the Board agreed. This was a god-send for me at the time. I buried myself in planning, promoting, raising funds, and recruiting volunteers.

We organized a "Family Fun Day" at Circle-C Ranch in conjunction with the groundbreaking exactly four months after Al went home. The day resembled a carnival utilizing all the water and sports activities available plus a dump-tank, face painting, cake walk, carnival games for all ages, and lots of good food.

The groundbreaking ceremony took place in a huge, brightly-colored tent. Music and testimonies preceded the moment when Board members turned the first shovels of dirt, followed by all of our family, then KCYFC Staff. The action-packed day ended too soon for the nearly 800 friends who participated.

Since completion, the beautiful Al Metsker Memorial Dining Hall/Snack Shop is a buzz of activity as teens take giant steps forward in their walk with the Lord on those grounds. Enhanced with beautiful landscaping, including a brick-paved memory garden and a large two-tiered deck overlooking the swimming pool, a common scene during camp is a group of teens studying their Bible or a cabin leader and teen having a private conversation in one of these picturesque spots.

The setting is just as Al would have wanted it.

CHAPTER 38

# New Life in Ministry

At this writing it has been more than seven years since Al went to be with his Father. Now he sees everything from an eternal view, as God does. I'm sure he is pleased to know this ministry has had a new birth and is continuing to win hundreds of students to Christ each year.

Since Al went to heaven in 1993, KCYFC has gone through a lot of changes. Some have been joyful and others have been difficult. Ronnie, who continues to be President, with his Leadership Team and staff, earnestly sought God's will in the tough decisions they had to make. Like a mother preparing to give birth, God took KCYFC through birth pangs that brought new life to the ministry.

It started with solidifying the mission and vision. The mission statement "To Bring Youth Into A Growing Relationship with Jesus Christ" is not stated in the exact words, but is essentially the same mission as the last 57 years. The vision is "To Provide World-Wide Youth Ministry Leadership." At the time the staff crafted this plan, I doubt that they had any idea to what extent God would use them to fulfill their vision.

Youth and the youth culture are quite different today than when we began 57 years ago. Consequently, youth ministry must be different to reach them. When we started Singspiration in 1943, there were no full-time youth pastors. Today, in Kansas City there are over 400 full-time youth pastors. When parachurch youth ministries—like Youth For Christ, Young Life, Campus Crusade and Fellowship of Christian Athletes—started years ago, they provided for the youth what an individual church could not. Now, churches have made youth a priority by hiring youth workers. With a passion to reach students for Christ,

Ronnie and the Leadership Team prayed and planned. They realized that the answer was to work along side the 400 youth pastors, uniting for a solid front with the gospel.

In 1994, Roy Bilyeu, a staff member for 25 years, started building networks of youth pastors in the Kansas City area. These youth pastors met regularly to pray for and encourage each other. By 1996, four networks of 15-20 youth pastors each met regularly.

At the same time, God burdened the hearts of students to reach their world. Even though the Supreme Court's 1984 "Equal Access Act" opened the door for Christian clubs in public schools, it wasn't until 1997 that Club121 started. Praise the Lord! Today, there are over 100 Club121s on public school campuses in Kansas City. The mission of Club121 is to connect students to Jesus and a church. A local youth pastor coaches each club.

I like the new name. Club121 stands for "one-to-one" evangelism. The world will be changed one person to one person to one person. Many scripture verses with 121 reference fit.

Deuteronomy 1:21 "See, the Lord your God has given you the land. Go up and take possession of it as the Lord, the God of your fathers, told you. Don't be afraid; do not be discouraged."

Philippians 1:21 "For to me, to live is Christ and to die is gain."

Hebrews 12:1 "Therefore, since we are surrounded by such a great cloud of witnesses, let us throw off everything that hinders and the sin that so easily entangles, and let us run with perservance the race marked out for us."

Psalm 121 The whole psalm is great! I'll let you look it up.

In less than three years, we went from having four networks of 15-20 youth pastors to 21 networks of 15-20 youth pastors. From these networks a Strategic Local Church Partnership has emerged. So the change has been from a para-church to a church-assisting organization. With this change came a new name on January 1, 2000, YouthFront. That got the attention of not only Kansas City, but also many other para-church youth organizations around the world.

I began to realize it was similar to how God had changed names when he started a new work. For instance, in Genesis 17:5 "No longer will you be called Abram; your name will be Abraham, for I have made you a father of many nations." And Jesus told Simon he would now be called Peter. So the name change signifies a new birth of the ministry built on the foundation of a 57-year heritage.

Rallies are now called "Impact" and are highly produced programs utilizing all modern electronic gadgetry with almost 100% teenagers on stage. Youth workers from all over the city bring vans, cars and buses full of students on Saturday nights. The auditorium is filled with 1200-1600 students at every program. After the gospel is presented, the opportunity is given and students still walk with their friends to the prayer room to receive Christ.

Circle-C and L-Bar-C are packed. New attendance records have been set the last three years. Soon after Al's memorial dining hall/snack shop was built, all 15 cabins at Circle-C were torn down and rebuilt. Also, all 22 cabins at L-Bar-C were renovated. Everything is now air-conditioned.

Because youth workers value the effect of the outward focus in a student's life, mission trips have become a vital focus. YouthFront facilitates countless groups and individual students to serve God on a mission trip. Based on Acts 1:8: "But you will receive power when the Holy Spirit comes on you; and you will be my witnesses in Jerusalem, and in all Judea and Samaria and to the ends of the earth." A student's "Jerusalem" is his friends and classmates. "Judea" is everything from helping in the inner city to volunteering as a teen staff at camp. "Samaria" is missions projects in other parts of our country, Mexico, and Jamaica. "Uttermost parts of the earth" include the overseas trips such as the many YouthFront have taken to places like Ireland, Russia, Romania, Australia, Hong Kong and other places around the world.

Student's lives are remarkably changed as a result of their experiences serving God on mission trips. Often the culmination is that they become full-time missionaries. I praise the Lord that thousands are continuing to be reached with the gospel today through the ministry God led us to start 57 years ago!

Recently I attended a meeting at L-Bar-C with 500 teen leaders—the sharpest teens you would expect to see anywhere! Never have I experienced the presence of the Holy Spirit more powerfully. At the end of the meeting those teens were spontaneously calling out to God, "I'm willing to pay the price!" From the depths of their souls they were admitting to be ready to die, if need be, for the cause of Christ. What greater dedication could they have!

Ronnie recently told this story.

"I've been working at painting our home—grabbing moments here and there to scrape, sand, and finally get on the ladder with a bucket of paint, a roller and a brush.

"I was perched on my ladder in a moment of painter's glory when the phone rang. No one else was home so I scrambled to answer it.

"Rather frustrated, I grabbed the phone and gruffed a hello. An excited youthful voice said, "Hey Ronnie, it's Jessica! Is it all right if I call a bunch of kids to come to your house Monday night to pray for school?"

"My heart melted in joy over her passion to see her school come to Christ," he continued. "For the next hour Jessica, a bubbly senior, and I talked about the prayer meeting and getting Club121 under way when school starts.

"The large group of students came together the first Monday in August to pray. Athletes. Cheerleaders. Student Body Officers. Band Members. All shared with each other their burden to win their school to Christ.

"It was Elliot's turn to share. Elliot trusted Christ as Savior at camp two years ago. He began, 'When I got saved I gave God my whole life to use as He wanted. This summer I went to Australia on a mission trip. While there I said, "God, where do you want me to go? I'm willing. Send me. I got my answer. He called me to America—my school!'

"This is only one of the stories I heard from those dedicated students. I rejoiced that God had called me to work with teenagers."

Week after week, those teens—with others joining them—sat on the carpet in circles at Ronnie's and Susan's house, praying. In the center of each circle was a school yearbook. Pointing to individual pictures and calling them by name, they prayed for every student in the school. Faculty and administrators were also objects of their passionate prayers. They claimed "target teens" for the Lord.

Even before school opened revival started. Unsaved students came to the prayer meeting. Friends were led to the Lord in various situations! Some administrators and teachers joined the Monday night prayer meetings. God hears and answers prayer—especially those of believing youth!

## The Vision Realized?

In almost every city in America, there exists some sort of para-church youth ministry and often a fledgling network of youth pastors. Already, word of the phenomenal success of the new model in Kansas City is spreading through professional youth ministry circles. Consequently, youth leaders are journeying to Kansas City from all corners of the country to learn how to duplicate in their area what is happening here. Whole cities are starting Club121's or other on-campus clubs. Traditional para-church organizations are beginning the transition to become a church assisting organization and helping to form a Strategic Local Church Partnership in their city. The words "one city, one church, many congregations" is a phrase used to capture the movement. This is remarkably similar to the early church in Acts. Even though Paul referred to the "church at Corinth," it was made up of several house churches, but they were all serving God together to build the Kingdom.

Additionally, teams of three or four of our leaders travel several times a year to overseas countries such as Romania, Hungary, Hong Kong, Jamaica and Cuba to conduct workshops. Groups of 200-300 native youth leaders enthusiastically drink in what they teach. Praise the Lord, victories are taking place around the world in reaching youth with the gospel!

Recently Mike King, now CEO of YouthFront, wrote a book, *Millennial Leap* introducing this concept. Already in its second printing, the book simply tells the story of the transition from KCYFC to YouthFront and the transition from a traditional parachurch to a Church Assisting Organization building a Strategic Local Church Partnership. He says: "I believe a new day has arrived when youth leaders from all denominations and youth organizations are joining together—abandoning their egos—to selflessly unite for one cause—to reach young people for Christ."

The story of what God has done in Kansas City is more than I can tell in this last chapter.

Perhaps you would like to read Mike's book, *Millennial Leap.*

Yes, names have changed, methods have changed and there are new faces on our staff of 80—but the mission is the same—reaching teenagers with the Gospel of our Lord Jesus Christ! The results are the same—winning youth for Christ and helping them grow spiritually to become dynamic witnesses for Him.

As I look back at the past 57 years, I realize that I have been simply along for the journey. The sense of fulfillment I have is indescribable. God started something through two people who were not qualified by the world's standards, but who were willing to be used to do "whatever had to be done". That "whatever had to be done" has not only brought thousands of teenagers to Christ, but is still, to this day, pioneering new methods in modern day youth ministry that will ultimately bring even more people into the Kingdom. I am so thankful to God for allowing Al and me to live the life he gave us. Truly not one person in the world can argue with a fulfilled life, except to say that—God did it!

ADDENDUM

# Family Fun
### "I have no greater joy than to hear that
### my children are walking in the truth." III John 4

First priority in our lives next to the Lord was our family, desiring to be good parents and leading our children in the way they should go. We tried to live Deuteronomy 6:6–9.

> Impress (these commandments) on your children. Talk about them when you sit at home and when you walk along the road, when you lie down and when you get up. Tie them as symbols on your hands and bind them on your foreheads. Write them on the door frames of your houses and on your gates.

Every moment of every day we tried to live for the Lord before our children. We wanted them to know that we were real – we lived at home the same as in public.

We were greatly disturbed when we heard a parent tell their child: "I said 'No' and my no is enough. Stop asking."

Our philosophy was don't say' No' unless you have a reason. If you have a reason, then tell your children why— thus teaching them how to make good decisions. If they are taught to make proper choices when they are *with* you, you can depend on them making the right ones when they are not with you. You can trust them!

From the beginning, we discussed openly in front of our children the heartbreak of someone getting into sin, what led to it and how it could be avoided. They learned by example from all our experiences—both trials and blessings. When we saw someone make a poor choice, we discussed it so they could learn from it. They also learned from people's good choices.

When they became teenagers we didn't have to lay down rules for them to rebel against. Instead, in answer to their request, we discussed what would be the value, benefit, consequences, and results both of doing or not doing whatever they asked. After discussing a situation they easily made their own correct decision. We seldom had to *order* them.

## Fun with Grandchildren

While our older grandchildren were growing up we lived across the road from Circle-C. One of their fun activities was to help Grandpa feed pellets to the fish in our lake. When he banged on a bucket, the water boiled as fish swished to retrieve the pellets. Fishing was fun, too.

Sometimes our whole family had great fun horseback riding through wooded trails or steering Honda trail bikes over our meadow. Exciting games of softball involved everyone from Grandpa to the youngest. We all played together in the games!

A favorite in the winter for the little ones was to play hide-and-seek inside our house. Mamas, Daddies, Grandma and Grandpa and all the little ones played. We were surprised how many nooks and crannies they could find to hide in. It was great fun! We loved to work jigsaw puzzles or play Monopoly, Pit, Rook, Croquet, Ping-Pong and so many other games.

When snow covered the ground, Grandpa Al tied ropes behind the tractor and we all piled onto sleds, holding the ropes. As he pulled us all over the meadow we screamed and laughed and we never had to pull the sled up a hill.

Even though we worked long hard hours, we made the most of every moment we had together with our family.

Sometimes on beautiful Sunday afternoons when Al and I were alone, we piloted our trail bikes (mine was a Honda 70 and his was a Honda 100) over the country gravel roads. Many times we traveled the 25 miles around Hillsdale Lake near our home. So relaxing and refreshing!

When our four oldest grandchildren were 11 and 12, a Board member, Ed Beason, called Al from Orlando.

"We'd like you and Vidy to fly to Orlando and take our motor home for a ten day vacation." Wow! What an opportunity! We weren't used to just taking off for a vacation but we hurriedly arranged to take our four oldest grandchildren—Topher, Liane, Michelle and Jennifer. They were enthralled with their first airplane ride and first view of the ocean. Disneyland and Epcot Center left them wide-eyed! What an incredible adventure!

Five years later we received another phenomenal gift. Beasons gave us that 32-foot motor home. So we took our six oldest grandchildren, now 17 to 12 years of age, on a three-week trip to California. People cringe when we tell that all eight of us traveled, ate and slept in our motor home for a 3,000-mile, three-week trip. What an incredible time we had!

Before we left Grandpa Al laid out the rules:

*No arguing or fighting

*Everyone would make their bed and keep their clothes picked up. Each one had his own drawer for belongings.

*Teams of two would be in charge of cooking and dishes each day. They could plan the menu, cook the food, and clean up.

It worked great! We traveled the northern route to San Francisco, visiting many attractions along the way, journeyed down the coast to San Diego, went across into Mexico for a day and returned the southern route. We survived the marvelous trip without any conflict and created marvelous memories.

## An Unusual Thanksgiving

Our Thanksgiving tradition was to give each person five grains of candy corn at the end of our dinner. Going around the table each person would tell something for which they were thankful for each grain of corn. Our "Thankful Time" often brought laughs, deepening love and tears of joy. This is a blessed time we cherish each year.

We were not prepared for Thanksgiving 1985. David was snowed under with television productions. Marilyn was busy with the LIGHT House. Dr. Don was delivering babies at the LIGHT House. Ronnie was overseeing the Rallies and Clubs. I was editing *Conquest Magazine*. Al was teaching CUBI, doing his daily Inside Story TV program and presiding over it all. We were all so busy we didn't even have time to think of Thanksgiving until the day arrived. Since we were all flexible and fun loving, we dreamed up a fun Thanksgiving.

Wearing grubby clothes, we met in the Rainbow Room where we cooked hamburgers on the big grill and made french fries in the deep fryer. The food didn't matter. We were having fun! After "lunch" we played hide and seek. There were no boundaries within the Auditorium and Rainbow Room. What fun! Our "Hide-and-Seek" game evolved into "Sardines." One person chosen to be "it" is allowed two minutes head start to hide. Then everyone searches for "it." When someone finds "it", they join him without letting others know. As others find and join "it" they are packed in like sardines and can't keep from giggling and attracting the attention of other seekers. We had a hilarious time!

Another time we took our five youngest grandchildren on a joyous adventure to St. Louis. Being ages 4 to 8, they raced from one thing to the next at the zoo, children's' museum, Magic House, and Train Museum. Even traveling down the highway was fun as they sat in a circle on the bed and played games or colored in coloring books.

These few highlights illustrate the loving relationship we had with all our family. How blessed we are!

For our friends who constantly ask where our family is today, the following will briefly bring you up to date on what God has done and is doing in their lives.

## Don and Martha Philgreen

Don and Martha have five children: Christopher "Topher", Michelle, Kevin, Jonathan, and Timothy.

Even though they lived an hour away in Ottawa, KS, they were still very involved in the KCYFC ministry. Their passion was to see the teens of Ottawa know Christ and grow in Him. They sponsored a YFC Club, coached a quiz team, and drove vanloads of kids to KC to participate in Rallies and music groups. Their home, which was dedicated to God, was always open to teenagers. Praise God, over 150 kids came to know Christ in their home during their 15 years in Ottawa. Don served as Choir Director, Deacon and Sunday School teacher in Ottawa Bible Church. He was on the School Board for a time in addition to his responsibilities at the hospital and his family practice.

When God moved them back to KC in 1985 as the LIGHT House was opening, (Chapter 35) the YFC staff and their families loved having Don as their staff physician. Don and Martha helped with the YFC Clubs where their teenagers were involved. Martha served the Lord as chairman of the KCYFC Luncheon and Dinner Club for 8 years.

After graduation from high school, Topher attended CUBI and married his YFC high school sweetheart, April Stanley. Topher joined the KCYFC staff in 1986. Having served in many capacities, he is now a Vice President of YouthFront and on the Leadership Team. The heavy responsibilities he carries is a perfect example of "to whom much has been given, much shall be required." Topher and April have three precious children: Cameron, Connor and Chloe.

Michelle, as well as Topher, was involved in Rallies, Clubs, Quizzing, Music Groups, and Camps while in high school. A student at Mid-America Nazarene University, Michelle was elected the first female Student Body President. She married Brian Gann whose passion is to serve God. An ordained lay pastor, he is part of a team who planted a new church. Michelle carries tremendous responsibility in the Children's Ministry as well as other areas of this alive, fast-growing church. She enjoys being mommy to their two darling boys, Joshua and Micah.

Jonathan, a senior at Kansas State University, is active in campus ministries and is on the Navigator Leadership Team, a ministry he shares with his cousin, Amy Metsker. He has been on several YouthFront mission trips, and on summer staff at Circle-C several summers. God has called him to the ministry.

Timothy loves the Lord with all his heart and is seeking God's will for his life. He has been active in church and working at Circle-C.

Don and Martha say God has used Kevin, their middle son, to remodel and remake their lives, God's sandpaper to smooth out rough edges. Kevin was born deaf and blind, with an enlarged heart, fused kidneys, breathing problems, genital and bone abnormalities, learning difficulties, and the list goes on. He wasn't expected to live many times along the way but at this writing he is 29. Everyone loves him. Don and Martha love to share what God has taught them through this experience. Kevin has kept them on their knees when all they could do was trust Him. God also used Kevin to burn in Don's heart the importance of every life, part of the journey to becoming so pro-life as to leave his practice to join the LIGHT House.

Don is now employed by Trinity Family Medicine and on faculty for their residency program. He continues to deliver babies for the LIGHT House as well as the Rachel House, another crisis pregnancy center.

In 1990, after Don's mother, Evie, suffered a stroke, they brought her to live with them. When God called Al home, they invited me to live with them also. Eventually we both sold our homes and built one together that would fit our special needs. Evie has the room she needs, I have a lovely apartment in the walkout basement, and Kevin's special needs are met as well. Who could ask for a greater blessing? We each have our own place yet we are together.

Full of compassion, Don and Martha are constant angels of mercy for many.

## David and Marilyn Lewis

David and Marilyn have four children: Liane, Jennifer, Delinda and David II. A stay-at-home mom, Marilyn constantly worked on YFC projects. With two small girls she had a graphics table set up in her basement where she produced the *Conquest* for a couple of years.

On staff, David spent the summers at Circle-C Ranch so his family was there also. Marilyn always kept busy. At times she was in charge of the Snack Shop. Other times she helped in the office, kitchen or wherever she was needed.

The summer of 1972 when their girls were 5, 3 and 1, an unforeseen event took away the head cook after two weeks. Ready to fit into any position, Marilyn became head cook for the remaining ten weeks of the summer. She did great! The teenage helpers loved to work for her because she made it so much fun.

Being a KCYFC employee meant a small salary. But David and Marilyn were resourceful. Several of their vacations were spent working on a "fixer-upper" house. They borrowed to buy a house, then worked around the clock redecorating it and sold it quickly. They usually made $2,000 to $5,000. This was a big boost to their economy and they enjoyed working together. They even had their small children painting in spots that didn't matter.

While their children were in Old Mission Junior High, Marilyn was a great Club Sponsor. Much of the time while their children were in their teen years, David was either Club Director or Music Director at YFC and their house was a beehive of activity. They never could anticipate how many would be there for a meal or even to stay overnight. All four of their children were star Bible quizzers, sang in YFC music groups and played dramatic roles.

In 1987 our hearts broke when they moved to Lynchburg,

VA where David went to work for Dr. Jerry Falwell for his TV satellite ministry. Our family had never been apart before this.

After several years, Dr. Falwell sold his satellite to the Southern Baptist Television Commission and David was the only employee they took with them. So Marilyn, David and Davey (he was the only one still home) moved to Ft. Worth, Texas. We were happy that they were closer to home.

For three years Marilyn was Secretary to the Pastor of a big Baptist Church. Their latest venture has been transforming a brick mansion into a romantic bed and breakfast, Lockheart Gables. More than a B&B, it is their ministry to married couples. This, David does on his off hours from his regular job and Marilyn does full time.

Liane and Jennifer both graduated from Liberty University. Jennifer married an Australian, Gavin Watson, whom she met at LU. Gavin recently completed his Masters in Biblical Studies at Dallas Theological Seminary. Jennifer continued with her schooling to receive her Bachelors decree in Nursing and works full time at Ft. Worth hospitals. They are active in their church.

Liane is on a team of three in charge of music and drama at Fellowship Church in Grapevine, Texas – with weekly attendance of 11,000-14,000. She arranges music for the band and worship team, leads rehearses, plays the keyboard and sings. I am thrilled to see her use the skills and knowledge she gained from her years in YFC music groups.

Delinda graduated from University of North Carolina, Charlotte with her Bachelors degree in Nursing. She married Bret Phillips whom she met at the university. They presented Marilyn and David with their first grandson, Henry. This brings my total great grandchildren to six so far! I am so blessed.

David II (Davey) played lead roles in all the musicals and dramas through his high school years. As a cadet at Texas A & M he graduated with honors and received a philosophy Fellowship at Notre Dame where he took his Masters degree. At this writing he is house parent to teenage boys at a children's' home in Ft. Worth.

## Ronnie and Susan Metsker

Ronnie and Susan have three children: Melody, Ronald II (Rusty), and Amy. It's hard for me to realize that they have been partners reaching young people with the gospel for 25 years. As they broke ground for their home in 1977 they rode the backhoe together. While Ronnie dug for footings, they prayed that hundreds of young people would hear the gospel and receive Christ there in their home.

Since 1981 students have been coming to their home for YFC Club, Quiz practices and prayer meetings. During those years, their small children saw teenagers receive Christ right there in their home and they "wanted to know Jesus just like the big kids." Ronnie and Susan had the privilege of leading each of their children to Jesus at the age of four.

While Melody, Rusty and Amy were teenagers; both junior high and senior high YFC Clubs met each week at their house—often more than 200 students a week came through their doors. During those years on Saturday nights, Ronnie drove a church bus by their house where a crowd of students packed into it and headed for Impact. Many of them received Christ.

All three children actively witness to their friends. Their summers are spent on mission trips and working as full-time staff at L-Bar-C Camp.

Right now I am a "Wildcat Grandma" as I have four grandchildren at K-State—all three Metskers and Jonathan Philgreen. This year Melody will complete her degree in Elementary Education/Special Education. She has been leader of youth in her church including leading Bible studies. On campus she has been active in Campus Crusade and was president of her residence hall, which gave her tremendous opportunity to take a stand for God. Melody believes God has called her into youth ministry.

Rusty is working on his degree to become a middle school social science teacher. He wants to be an example of a "godly man" before youth. He leads Bible studies in his fraternity house, Theta Xi and is leading his "brothers" to Christ. He has been on summer staff at L-Bar-C several summers as well as sandwiching in a thriving lawn business.

Amy was a cheerleader for six years and as a senior was president of Shawnee Mission North high school student body. She now leads a Bible study in her Kappa Kappa Gamma sorority house. She serves on the Navigator Leadership Team with cousin Jonathan Philgreen. Amy is pursuing a degree in Communications/Public Relations, which she hopes to use in ministry.

Susan serves alongside Ronnie at YouthFront mostly in Development and Public Relations. Students still come to their home to pray and plan for Club121.

Ronnie and Susan have always been intensely involved in their children's schools and in the community. They were PTA presidents and Susan served on the Advisory Board for the Shawnee Mission School District for several years. In 1999 Susan was elected to the School Board – a district of 31,000 students in over 50 schools. For the 2000-2001 school year, the board voted unanimously for her for Vice-President of the Board. She views this as an incredible opportunity to be "salt and light" for the sake of the Kingdom and the community.

I have shared about our family in praise to God for answering prayer and as a testimony that God is faithful. As each child was born we gave them to God and asked that He would keep them from sin and bring them to Himself. There is no question—God did it!

# Appendix A

## Soul Winning Course

Here is Al's simple basic outline.

### Three Requirements of a Soul-Winner

*A soul-winner must know Jesus as Savior.

*A soul-winner must live a clean life.

*A soul-winner must have a burden for the lost.

### Five Points

Several scriptures are given for each point. Memorize them all and follow God's leading which ones to use for each person, according to their needs.

1 - **All have sinned.** Romans 3:23, Romans 6:23, Titus 3:5, Isaiah 53:6, Isaiah 64:6

   The gap between God and Man is created by sin.

2 - **Christ died for us.** 1 Peter 3:18, Romans 5:8, 1 Peter 2:24, Romans 5:19

   Jesus Christ bridges the gap of sin.

3 - **We must repent.** Luke 13:3, Acts 3:19

   **Repent** means to be sorry for your sin, turn your back on sin, change your attitude.

4 - **We must believe.** Romans 10:9-10, John 1:12, John 3:16, John 3:36, Revelation 3:20, Ephesians 2:8-9, John 6:47

   **Believe** means receive, commit, trust completely as when you sit on a chair, you trust it completely to hold you. Salvation is by **grace** through **faith** in Christ. We must stand on God's unchanging Word, not feeling or emotion.

   Explain that **prayer** is just talking to God – just like you are talking to me. "Open you heart to Him in your own words and tell him you know you are a sinner, you are sorry for your sin and want Him to forgive you, come into your heart and give you eternal life."

348

**5 - Assurance of Salvation**—1 John 5:11-13, John 5:24
Assurance of salvation is necessary to grow.

### Beginning Steps to Help Spiritual Growth
*Ask your new convert to tell you in his own words what he has just done. Get a testimony from him/her. Help him/her know how to say it.
*Tell him what he must do to grow spiritually.
1 – Read your Bible. (Start reading the book of John first.)
2 – Witness. (give your testimony)
3 – Get involved in a Bible preaching church.
*Go with him to tell someone else his testimony
*Follow him up with phone calls, meetings, etc.

We believe bringing a new baby into God's family is every bit as serious as a physical birth. It is important that there be no casualties. A born-again baby Christian needs to be nurtured and cared for just as a new physical baby. So Al taught how to help and encourage the new Christian.

Consequently, there was a test to make sure those who took the course really knew how to lead someone to Jesus. First, they had to pass a written test followed by a demonstration of how to lead someone to Jesus. An experienced counselor played the part of a seeking sinner and the student had to lead them to Jesus. If they didn't do a good job, they were given pointers. Sometimes they studied more and took the test again. After passing the test, they received a "Certified Counselor" card.

Through the years teaching the Soul Winning Course has been a staple of our ministry. It was our goal that every teenager involved in KCYFC learned how to lead their friends to Christ using proper scriptures. A large percent have done this.

Eventually the name changed to Basic Counseling Course and then to Basic Training for Evangelism—but it's basically the same course—expanded some now. Thousands upon thousands have taken and used it. The whole premise: "Teens telling teens!"

## Prayer Room Procedure

Equally important to us was our prayer room procedure, which I think was unique to us. We were determined that a new baby Christian would give his/her testimony at least three times before leaving to go home for two reasons:

1. If they had trouble saying it right, we helped them. (For instance, one might say, "Bob just saved me." Even though we made it clear that Jesus saves them, it's easy for a new convert's terminology to get mixed up and refer to their counselor.) We wanted to make sure they said it right.

2. Each time they gave their testimony they grew. This practice made it easier for them to give their testimony to skeptical family or friends.

The counselor first asked, "Tell me in your own words what you have just done." That was their first testimony.

A Chief Counselor in the prayer room would be the next one to ask that question. This would be their second testimony.

The counselor was taught to then take the convert to the friend or family he/she came with and say, "Tell (your friend) what you have just done." This was the third testimony. By this time they knew how to say it.

Every convert, we prayed, would go home with complete assurance of his/her salvation and become a growing Christian.

# Appendix B

# TIMELINE OF KCYFC/YouthFront

1943 KCYFC founders, Dr. Al and Vidy Metsker held the first
KCYFC Saturday event–called "SINGSPIRATION."

1944 Al developed and started teaching his SOUL WINNING
CLASS.

1945 HIGH SCHOOL BIBLE CLUBS were started in Kansas
City, originally called "Youth on the Beam."

1946 Third Anniversary SUPER RALLY in Municipal
Auditorium.
First KCYFC "CAMPSPIRATION" at Lake Afton
near Wichita, Kansas.
BIBLE QUIZZES began.

1948 BIBLE CLUBS put out of schools—bought MOBILE
CHAPELS.

1949 Al started his YOUNG PREACHERS' CLUB.

1950 CITYWIDE CRUSADE in Municipal Auditorium
with Merv Rosell.

1951 YOUTH FOR CHRIST HOUR RADIO program began.

1952 EVANGELISTIC CRUSADE in Municipal Auditorium
with Jack Shuler.

1953 Purchased first HEADQUARTERS building at 4500
Walnut.

1956 Moved to new HEADQUARTERS building at 4715
Rainbow Blvd.

1957 Started MOTHERS' CLUB.

1959 Built DORMITORY.

1966 First Rally in new 1600-seat AUDITORIUM.

1966 Started LUNCHEON and DINNER CLUBS

1967 Al received HONORARY DOCTORS DEGREE from
John Brown University.

1970 CIRCLE-C RANCH opened.

1972   Launched weekly 30-minute "CHRIST UNLIMITED" TELEVISION SHOW.

1973   SUPER RALLY in Royals Stadium (Kauffman Stadium) with Pat Boone Family.

1975   CHRIST UNLIMITED BIBLE INSTITUTE started

1976   SUPER RALLY at Arrowhead Stadium with Johnny Cash

1978   KYFC TV-50 went on the air. (TV-50 was sold in 1996 so KCYFC could focus totally on the mission of bringing youth into a growing relationship with the Lord Jesus Christ.)

1979   FIRE at Circle-C Ranch destroyed the Lodge – was rebuilt in eight days.

1980   EVANGELISM EXPLOSION on TV-50.

1982   L-BAR-C Ranch opened.

1985   LIGHT House opened—a Crisis Pregnancy Center. PIZZA BLAST in Municipal Auditorium with Jerry Johnston preaching.

1986   REV. RONNIE METSKER succeeded Dr. Al as EXECUTIVE DIRECTOR.

1988   First STUDENT MISSIONS TRIP.

1990   LIGHT House was graduated as an independent ministry.

1992   KYFC-TV received STATION OF THE YEAR award from NRB. Over 5,000 teens prayed at SEE YOU AT THE POLE in Kansas City.

1993   "SEE YOU AT THE PARTY" at Bartle Hall with 12,000 attending. Over 800 received Christ as Savior.

1994   Distribution of 20,000 BIBLES in Russian language by KCYFC teenagers on a mission trip.

1995   DOWNSTAGE CAFÉ, a Christian coffeehouse started at KCYFC.

1997   KCYFC began the International Youth Worker Training Conference. At this writing more than 500 from 23 countries have been trained in effective youth ministry methods.

Appendix

*KCYFC organized church YOUTH WORKER NET
WORKS and started CLUB121.

2000    Changed name to YouthFront.

# Appendix C

## YouthFront

YouthFront, formerly Kansas City Youth For Christ, is a youth ministry in Kansas City that has made the philosophical leap from being a traditional para-church ministry to a church assisting ministry. Along with 21 networks of youth pastors, YouthFront is uniting the youth church of Kansas City for strategic ministry. Over 400 churches in Kansas City are working together with YouthFront.

You can read about the journey of KCYFC to YouthFront through a recently released book, *Millennial Leap*, by CEO Mike King. The book is available online at www.youthfront.com, or by calling 1-800 880-5932.

All official documents are still valid for the name Kansas City Youth For Christ.

**Current programs of YouthFront:**

**Club121** - 110 in Kansas City area

**Impact** - first and third Saturday nights of the school year

**Drama Teams** - Made up of students who perform at Impact and around the country

**Impact Band** - Made up of students who perform at Impact and around the country

**City-Wide Events** with the Church of Kansas City

**Circle-C Camp** - All summer long and winter conferences

**L-Bar-C Camp** - All summer long and winter conferences

**Local Missions** in Kansas City - All year around

**Outlying Missions** in Mexico and Jamaica - Over 20 groups each Spring and Summer

**Overseas Missions** in Europe, South America, the Middle East, Australia and Asia

**Training** for local Youth Pastors for effective youth ministry

**Training** for leaders of new Church Assisting Organizations who are building a Strategic Local Church Partnership in their city

**Youth Ministry Products and Resources** - Sold mainly online at www.youthfront.com

**You can reach YouthFront in Kansas City:**
YouthFront (KCYFC)
4715 Rainbow Blvd.
Shawnee Mission, KS 66205
(913) 262-1700
(913) 262-3900
1-800-880-5932
www.youthfront.com
www.youthfrontzone.com
www.club121.com

# Appendix D

# DR. AL'S QUOTES

*These are some statements Dr. Al quoted often.*
*I don't know if they are original but they were a part of him.*

What you will be, you are now becoming.

The *Word* of God does the *work* of God.

Major on ASSETS—Minor on LIABILITIES.

You can GIVE without LOVING—but you can't LOVE without GIVING.

People will not care how much you KNOW—until they know how much you CARE.

The world has always made room for a desperate man or woman.

What you DO speaks so loud, I can't HEAR what you're saying.

There is no limit to the good a person can do if he/she doesn't care who gets the credit.

Happy is the person who dreams dreams—and is willing to pay the price to make them come true.

Praise in public; Criticize in private.

Lead, follow or get out of the way.

If you're going to be blue—make it a bright blue.

You are what you are when no one is looking.

I cannot lead someone where I have not been.

The Bible is our final authority. Memorize it. Quote it. Put full trust in it.

God can turn my bungles into blessings.

You can help a teenager only to the extent you know him/her personally.

If it's doubtful, it's dirty.

Don't criticize someone until you've traveled a mile in his shoes.

There is no room for improvement in God's plan for my life.

The devil's chief tool is discouragement.

With God's help—the difficult we do immediately. The impossible takes a little while.

Attempt great things FOR God—expect great things FROM God.

If you don't stretch yourself, you won't grow.

Change your methods—but never change your message.

To order additional copies of

# God
# Did
# It!

**Vidy Metsker**
**P.O. Box 27214**
**Overland Park, KS 66225-7214**

Send $19.95 for Hardcover;
$14.95 for softcover
plus $3.00 S&H

**OR**

Have your credit card ready and call

**Toll free: (877) 421-READ (7323)**

or send $19.95 for Hardcover;
$14.95 for softcover each plus S&H*

Your Choice: $5.95 - USPS 1st class
$4.95 - USPS Book rate
to
WinePress Publishing
PO Box 428
Enumclaw, WA 98022

* Add $1.00 S&H for each additional book ordered.